POLICING ACROSS NATIONAL BOUNDARIES

POLICING ACROSS NATIONAL BOUNDARIES

EDITED BY
Malcolm Anderson
Monica den Boer

Pinter Publishers
London and New York

Distributed in the USA and Canada by St. Martins Press, Inc.

Pinter Publishers
25 Floral Street, Covent Garden, London, WC2E 9DS, United Kingdom

First published in Great Britain in 1994

Distributed Exclusively in the USA and Canada by St. Martins Press, Inc., Room 400, 175 Fifth Avenue, New York, NY10010, USA

British Library Cataloguing in Publication Data

A CIP catalogue record for this book is available from the British Library
ISBN 1 85567 195 6

Library of Congress Cataloging-in-Publication Data

A CIP catalog record is available from the Library of Congress

*HV
8194.5
A3
P65
1994*

Typeset by Florencetype Ltd, Kewstoke, Avon
Printed and bound in Great Britain by Biddles Ltd of Guildford and King's Lynn

CONTENTS

DATA PROTECTION

CONCLUSION: IDEOLOGY AND DISCOURSE

CONTRIBUTORS

Professor Malcolm Anderson, Professor of Politics, Department of Politics, Dean of the Faculty of Social Sciences, University of Edinburgh

Martin Baldwin-Edwards, Lecturer, Department of Social Policy, University of Manchester

Professor John Benyon, Director of the Centre for the Study of Public Order, University of Leicester

Professor Didier Bigo, Professor of Politics, Institut d'Etudes Politiques, Paris, Chief Editor of *Culture et Conflits*

Dr Monica den Boer, Research Fellow, Department of Politics, University of Edinburgh

Dr Frank Gregory, Senior Lecturer in Politics, Director of the Police Research Unit, Mountbatten Centre for International Studies, University of Southampton

Bill Hebenton, Lecturer, Department of Social Policy, University of Manchester

Dr Mike King, Lecturer, Centre for the Study of Public Order, University of Leicester

Charles D. Raab, Senior Lecturer, Department of Politics, University of Edinburgh

Dr Kenneth G. Robertson, Director of Studies, Graduate School of European and International Studies, University of Reading

Lynne Turnbull, Research Assistant, Centre for the Study of Public Order, University of Leicester

Dr Neil Walker, Senior Lecturer, Department of Public Law, University of Edinburgh

Dr Andrew Willis, Director of the School of Social Work, University of Leicester

Dr Rachel Woodward, Research Fellow, Centre for the Study of Public Order, University of Leicester

ABBREVIATIONS

ACPO	Association of Chief Police Officers
CE	Council of Europe
CEC	Commission of the European Communities
CELAD	Comité Européen de la Lutte Anti-Droque
CELAT	Comité Européen de la Lutte Anti-Terrorisme
CERI	Centre d'Etudes et de Recherches Internationales
CIA	Central Intelligence Administration
CID	Criminal Investigation Department
CIS	Commonwealth of Independent States
CNG	Central Negotiating Group
CNIL	Commission National de l'Informatique et des Libertés
CRS	Compagnies Républicaines de Sécurité
CSFR	Czech and Slovak Federal Republic
CSPO	Centre for the Study of Public Order
DA	District Attorney
DEA	Drug Enforcement Administration
DNA	Deoxyribonucleic Acid
EC	European Community
ECHR	European Convention of Human Rights
ECJ	European Court of Justice
EDU	European Drugs Unit
EEA	European Economic Area
EFTA	Economic Free Trade Area
EIS	European Information System
ENP	European Network for Policewomen
EPC	European Political Cooperation
ETA	Euskadi Ta Askatasuna – Basque Separatist Movement
FBI	Federal Bureau of Investigation
FCO	Foreign and Commonwealth Office
HL	House of Lords
HM	Her Majesty's
IGC	Intergovernmental Cooperation
INSEE	Institut Nationale des Statistiques Economiques
JAU	Joint Assistance Unit
KGB	State Security Police of USSR since 1945
MAG '92	Mutual Assistance Group '92
MLA	Mutual Legal Assistance
MNS	Migration News Sheet

MVD	Soviet Internal Security Service
NATO	North Atlantic Treaty Organization
NCB	National Central Bureau
NCIS	National Criminal Intelligence Service
OECD	Organisation for Economic Cooperation and Development
QPM	Queen's Police Medal
SB	Secret Branch (Political Police)
SCTIP	Service Cooperation Technique Internationale de Police
SEPAT	Stupéfiants Europe Plan d'Action à Terme
SIS	Schengen Information System
SOCOS	Scenes of Crime Officers
SWAT	Special Weapons and Tactics
TEU	Treaty on European Union ('Maastricht' Treaty)
TIR	Trans International Routier
Trevi	Terrorisme, Radicalisme, Extremisme et Violence Internationale
UCLAF	Unité de la Coordination de la Lutte Anti-Fraude
UISP	Union International de Syndicats de Police
UN	United Nations
UNHCR	United Nations Higher Council for Refugees
WEU	Western European Union

PREFACE

Malcolm Anderson and Monica den Boer

This collection of chapters originated in a workshop held under the auspices of the European Consortium for Political Research held in Limerick in the Republic of Ireland at Easter 1992. They are an early contribution, predominantly from a political science point of view, to a difficult debate, the outcome of which will have a profound effect on all the citizens of the European Community countries. It is a debate which will help to shape what it means to be a citizen of Europe as well as influence the treatment of non-EC citizens who cross the external frontier of the EC. But it is about many things – civil liberties, data protection, criminal law procedures, accountability and the raw struggle for power, influence and resources.

The very word 'police' has different meanings and has divergent resonances in the twelve EC member states; policing is done in different ways according to different laws in the complex societies which make up the Community. Yet there is a common belief that the police are the guardians of internal tranquillity, order and security; just as the armed forces are the guardians of security from external military threats, they are seen as an essential part of 'state sovereignty'. The permanent alliance and the integrated command structure of NATO represented a remarkable shift away from the unfettered independence of action which had previously been such a feature of sovereignty in the military realm; stable and institutionalised police cooperation offers the prospect of an equivalent change in the authority of the state in the domain of internal security.

These general considerations about the implications of police cooperation, in theory and in practice, are the subjects of Malcolm Anderson's introductory chapter which sets the context for more specialised subjects which are dealt with by other contributors. Neil Walker explores in more detail the relationship between police cooperation and European integration, and between policing and the nation-state. As such, he develops a theme already referred to by Malcolm Anderson and, suggesting that policing is a quasi-autonomous social field. This is followed by a chapter written by John Benyon and others, which suggests both the need and the difficulty of advancing research in the field of police cooperation. This chapter proposes a framework for explaining the nature of the developing system of cooperation by a mapping of the structures, institutions and arrangements involved.

The next chapters are concerned with specific police cooperation issues which, nonetheless, have wide implications for European societies and the relationship between the EC and the wider world. The first two concern relations with central and eastern Europe. Mike King considers the construction of the so-called 'Fortress Europe' in the area of the policing of refugees and asylum seekers. The control of these persons involves a common visa policy, an enforceable distinction between asylum seekers and 'economic' refugees as well as a reinforcement of the policing of the external border. The 'threat from the East' is seen here as an important internal security problem for EC countries. Frank Gregory pursues this further in exploring the crime explosion in the former communist states and the problems this poses for cooperation between eastern and western law enforcement agencies. One of these problems is the sharing of police intelligence and Kenneth Robertson explores this conceptually murky and little investigated field. Police intelligence may serve strategic or tactical purposes but it should be distinguished from mere information, such as the licence number of a stolen car. Information is relatively easy to share between police forces but the sharing of intelligence poses difficult ethical, political, operational and sometimes legal problems.

Data protection rules and legislation are one potential obstacle to the sharing of information and intelligence. In police cooperation, as Charles Raab shows, data protection is not only a civil liberties issue about whether or not an individual has the right to verify information held in data banks and transferred on request to another jurisdiction. It is also an issue of the quality of the information passed through police information systems. Agreement on police data has been slow to reach because is an appendage to a wider debate on data protection in which powerful commercial interests are involved. Martin Baldwin Edwards and Bill Hebenton exemplify the workings of the Schengen Information System in the light of national data protection legislation and the Council of Europe Convention on Data Protection.

From the particular we move back to the more general with the chapter of Didier Bigo, who provides a radical and somewhat pessimistic assessment of the political battles now taking place (and which will continue in the future) in the field of internal security. Bigo describes a scenario of ideologies linked to police agencies and ministries whose struggle for position and influence can only with great difficulty be subject to democratic control. Finally, Monica den Boer contributes a concluding chapter, a coda for the volume as a whole, which examines police cooperation as a discursive field shared by the members of a policy community. Although the policy debate is characterised as lacking a clear sense of purpose, analysis of stereotypical arguments reveals a more coherent ideology about the internationalisation of crime, the effectiveness of border controls, and the replacement of old threats to Europe's internal security by a new threat, namely immigration.

These are not the only problems posed by the ever-changing agenda of police cooperation. There are many topics and perspectives which are inevitably omitted from this volume, such as the co-operative efforts against international fraud, money-laundering and terrorism, and the legal or socio-economic perspectives on these problems. We believe that the most important issues are discussed in the pages which follow. If others can be provoked into disagreement and argue that the real issues are elsewhere, this volume will have served its main purpose.

Malcolm Anderson
Monica den Boer
Edinburgh, July 1993

ACKNOWLEDGEMENTS

The editors would like to thank the European Consortium for Political Research for supporting a workshop entitled 'Police Cooperation in Europe after 1992' on which this volume is based.
Malcolm Anderson, Monica den Boer, Neil Walker, and Charles Raab would also like to acknowledge financial support from the Economic and Social Research Council, and from the Jean Monnet Project of the European Communities, which have supported a research project in the University of Edinburgh on European Police Cooperation.

GENERAL PERSPECTIVES

1

THE AGENDA FOR POLICE COOPERATION

Malcolm Anderson

This chapter sets out the main elements of the intellectual debate and of the political agenda for police cooperation in Europe; the aim is to provide a framework for the more specialised discussion of particular issues in subsequent chapters. As Didier Bigo points out in chapter 9, official definitions of the issues and problems must not be uncritically accepted. But the starting point of current discussion must be the general recognition by governments (through their agreement to the Palma document in 1989, the Trevi Action Programme of 1990, and the articles on Home Affairs and internal security in the Maastricht Treaty on Political Union) that further progress towards European integration requires an improvement in the quality of police cooperation. Quality means the achievement of practical objectives of crime control and the promotion of certain values such as individual liberties, security and cross-border solidarity. Even though police cooperation and mutual legal assistance in criminal matters are not yet formally within the Community institutions, progress in these areas is an important indicator of the integration achieved in the European Communities.

Six interrelated topics are discussed in this chapter. The first is the various theories aimed at understanding the process of European integration. These theories are one step removed from the second topic – the arguments used by decision-makers to promote policy objectives. The words and phrases used in everyday political debate are often derived from complex theories mediated through the press and broadcasting, and even through social conversation. Persuasive justifications (rhetoric) are usually the *sine qua non* of successful policy implementation. In the case of police cooperation these justifications must mobilise broad political support as well as professional police opinion. The third topic is the practical steps towards improved systems of cooperation which do not start from a *tabula rasa* but which build, where possible, on existing domestic and international arrangements. The fourth topic is the recent history of policy in this area; some aspects of this history are partially hidden until confidential official papers are made available but the main features are in the public domain. The fifth topic concerns the potential impact of closer cooperation on law enforcement and the administration of justice. Finally, some conclusions are reached about the politics and present trends of police cooperation.

The political theory of European integration

Theories of European integration remain very much those of the 1960s although the time is ripe for renewed theoretical inventiveness. The prospect of institutional cooperation in the field of internal security should be a stimulus and ideas concerning the 'post-Hobbesian state', that is to say a state which is no longer primarily regarded as the guarantor of internal and external security, are already being advanced.

The theories which prevailed during the first phase of European integration in the 1950s and 1960s led to a rejection in the following decade, as these theories began to have a shop-soiled look, encapsulated in the title of a book, *The Obsolescence of Regional Integration Theory*, by E.B. Haas (one of the major contributors to the first phase of theorising). This rejection and the theoretical 'pause' which followed it reflects the lack of qualitative change in the activities of the Communities themselves. No developments occurred which could provide a substantial enough handle for renewed speculation. In the light of all the activity in the 1970s and 1980s – the expansion of the EC, the introduction of the Exchange Rate Mechanism, the Single Market Programme, direct elections to the European Parliament, and the remarkable development of European Economic law – this is a debatable assertion. But there was no practical test of the theories put forward in the 1960s and therefore no dominant conceptual framework emerged.

But the events surrounding the 1992 Maastricht intergovernmental conferences have given a topical relevance to the original clash between the functionalist, neo-functionalist, pluralist and federalist perspectives (to use the categories set out by Charles Pentland, 1973) on the dynamics of European integration. The functionalist view, which derives much from Marx and Comte, although sometimes explicitly disclaiming their determinism, is one which sometimes underlies discussions of police cooperation. The frequently made assertion that the development of modern communications and of mass transportation systems require closer transfrontier police cooperation because they have rendered traditional frontier controls ineffective is based on rather crude functionalist premises. The assumption of functionalists is that economic and technological factors are the motors of change in the international system. The most straightforward example of this position, and one of the most persuasive, is in the work of John Herz (1959, 1968) who suggests that the basic political unit throughout history is the one which provides military security and this basic unit changes depending on the military technology available. The structural-functionalist theories developed by anthropologists which have now influenced the other social sciences are the most sophisticated expression of this world view. Functionalism is also a practitioners' perspective in that many international and European public servants see themselves as contributing to the solution of human welfare problems which are the direct outcome of technological and economic change. These public servants, expressing different functional analyses, are divided between those who regard the European Communities as fulfilling the general functional requirements of the whole system, such as balanced economic growth and internal and external security, and those who consider they provide for the functional needs of particular large groups of individuals, such as producer or consumer groups or bureaucracies.

Those who hold the former view would argue that closer police cooperation arises directly from the functional needs of policing contemporary society – in other words, the geographical mobility of large numbers of people requires that policing is closely coordinated across internal frontiers in order to maintain adequate levels of crime control; the police function as well as the revenue function of customs has to be displaced to the external frontier of the European Community and to the interior of the member states. In both cases this requires closer cooperation between the customs and police of the member states in order to maintain the same level of internal security; fraud against the European Community requires close cooperation between a Community fraud intelligence service and the anti-fraud services of the member states; and so on. In this view, no further political justification is required – closer cooperation is a result of changing circumstances and the demand for law enforcement. Those who hold this latter view consider that policing arrangements will protect the activities of dominant functions such as agricultural production, industrial production, communications, transport, education, training, government and administration. Since the requirements of these functions sometimes conflict there has to be a compromise on police priorities; but most of these functions share a need for public tranquillity and, therefore, require efficient public order policing.

The two functionalist perspectives can appear virtually identical in some circumstances but they are easily distinguished from neo-functionalists. The latter regard the intermediaries – governments, ministries, agencies, political parties, interest groups, international organisations – as playing a crucial role in the integration process. They articulate the various functional requirements of the system but it is their interaction, in certain conditions and circumstances, which results in political integration. Loyalties and political activities shift from the national to the European level because of bargains struck between the various parties involved who are under pressure from certain functional requirements. What Ernst Haas, the most celebrated exponent of neo-functionalism, attempted to identify was the basis of the 'authority-legitimacy' transfer from one level of government to a new level. In the EC context, this means that, for many purposes, the states continue to exist but the European level is viewed as a legitimate arena for action and decision. In terms of contemporary

policing problems, governments and police authorities see a functional
requirement for closer European police cooperation with the completion
of the internal market and the abolition of many controls at the frontier.
However, they are engaged in a process of bargaining within the framework of medium- and sometimes long-term strategic goals, from which
both the scope of cooperation as well as the institutional form of cooperation will emerge. Neo-functionalism helps to provide a framework for
explaining the timing and nature of new initiatives with rather more
plausibility than the functionalist position.[1]

   Jean Monnet, one of the great 'fathers of Europe' often seemed to
operate from neo-functionalist premises although he was, above all, a
pragmatic statesman striving to achieve practical ends. His idea of
spill-over, taken up by Lindberg (1963) and Haas (1975), fits these
premises – that action in one sector of policy leads to changes in other
sectors partly as a result of practical pressures and partly because of
policy-makers' perceptions that the situation has changed. The 1990 Trevi
Action Programme may be explained along these lines. The Single
European Act and the Cockfield White Paper of 1985 envisaged the completion of the internal market and the end of systematic frontier controls
on persons and goods. Before any practical effects of this were felt, it
created the perception of a new situation to which police agencies had to
react. Some countries wished to proceed more quickly than others in the
dismantling of frontier controls and from this emerged the two Schengen
agreements, in which first five and eventually nine countries were involved.
However, all EC countries agreed an action programme of police
cooperation in June 1990 through Trevi. In this case, the most important
factor was the perceptions of policy-makers about a situation rather than
pressure of practical problems. This is an example of the neo-functionalist
contention that the 'subjective' preferences of the decision-makers may act
on the 'objective' conditions. Practical problems, serious enough at the
local level, such as the exposure of the external frontier of the EC to mass
migration of Albanians to Brindisi and from Eastern Europe into
Germany, were, of course, exercising very strong pressure on some
governments to arrive at a common European policy on the policing the
external frontier.

   The pluralist position is associated with the Gaullist vision of '*l'Europe
des patries*' – power remains dispersed among the states. But states which
cooperate closely for certain purposes can become a 'security community'
in which the resolution of conflicts by force becomes inconceivable. The
realist school of international relations is linked to pluralism because it
rests on the axiom of the fundamental reality and the permanence of the
sovereign nation state pursuing its interests in an anarchic society of other
nation states; the search for security may lead to highly developed forms of
cooperation between them. There are many varieties of this position but
all give priority to the international security arena and to the exclusive role
of the sovereign state in this arena. The familiar division, proposed by
Stanley Hoffman, between high politics and low politics, is based on this
position; the former refers to the noble or regalian aspects of policy,

foreign affairs and defence, the latter to mundane matters of taxation, trade, industrial policy and so on, grandly described by de Gaulle as *'l'intendance'* or housekeeping. The former must be in the hands of the states as the effective controllers of armed force and the basic political focus of loyalty. By contrast, the latter could, by inter-state agreement, be managed by an international agency or organisation; the actions of these international agencies could be repudiated if they acted in a way contrary to the interests of the states. This view of the world does not exclude the possibility of European political unity – the *'Europe des patries'* could become the *'patrie européenne'*. This would happen only when Europe became the accepted security community in the sense that its inhabitants regarded it as the guarantor of their physical security and as the primary focus of their loyalty. This perspective influenced Brodeur's (1983) distinction between 'high policing' and 'low policing', with high policing relating to state security and low policing dealing with ordinary criminality and petty offences. But the main propositions which derive from the realist/ pluralist position is that some forms of policing can be assigned to the realm of low politics and may be dealt with by European/international agencies whilst others must be kept within the domain reserved to the state. In the terms of this position, there are no problems about transferring to a European agency the police role of customs, the circulation of intelligence about ordinary crime, fugitive criminals and similar matters but control of public order police and the protection of the constitutionally established public authorities must remain with the state. This is not so much a judgment about what is right and appropriate as a pragmatic judgment about what is required to preserve the integrity of the state.

There are significant overlaps between pluralist and at least one sort of federalist approach to the process of the ever-increasing union between the European peoples. Two strands in federalist thinking, the legal/ constitutional and the sociological, have been identified (Pentland, 1973: 147–192).[2] The legal/constitutional is the oldest approach to the integration process because it is embedded in theories of social contract in terms of which previously sovereign entities come together to recognise a new higher authority. In the schemes for perpetual peace, such as that of the abbé Saint Pierre in the eighteenth century, states should do this in order to avoid wars between them. The classic example of building a federal constitution according to the contractual model is that of the Philadelphia convention which drafted the constitution of the United States. The sociological approach to federalism, the most distinguished exponent of which is Carl Friedrich (1968), has almost the same definition of the nature of federalism, although it uses the language of power and political values, rather than the legal language of authority and competences; sociological federalism is also more concerned with the social organisation which sustains federal arrangements and proposes that sociological rather than legal tests must be employed to assess the degree of federalism within a system.

Both strands are concerned with federation as the end product of European integration. Federation is neatly defined by Wheare (1963: 10):

'By the federal principle I mean the method of dividing powers so that the general and regional governments are each, within a sphere, coordinate and independent.' The only way in which this arrangement can be arrived at is through an explicit political bargain. Federalism means that there are some federal laws, some state laws and some which both levels have the right to adjudicate. In principle, in a federation, it would be possible to have all law enforcement or police in the hands of the states; this is inconvenient and hard to sustain in the long run as the examples of the USA, Germany and Australia illustrate – all of whom have gradually developed a federal policing capacity despite an initial intention to vest police powers in the states, *Länder* or provinces. In general the debate over police powers is likely to be parallel but not identical with the development of legislative/judicial authority at the federal level – the more federal legislation is enacted the greater becomes the pressure for a federal law enforcement capacity. This is reflected in recent European experience where the debate over Europol and closer European police cooperation has taken place partly as a response to practical problems of law enforcement and partly as a consequence of the growth of European law.

All these four approaches seem to offer some guidance about the nature, form and direction of police cooperation in Europe and all four seem to find echoes in practical discussions.[3] Although some aspects of, for example, sociological federalism and neo-functionalism are similar, there are also significant differences between the four approaches. There is a basic clash between those who believe, like many functionalists,[4] that there is an irresistible dynamic leading to European union, based on underlying systemic factors and those who reject this assumption, believing that European union, if it is ever achieved will result from a series of steps in constitution building and, at some point, one big step into federal union. In the field of the 'noble' or regalian functions of the state – foreign affairs, law-making, external and internal security–federal solutions have not yet been adopted in Europe.

The citizenship chapter of the Maastricht Treaty on Political Union was a significant step in a federal direction which has implications for policing. The Treaty defines certain political rights in the EC, adding to the economic and social rights set out in the Treaty of Rome. A core problem in fully developing EC citizenship is the belief, almost universally held, that there is something special about fellow countrymen/women (Goodin, 1988). The difficulty for European federalists is how to revive old notions of dual, or multiple, loyalty and obligation, commonplace in medieval Europe but alien to modern secular thought. For effective criminal law enforcement in the new Europe, obligation to assist police in all 12 jurisdictions should be felt by the whole population of the European Community. This obligation must be based, first, on trust in the police institutions of other EC countries and, second, on a convincing justification for having this obligation.

The rhetorical justification of police cooperation

The shallow nature of the arguments for further improvements in the quality of police cooperation, often proposed by ministers and police agencies with their own agendas, is a particular illustration of the necessity of new conceptions of the European Community. Creating fantasies and fears about potential threats to internal security concerning a flood of illegal immigrants bringing with them drugs, arms dealing, organised crime and racketeering may have a certain populist appeal but it is not an adequate substitute for ethical arguments on which to base new obligations.

Threats to internal security posed by criminal activities are real but often temporary. The first stimulus towards EC police cooperation, the setting up of the Trevi group in 1975, was in the area of political crime or terrorism. This had echoes of the 1898 secret anti-anarchist conference which the Italian government convened in Rome to help to secure intergovernmental cooperation in tracking down anarchists (Jensen, 1981). In the 1970s 'international terrorism' was regarded as a scourge in much the same way as anarchism in the late nineteenth century. The unpreparedness of governments and the shock created by such incidents as the massacre of Israeli athletes at the 1972 Munich Olympics provided a simple and clear issue to gather support for police cooperation. 'The fight against international terrorism' is too narrow and difficult an issue to develop broad operational cooperation between police forces. Moreover, terrorist incidents, particularly those associated with the Middle East, have been in decline since the mid-1980s.

Terrorist acts profoundly alarm public opinion in Western Europe and have been used on many occasions to plead the case for greater international police cooperation. For example, on 10 March 1987, President Mitterrand said on Spanish television: 'Since terrorism is international, investigation, prevention, repression and sanctions should also be international.' Numerous statements have been made by government leaders suggesting that terrorism has become genuinely international through informal links and mutual aid between terrorist groups, and through state sponsorship of terrorism – especially by Libya, Syria and Iran. Outrage over terrorism has supported several initiatives in international cooperation – in addition to the Trevi group, notable examples are the 1977 European Convention on the Suppression of Terrorism, the 1979 EC Dublin Declaration on Terrorism, and the 1984 decision by the General Assembly of Interpol to accept messages concerning terrorist acts through its communications network. Cooperation on counter-terrorism is a difficult area partly because counter-terrorist action within states invariably includes the security services. Coordination between police and security services within states is usually *ad hoc*; security services are bound to maintain their own international networks about which the police have no knowledge. Institutionalised cooperation both within and between states poses problems. Also, terrorist acts have a political context which usually defies attempts by governments and law enforcement agencies to separate the 'criminal' acts from their 'political' background. A change in political circumstances or the resolution of a political problem often results in the decline or the ending of terrorism which is not usually the case for other forms of criminality. Nonetheless, the issue of terrorism has done much to make familiar the idea of the European Community as a security community and initiate the first moves to giving it a practical form.[5]

The second area of criminality with the potential to legitimise close cooperation is the increasing traffic in narcotic and psychotropic drugs. In most EC countries, public opinion seems unequivocally to support a hard-line repressive policy on drugs (although this may be changing). Intensive consultations on drugs policies have been carried on since the early 1970s through the Council of Europe's Pompidou group. However, in both police circles and public opinion it is generally recognised that this is not a specifically European problem for which there can be European solutions. The most profitable forms of trafficking involve drug production in poor countries for export to rich countries, and profits are often laundered through off-shore financial institutions. Although the existence of a market for drugs in the rich countries is the cause of the traffic, the emphasis in the developed world has been on police action and repression of the traffic. Presidents Reagan and Bush have announced a 'war on drugs', even mobilising the military and the CIA in the fight, and the 1988 United Nations convention on drugs is almost entirely devoted to harmonisation of repressive measures. Drug trafficking is often carried out by complex criminal conspiracies and this provides a broader basis for international, although not necessarily intra-European, police cooperation than terrorism.

The specific justification for European police cooperation given most prominence recently and the underpinning of the Trevi Action Programme of June 1990, is the necessity of *'actions compensatoires'* (compensations) to make up for the loss of frontier controls. A plausible assumption was that certain kinds of criminality would be facilitated by the dismantling of frontier controls. However, it is difficult to mobilise opinion about hypothetical possibilities by contrast with the ease with which opinion is aroused by current feelings of insecurity (Walker, 1991: 43–44). This partly explains, within the context of the police and criminal justice debate, the emphasis on the dangers of free movement of persons in the Communities as they relate to immigration of non-EC nationals. The issue of non-EC immigrants disturbs all the electorates in the Community countries, especially in Germany which is open to asylum seekers and economic migrants from the East Central European countries and further afield. The Maastricht Treaty includes a commitment to move towards a coordinated approach on matters such as asylum, external border crossings and immigration policy, and the EC Commission can take an initiative on these matters. A coordinated approach to them clearly requires law enforcement cooperation, although this is excluded from the competence of the EC Commission.[6]

One advantage of focusing opinion on the immigration issue for law enforcement cooperation is that it coincides with the EC Commission's concern to promote a secure external frontier for the Community when controls at internal frontiers are dismantled. This 'ring-fence' solution, encapsulated in the Palma document and more recently by the Report on the *Ad Hoc* Group on Immigration prepared for the Maastricht Conference,[7] has implications wider than immigration. The immigration issue, however, makes it comprehensible and popular to millions of citizens in the EC member states. Severe immigration restrictions are, of course, condemned by liberal, leftist and third world orientated groups as an expression of 'fortress Europe' – an irresponsible attempt to seal off the European Community from the troubles and problems of the rest of the world. Defenders of civil liberties are also concerned that 'fortress Europe' will lead to non-accountable policing of migrants from non-EC countries (Spencer, 1990; den Boer, 1993). These contrary views can mobilise only small minorities and loud expressions of them almost certainly mobilises opinion against them which could strengthen support for closer police cooperation.

Recent European Councils have invariably coupled immigration and criminal justice issues in their post-Council programmes of action and this is likely to persist in the future. Specific examples of criminal law-breaking, particularly in the drugs and terrorist fields, will also be used to reinforce the case for police cooperation in the European Community from time to time but they lack the advantages of immigration as a continuing *leitmotif*. Since immigration concerns the movement of persons originating from outside the European Community, this theme also has a link with racism which could result in serious political and social difficulties.

Recent history and unresolved questions

The history of practical police cooperation in Europe can be briefly told. Until recently, it is a story of pragmatic responses to particular pressures. The main instrument of cooperation has been and, at the operational level, still is Interpol. The message traffic passing through Interpol has always been overwhelmingly European in origin and in destination. Steps towards creating a 'Europol', a specifically European form of police cooperation, were first taken within Interpol itself.

Moves within Interpol to establish a European regional tier began in the 1970s when the SEPAT (Stupéfiants Europe Plan d'Action à Terme) was introduced and led to the introduction of police liaison officers for each of the major European countries in Interpol Headquarters to assist with requests for information concerning their own countries (Anderson, 1989: 118, 169–171). A European Regional Conference was also established; at the 1981 meeting of this conference the German delegation proposed the setting up of a European Regional Bureau. A group – the Technical Committee for Cooperation in Europe – was set up to examine the feasibility of this proposal. This committee has met regularly ever since and, inter alia, has proposed a European secretariat within

Interpol Headquarters (established in 1986). But various frustrations about Interpol resulted in the term Europol being associated with setting up an organisation entirely outside Interpol (Fijnaut and Hermans, 1987: 38–39).

Two institutions unconnected with Interpol have been established – the Trevi group and the Schengen system. Both operate outside the framework of the Communities as intergovernmental arrangements; the first came into existence in 1975 under the authority of European Political Cooperation, the second is based on two agreements reached in Luxembourg in 1985 and 1990, whose signatories now include 9 of the 12 members of the EC. The Trevi system is in transition (and will probably disappear after the full ratification of the Maastricht Treaty) but at the time of writing only one of the committees of the Trevi group has had a direct operational role: Trevi I, the original core of the institution, contained a secure communications link between the relevant ministries in the Community countries for passing sensitive anti-terrorist intelligence between them. The other Trevi groups are essentially consultative groups, although informal policy coordination has been achieved through them with Trevi IV – the 1992 committee – which played an overall coordinating role until it was disbanded.

The recent basis of Trevi activities is the Action Programme of June 1990. This programme was a synthesis of all measures on which the 12 were agreed (without always having the legal instruments in place to carry them out). The order of the subjects in the programme gives some indication of the relative importance attributed to them. After a preamble stating that the Trevi system does not prejudice previously established agreements and systems such as Interpol, the first topic is 'combating terrorism'. The question now raised by this paragraph is whether the 'rapid and protected communications system which the Trevi Group Conference of ministers decided to establish in London on 25 September 1986' will continue to have a separate existence in the light of other established and planned systems of communication.

Paragraph 3 on combating drug traffic contains an impressive list of areas and forms of cooperation, including controlled delivery, the use of joint teams, and training and research programmes. The European Drugs Intelligence Unit (abbreviated to the European Drugs Unit before it was transformed into Europol) is agreed in principle in this paragraph, although not yet established because no decision has been taken on its location. This is essentially a clearing house for information held by national drugs intelligence units and would ensure the effective communication among them of all matters related to investigation, repression and prevention. The European Drugs Unit is the basis on which Europol is to be initially developed and it would be relatively easy to broaden its remit to include cross-border serious and organised crime, a subject treated in paragraph 4 of the Trevi Action Programme.[8] A second basis is through the development of the liaison officer system possibly in conjunction with the European Information System[9] envisaged in paragraph 15 of the Action Programme. The system of liaison officers receives relatively detailed attention in paragraph 9. This paragraph carefully preserves the principle of sovereignty but encourages the full cooperation of national authorities with liaison officers from other European Community member states, even going as far as giving them access to national criminal intelligence computer files. Paragraph 10 also envisages close coordination of the activities of the liaison officers of member states operating outside the European Community.

The inter-ministerial agreement on Europol, concluded between the governments of the Twelve in 1993, gave a restricted remit to gather and exchange information about drug trafficking. In the longer term, Europol may be established with broad terms of reference covering all aspects of internal security and bringing together all the existing operational arrangements contained within Trevi and Schengen, and include new forms of cooperation such as a European Police Institute. At the moment, the future is uncertain because of unwillingness on the part of the northern periphery of the European Community (Denmark, Ireland and the United Kingdom) to accept significant moves towards institutionalised and formalised police cooperation which goes beyond information exchange.

These same three countries are not signatories of the Schengen Agreements (den Boer, 1991). The operational facility, the Schengen Information System – a data-base giving basic information about criminal matters (wanted persons, stolen cars, etc.) and about prohibited immigrants to which the national police of the member countries will have on-line access – is complemented by an emergency system called Sirène – national offices (staffed by lawyers as well as police officers to check on the legality of the action requested) receiving calls for immediate operational assistance. France was the only country to ratify Schengen without delay,[10] but the contract for the computer facility necessary for the Schengen Information System located in Strasbourg was agreed in a meeting in Rome in December 1991, and the Sirène system could be introduced in most countries by executive action. However, the new 1993 right wing government in France caused considerable dismay in the Schengen countries and in the EC Commission by adjourning *sine die* the abolition of frontier controls, and thereby undermined the reason for having the Schengen Agreement. The reasons given were lack of confidence in Italian immigration controls and objections to the drugs policy of the Netherlands which facilitated the import of drugs into France.

The Maastricht agreement and police cooperation

The reason why the word 'federal' became such an issue for the United Kingdom in the period before the Maastricht intergovernmental conferences was that the Major government, or at least an influential section of the Conservative party, objected to the EC acquiring some of the characteristics and competences of a state. Some argue that this was already the case because EC law is directly applicable in the member states and takes precedence over national law, because the EC Commission has genuine executive authority in international economic negotiations, and because Community regulations are directly enforceable in the member states. But the British government can maintain that, as long as the Council of Ministers is the legislative body for the Community and as long as the Communities have a severely limited role in the 'noble' areas of state action, the EC is an intergovernmental organisation. Opponents maintain their view that the European Communities are much more than an intergovernmental organisation; they have autonomous authority which is steadily growing and will continue to do so until a state of political union is reached. In the context of rapidly evolving global relationships, this difference between the UK and its European partners may be marginalised or may be confirmed as a fundamental clash of political outlook or may expose the British position as a political bluff or tactic.

The European Community agenda remains open despite apparently the important decisions of principle taken at Maastricht such as the fixing of a timetable for a single currency. The openness is particularly apparent in the field of home affairs and police cooperation. On this subject, the text approved by the Maastricht conference on 13 December was virtually a blank page on which a text would have to be written subsequently. Opposition to the Article on police cooperation was therefore muted. The Netherlands was critical before the meeting but because it held the Presidency of the conferences it stayed silent in the interests of getting an overall agreement, while the UK was critical but willing to accept the Article because it seemed not to go beyond intergovernmental cooperation.[11]

The declaration of the Conference explicitly acknowledged the German lead[12] on police cooperation by confirming the agreement to the German delegation's proposals at the European Council Meeting in Luxembourg on 28–29 June 1991. The headings under which support was affirmed were:

- support for national criminal investigation and security authorities, in particular in the coordination of investigation and search operations;

- creation of data-bases;

- central analysis and assessment of information in order to take stock of the situation and identify investigative approaches;

- collection and analysis of national programmes for forwarding to member states and for drawing up Europe-wide prevention strategies;

- measures relating to further training, research, forensic matters and criminal records departments.

The Conference further agreed that it would consider on the basis of a report during 1994, at the latest, whether such cooperation should be extended.

The general effect of Maastricht was to sanction discussions which were already proceeding. The Treaty did not mark any bold initiative which would clearly establish the future direction of police cooperation. But Maastricht presaged the eventual amalgamation of the Trevi group into a committee with a wider remit, known as the 'K4 Committee' after the article of the Treaty. Maastricht also gave the Commission very limited rights of initiative in areas which impinge directly on policing – asylum, visa policy, control of the external frontier; in future, this toehold will doubtless be exploited to the full. The overall effect, largely thanks to Chancellor Kohl, was to move the issue of police cooperation higher on the political agenda with every chance that it will remain there. But an operational Europol with executive power is still a long way off. As van Outrive, the *rapporteur* on Europol for the Committee on Civil Liberties and Internal Affairs, stated in the European Parliament: 'At present we do not have the political, legal and procedural structures we would need for an operational European federal police force.'[13]

Implications of closer police cooperation on domestic policing and criminal justice

The potential impact can be assessed only on the basis of uncertain assumptions such as that the Scandinavian countries, Switzerland and Austria will become members of the Community around the end of the century but that the East Central European countries and Turkey will not; that Britain and Ireland will be drawn within the Schengen system via a modification of the European Information System; that there will be no social conflict in the Community which will lead one country to adopt internal security policies radically different from the others (for example, France in relation to recent changes in Algeria); that no major member state will commence or will persist in distancing itself from European integration and that changes in the global system will not have severely disruptive effects on the European Communities. Future trends can only be assessed within the framework of one of the theories outlined in the first section of this chapter. The neo-functionalist position is adopted here – the decision-makers make policy subject to certain pressures because of the functional requirements of the system as a whole, as well as certain sub-systems within it.

The first pressure which may be felt is in the direction of harmonisation of criminal justice procedures. It will be hard to resist the practical arguments in favour of automatic extradition; the UK and Ireland may resist, if past history is any guide: it took the UK 32 years to ratify the European Convention on Mutual Legal Assistance and 34 years to ratify the European Convention on Extradition. Other countries, lacking a historical practice of extraditing their own nationals may also have hesitations. In the longer run, and provided that the UK does not retain the panoply of its frontier controls, the island members of the EC may be expected to fall in line. If fugitive criminals can pass frontiers without let or hindrance, there is an overwhelming argument for returning them without delay. There will also be arguments in favour of some harmonisation of criminal law procedures in other areas such as the rules concerning the transfer of evidence.

This first form of pressure may lead to a second – a move towards identifying serious crimes, as 'Eurocrimes', subject to similar penalties and capable of being proscribed anywhere in the Community. This would open the way to a Europol with police powers. But influential opposition to this kind of harmonisation may be expected. Lord Mackay of Clashfern (1992), the Lord Chancellor of Scottish origin who is head of the judiciary in England and Wales, specifically and strongly rejected moves towards overall criminal law harmonisation in a speech in Strasbourg in January 1992.

A third pressure is one immediately felt by the Schengen system and Europol – the necessity for agreed general rules on data protection. The criminal intelligence dimension is only one of many aspects of data protection which are being confronted in the process of completing the single market, but here civil liberties issues are most acute. As Charles Raab illustrates in his contribution, the draft convention on data protection is being driven by pressures other than those arising from law enforcement.

A fourth pressure will be for a standard form of central facility in each country which the police forces of other countries can contact directly, along the lines of the *Sirène* bureaux in the Schengen system, and these may well be coordinated with the Interpol NCBs. This could generate a demand for the 'officialisation' of the informal police force to police force contacts which already take place, as direct personal contact will increase in the investigation of complex crimes by police forces in different countries. One area in which this is likely to take place on a greatly expanded scale is financial fraud, and this poses serious problems because of the very different approaches to fraud in the legal systems of the member states.

A fifth pressure will be for an increased level of exchanges between police forces, common training facilities for officers heavily involved in European cooperation, training modules for all officers in the implications of the closer contacts with other European countries and so on. This could be associated with a move to define a European-wide police deontology or code of professional/ethical standards. This has hardly been discussed in the run-up to 1992 but it could be associated with ideas about a European Police Academy or Institute (van Reenen, 1992). It could emerge as a pre-emptive move by the professional police milieu to shape the form which police accountability may take at the European level.

A sixth form of pressure will be for accountability of police officers involved in European cooperation. Exchanges of services or favours across frontiers can lead to abuses, for example, of the civil rights of immigrants and of the unauthorised communication of sensitive information about individuals. This, in conjunction with general suspicions of the police, will lead to demands (already being made by the Committee on Civil Liberties and Internal Affairs of the European Parliament) for an effective European complaints system, complete transparency of the systems of cooperation and, at least indirect, accountability to the European

Parliament. It is hard to envisage any parliamentary accountability being particularly robust and a well-conceived individual complaints mechanism (perhaps modelled on Interpol's supervisory board; Anderson, 1989: 65–66) could partially fill the gap. There could be pressure from the police themselves for some system of accountability to deflect political attacks from the political left and civil liberties groups which could gain wide credence if there were abuses. The attack on police cooperation has already started, well exemplified by a meeting of the Greens in the European Parliament, the Greens in the Bundestag and others held on 12 and 13 July 1990.[14]

The final form of pressure is the changing pattern of criminality and the police and societal responses provoked by them, which is largely unpredictable. A plausible assumption is, however, that increasingly crimes against persons and against property will have transfrontier aspects and implications. This will increase public acceptance of close police and judicial cooperation but it will also create greater sensitivities about the ways in which nationals of one country are treated by the authorities in another. Press and public comment about practices in other jurisdictions are likely to increase.

Conclusion

The momentum to create Europol is now underway. Eurosceptics have not made it a target of their hostility, despite the encouragement given to their views by Raymond Kendall, the Secretary General of Interpol, at a meeting at the House of Commons in January 1992. The agreement to establish Europol in the Maastricht Treaty and in the draft Europol convention is provisional; it provides a framework within which more detailed arrangements may be worked out later. There remain more questions than answers about Europol. The location of its secretariat and headquarters staff has proven controversial. The relationship between the Europol convention and other conventions and agreements such as Schengen and the External Borders Convention, as well as between Europol and the information collection and intelligence exchanges, envisaged by the European Intelligence System (EIS) and the Schengen Information System (SIS), remain unresolved. The division of tasks between Europol and Interpol will become an issue in the future. Whether Europol can act as an effective liaison with agencies outside the EC such as the US Drugs Enforcement Administration (DEA) and the Central and Eastern European police forces has to be decided. One problem with the slow start of Europol is the potential damage to its credibility as an effective instrument of law enforcement cooperation in police forces. Partly as a consequence, operational cooperation may come from outside Europol through cooperation between, for example, serious fraud offices and other specialised police agencies, leaving Europol confined to the drugs field – and political consensus on drugs policies in the repression of drug-trafficking.

Several political 'layers' will influence the development of police cooperation. Provided there is political harmony the professional law enforcement layer will be a crucially important one because police practices will gradually evolve which are more or less acceptable to governments and public opinion. The emerging system of police cooperation will not operate simply according to officially sanctioned formal rules. Informal systems of doing business will inevitably emerge: networking, apparent in all areas of European Community endeavour, will spread in the police milieu; unexpected crime problems will emerge which require the adaptation of practices. The values, perceptions and attitudes of police officers within the states will affect the nature and quality of cooperation. Some police forces and law enforcement agencies will be enthusiasts for cooperation whilst others will be reticent.

However, it is much more likely that internal security will be a high-profile political issue because policing a very diverse social and cultural area such as the EC is inevitably going to cause controversy. This will result in high-profile intervention of other political 'layers' – governments, parliaments, parties, organised groups, loose networks, street agitators and the media. Questions concerning racism and xenophobia, the policing of ethnic minorities, strikers and protesters cannot be politically neutral. Certain policing methods and techniques such as identity checks, electronic surveillance devices and the use of firearms, as well as differences in criminal procedure, sentencing and penal policy are highly controversial within the EC. As the EC jurisdictions draw closer together, these controversies will become transnational. This will create pressures for governments to take action to reduce conflicts and tensions; this action will often have to be at the collective European level.

Effective police cooperation should be based on a belief that it contributes to the improvement of the security of the citizens, defends their rights and liberties, and is essential for effective repression of important categories of crime. This can only happen when there is a broadening of the notion of European citizenship. The majority of the population must be convinced they have rights and duties in the EC as a whole as well as in their own country. The economic and social rights guaranteed to individuals by the Treaty of Rome have now been supplemented by political rights. This citizenship carries with it the right to vote and to stand for election in municipal and European elections for every EC national resident in another country of the Community; it is probably only a matter of time before reciprocal rights to vote in national elections are accorded. Individuals have acquired the beginnings of a dual citizenship – citizenship of their own country as well as the European Community – with the strong possibility that it will develop into full dual citizenship. Already the British police in dealing with a French national are no longer dealing with an alien but, in the terminology of the Maastricht Treaty, with a fellow citizen. In the new Europe, it is difficult to argue, as Walzer (1983) has done that the sphere of justice is limited to the boundaries of the state.

Explanatory theories, tinged with positivism, of European integration – the preponderant form of theorizing in the first phase of the EC – are insufficient for the purposes of analysing, or indeed effectively promoting, police cooperation. Both for intellectual and for practical reasons, the difficult issue of citizens' duties and obligations beyond the frontiers of the states must be engaged. There are many strands of political and legal theory which are relevant to this issue. There is not one but several justifications of closer police cooperation – practical, moral, political; the key actors in the policy-making process are unlikely to be agreed on a particular justification because of differences in their political, social and cultural backgrounds. Whether closer police cooperation happens depends on whether there is broad support in the governments and administrations of the EC and on whether key decision-makers are determined to see it happen. The crucial steps in the medium and long term are some harmonisation of the criminal law and criminal law procedures and an operational role for a European police. These will meet strong resistance but they are a more important test of the commitment of European governments to a genuine union of European states than any integration of economic policies.

Notes

1 This is particularly the case with more recent formulations of the neo-functionalist position such as Keohane and Hoffman (1990).
2 There is a third strand which has been influenced by Proudhon which considers that federalism can be an all pervasive principle of social organisation. Some partisans of European integration such as R. Pelloux and Henri Brugmans are very much in this tradition.
3 The various arguments of the 'Eurosceptics' are, for the purposes of this paper, ignored. In the domain of police cooperation, however, one is worth taking particularly seriously. This is the view that there are various powerful forces underpinning global integration but it is not possible to predict with any certainty the direction that this will take – the possibility that any tidy scheme of the European Union being realised is not very great because all blueprints and reasonable schemes are likely to be derailed by global developments.
4 Not all do. The recent revisionist analysis by Streeck and Schmitter (1991), which could be classed as functionalist, takes the contrary view.
5 This theme is impressively developed in a paper (with a restricted circulation) by Didier Bigo presented at a seminar on the Schengen Agreements and the Trevi group at the Fondation nationale des sciences politiques, Paris 25 October 1991.
6 See annex 2 of the Treaty on Political Union.
7 *Report from the Ministers Responsible for Immigration to the European Council meeting in Maastricht on Immigration and Asylum Policy*, Brussels 3 December 1991 SN 4038/91 (WGI 930).
8 *International Enforcement Law Reporter*, January 1992, 8 (1), 14–16. One major problem will be defining exactly what is covered by 'cross border serious and organised crime.'
9 The development of the EIS is coordinated by the French – its relations with SIS are, as yet, undecided.

10 A Schengen 'control committee' of the French Senate set up on 26 June 1991 made a highly critical report of the agreements published on 18 December 1991; this was too late to affect the French government's position but may have influenced parliamentary opinions in other countries. *Agence Europe* reported a meeting in December 1991 of MPs from the eight countries who had joined Schengen in order better to inform themselves of its implications.

11 *NRC Handelsblad*, 10 December 1991.

12 Voices had been raised in Germany since the 1970s proposing a European police agency (Cullen, 1992: 78).

13 *Debates of the European Parliament*, 21 January 1993, No. 3–426/281.

14 For a report see *Les Cahiers de la sécurité intérieure*, 1990, 1 (2), 220–221.

References

Anderson, M. (1989), *Policing the World. Interpol and the Politics of International Police Cooperation*, Oxford, Clarendon Press.

Boer, M. den (1991), *Schengen: Intergovernmental Scenario for Police Cooperation*, A System of European Police Cooperation after 1992, Working Paper V, Edinburgh.

Boer, M. den (1993), *Immigration, Internal Security and Policing in Europe*, A System of European Police Cooperation after 1992, Working Paper VIII, Edinburgh.

Brodeur, J.P. (1983), 'High Policing and Low Policing: Remarks about the Policing of Political Activities', *Social Problems*, **3**, 5, 507–520.

Cullen, P. (1992), *The German Police and European Cooperation*, A System of European Police Cooperation after 1992, Working Paper II, Edinburgh.

Fijnaut, C. and Hermans, R.H. (Eds.) (1987), *Police Cooperation in Europe*, Lochem, Van den Brink.

Friedrich, C.J. (1968), *Trends in Federalism in Theory and Practice*, New York, Praeger.

Goodin, R.E. (1988), 'What is so Special about our Fellow Countrymen?', *Ethics*, **98**, 4.

Haas, E.B. (1975), *The Obsolescence of Regional Integration Theory*, California University, Institute of International Studies, Research Series no. 25.

Herz, J.H. (1959), *International Politics in the Atomic Age*, New York, Columbia University Press.

Herz, J.H. (1968), 'The Impact of the Technological-Scientific Process on the International System', in A.A. Said (Ed.), *Theory of International Relations*, Englewood Cliffs, Prentice-Hall.

Jensen, R.B. (1981), 'The International Anti-Anarchist Conference of 1898 and the Origins of Interpol', *Journal of Contemporary History*, **16**, 323–347.

Keohane, R. and Hoffman, S. (1990), 'Community Politics and Institutional Change', in W. Wallace (Ed.), *The Dynamics of European Integration*, London, Pinter.

Lindberg, L.N. (1963), *The Political Dynamics of European Integration*, Stanford, Stanford University Press.

Lord Mackay of Clashfern (1992), *Diversity in Unity – European Laws*, 1992 Churchill Memorial Lecture.

Pentland, C. (1973), *International Theory and European Integration*, London, Faber.

Reenen, P. van (1992), 'Today's Training: A European Police Institute', in M. Anderson and M. den Boer (Eds.), *European Police Co-operation. Proceedings of a Seminar*, Department of Politics, University of Edinburgh, 131–145.

Spencer, M. (1990), *1992 and All That; Civil Liberties in the Balance*, London, Civil Liberties Trust.

Streeck, W. and Schmitter, P.C. (1991), 'From National Corporatism to Transnational Pluralism: Organised Interests in the Single European Market', *Politics and Society*, **19**, 2, 133–165.

Walker, N. (1991), *The United Kingdom Police and European Police Cooperation*, A System of European Police Cooperation after 1992, Working Paper III, Edinburgh.

Walzer, M. (1983), *Spheres of Justice*, Oxford, Blackwell.

Wheare, K.C. (1963), *Federal Government* (4th edn), London, Oxford University Press.

2

EUROPEAN INTEGRATION AND EUROPEAN POLICING: A COMPLEX RELATIONSHIP

Neil Walker

The aim of this chapter is to examine the precise nature of the relationship between new transnational and supranational initiatives in the police sector on the one hand, and macro-political trends towards integration within the European Community (EC) on the other. The issue is one of profound theoretical and practical significance.

Any debate over the future of policing in the European Community raises the question of the relationship between the forms of policing and the forms of political life. In its most general formulation this question asks to what extent, and in what manner, policing arrangements within a community are informed by, and informative of the broader institutions, practices and ideas in terms of which that community constitutes itself as a political entity. When social scientists and social theorists conduct this inquiry, they usually do so in either historical or counterfactual terms. They may engage in retrospective analysis of the manner in which the unfolding forms of political life within different societies have become interwoven with the development of a policing capacity (Robinson and Skaglion, 1987). Alternatively, they may proceed by means of hypothetical discussion, attempting to gain insight into the broader significance of policing institutions by asking what difference it would make to the wider polity if such institutions had not evolved in their present form (Bittner, 1971; Cohen, 1985; Klockars, 1985). Both methods have their limitations – their analytical blind spots. The historical method risks confusing consequences with causes (Brogden, 1990); just because police institutions develop in response to a particular configuration of social and political pressures does not mean that the contemporary relationship of these institutions to the wider political domain remains explicable in these original terms. By contrast, the counterfactual approach focuses more closely upon the contemporary relevance of policing institutions. However, the attempt to make sense of the world as it is by reference to other possible worlds is by definition a speculative enterprise; the answers to the 'what if' questions – the causal models in terms of which alternative scenarios are constructed – are not susceptible to empirical refutation.[1]

If, instead, the inquiry were directed towards current developments in policing institutions occurring against a backdrop of structural change in the wider political sphere, the pitfalls of historical and counterfactual approaches alike could be avoided. On a global canvas, the underlying institutional and conceptual grid which shapes policing remains embedded in the traditional structures and ideologies of the nation state. But the developing mosaic of the EC provides an outstanding exception. As a novel form of political order the EC has begun to challenge the hegemony of the nation state and has come to rank alongside the latter as a key unit of political organisation. Hence, the shifting pattern of mutual influences, of legal and political competences, and of competing claims to legitimacy, which characterises the relationship between the new political order and its more traditional rivals.

Inquiry into the relationship between police development and political development in contemporary Europe also has a pressing practical significance. Some critics have bemoaned the piecemeal, incremental quality of police institutional development in the new Europe (van Reenen, 1989; Benyon et al., 1990). The internal market programme, triggered by the Single European Act, may have indicated a more coherent approach to internal and external economic relations, but it rendered even more patternless institutional development in the form of 'spillover' (Lindberg, 1963: 289) into areas such as social policy and police and criminal justice cooperation. The explanation for this and its implications for future development are complex and multi-faceted (Streeck and Schmitter, 1991); but in the police and criminal justice sector one associated cause and effect is a sense of *structural fatalism* which is often subscribed to within the professional and policy-making community (van Reenen, 1989; Bentham, 1992). This perspective rests upon an inference that the final shape of policing in the Community depends upon the final shape of the Community itself as a political entity, and that since this wider vision remains hazy and contested it would be pointless to advocate new policing practices and mechanisms on anything other than a provisional, flexible, and modest basis.

An alternative attitude towards police cooperation prevalent within the professional and policy-making community is what might be termed *naive separatism*. From this perspective, models of police cooperation are assessed and evaluated independently of wider political forces. The requirements of international law enforcement are seen as paramount and little attention is given to the *realpolitik* of international relations and how this might impede the development of optimal systems of cooperation. For example, Fijnaut has noted a tendency for blueprints for European police cooperation to set unrealistic timetables and to adopt over-ambitious standards (Fijnaut, 1991). The Benelux Agreement, the Schengen Accord, the security aspects of the 1992 Programme, and, most recently, the Europol initiative, are all testimony to the disappointed expectations of policy-making élites who believed that matters intrinsic to law enforcement could be cordoned off from wider political concerns.

It would seem, therefore, that the two forms of conventional wisdom within professional and policy-making communities as to the relationship of policing to developments beyond the nation state have evinced opposite errors. While structural fatalism treats policing as the dependent variable, naive separatism fails to acknowledge sufficiently the inevitable inter-penetration of policing and wider political matters. Furthermore, although diametrically opposed in theory, these two perspectives may be closely related in practice. Naive separatism tends to beget policies which become politically marginalised, so encouraging structural fatalism. As suggested above, however, the new circumstances of *fin de siècle* Europe should provide an opportunity to challenge such attitudes. The embryonic development of new forms of policing and politics in the EC should not be seen as an occasion to apply old orthodoxies in unreflective fashion, but as an opportunity to gain fresh insights and to place the debate on the future of policing in Europe on a more positive and informed footing.

Policing and the nation state

The nation state is the most powerful reference point for our present understanding of the wider political relevance of policing institutions, and so it is to the concept of the state that we first turn. Despite much debate in social science and social theory during the past twenty years, the state remains an essentially contested concept (Gallie, 1956), for two main reasons. First, within explanatory theory the modern state typically comprises a broad network of institutions and capacities, whose apparently heterogeneous nature allows scope for theorists to reach divergent conclusions in their attempts to locate within its broad framework an underlying operational unity. Second, within normative political theory, conceptions of the state are so bound up with rival notions of the good life as to provide a significant secondary battleground for opposing political ideologies (Jessop, 1990: 339–340).

Nevertheless, there remains an 'overlapping consensus' (Rawls, 1987) across a broad spectrum of opinion as to some of the salient characteristics of the state. This consensus has its philosophical roots in Jean Bodin and Thomas Hobbes' realist account of the absolutist state of the sixteenth and seventeenth centuries, and later sociological roots in Max Weber's analysis of the maturing nation state of the early twentieth century. In particular, Weber's characterisation of the modern state as 'a human community which (successfully) claims the *monopoly of the legitimate use of force* within a given territory' (Weber, 1948: 78) still provides a popular analytical point of departure (Giddens, 1987: ch. 7; Hall and Ikenberry, 1989: ch. 1; Held, 1989; Jessop, 1990: 343; Poggi, 1990: ch. 1). For Weber and others who subscribe to the theory of the *Machtstaat*, it is the direct control of the means of internal and external violence which is *the* distinguishing feature of state power.

A more teleological conception of the state has remained faithful to the Hobbesian tradition insofar as it perceives the 'finalities' (Poggi, 1990: 15) towards which the state is directed as resulting from its possession of a monopoly coercive power. For one writer, the state's coercive power allows it to achieve an 'administrative monopoly over a territory with demarcated boundaries' (Giddens, 1987: 171). To take another example, this power may be viewed as enabling the state 'to define and enforce collectively binding decisions on the members of a society in the name of the common interest or general will' (Jessop, 1990: 341). From this perspective what the state, through its dominant interests, strives most assiduously and effectively to achieve is the consolidation of its own power-base and the maintenance of its own integrity *qua* state.

There are parallels in both form and substance between theories of police and state theory. As to form, policing theory, like state theory, embraces both means-centred and teleological analysis, with the latter emphasising the intimacy of the connection between the ends of police work and the distinctive means available to police agencies. As to substance, key features of both the means and ends of the modern state as conventionally conceived are, within the domain of policing theory, claimed as specific attributes of the police function. Thus, means-based analysis of policing has stressed the position of the police as 'a mechanism for the distribution of non-negotiably coercive force' (Bittner, 1971: 46), and as 'the specialist repository domestically of the state's monopoly of legitimate force' (Reiner, 1992: 49). In short, police is the label and policing the means used by the state when asserting its exclusive title to the use or threat of force against dangers from within its territory. Within the teleological approach there is similar convergence of state theory and police theory. Marenin, for example, has claimed that the role of the police is to protect both 'general and specific order' (Marenin, 1982: 258), the former referring to preserving public tranquillity and the latter to protecting the interests of those in a dominant political and social position.

A more detailed examination of the key themes of police theory reveals an even closer connection between the police function and the broader function of the state. Of the two forms of order which policing protects, the link to the interests of the state is plainly more direct in respect of specific order. Thus Brodeur talks of the tradition of 'high policing', characterised by its propensity to 'reach ... out for potential threats in a systematic attempt to preserve the distribution of power in a given society' (Brodeur, 1983: 513). High policing is about the preservation of the specific forms of order upon which the security of the state most immediately rests, whether through combating terrorist organisations and activities, or through gathering comprehensive information on political dissidence, or through laying contingency plans for the widespread breakdown of public order.

Since the protection of general order involves the preservation of those minimum standards of private security and public peace necessary for the working of *all* societies and from which all social actors benefit, it is difficult to see any more precise connection between this aspect of policing and state interests. However, such a superficial conclusion would be misleading for three reasons. First, although specific order and general order are analytically distinct, in practice particular police activities may achieve both. Activities which pose a direct challenge to the state, such as urban disorder or terrorist attacks on civilians, also threaten the general order of the wider population. Conversely, mainstream policing activities more closely concerned with the maintenance of general public security, such as preventive patrol or detection of criminal offences, are prerequisite to a more specific form of order. Further, such general policing tends to benefit disproportionately those groups whose interests are more closely identified with specific order.

Second, quite apart from this conceptual common ground, the boundaries between specific order and general order may be blurred or broken in certain places. Particular crimes such as drug-trafficking may straddle the border between specific and general order, while criminal networks may embrace a range of practices located at either side of the divide. A third argument which ties the police goal of general order to the interest and authority of states *per se*, and not merely to some abstract, universal interest in stable social order, involves examining means rather than ends. Since the maintenance of order is such an extraordinarily diffuse notion it can involve police officers in an unpredictable range of situations whose only common feature is the need for authoritative resolution, if necessary by coercive means. As we have seen, only the state, with its claim to exclusive control of a distinct territory, possesses the resources to give the police the manpower, equipment and legitimacy necessary to wield this enormous, often discretionary power. The monopoly of coercive power also points to the key role of the police as the residual, or 'stand-in' authority within the state (Cohen, 1985: 37).

This role has to be understood in the light of the broader claim of the state to 'administrative monopoly' within a territory. The overall administrative apparatus of the state may be viewed as a series of policy sectors – education, social welfare, industry, transport, etc. – each subject to a degree of overall appraisal and planning at the macro-political level with reference to matters of broad ideology and questions of deployment of scarce economic resources, but each to some extent autonomous (Dunleavy, 1989). As an activity which transcends narrow sectoral boundaries, policing is exceptional within this vertical division of labour. Police intervention may be required to deal with threats to or breaches of general order as they occur across a range of social activities, many of which are normally governed by a quite separate framework of social control but which periodically experience an 'authority vacuum' (Cohen, 1985: 38). As Cohen argues, '[s]ocial workers, medical personnel, teachers, probation officers, judges, parents and others in identifiable social roles have a wide range of authority they may fail to exercise for one reason or another'; in such circumstances it typically falls to the police, given their general capacity to provide an authoritative solution and their round-the-clock availability, to plug the gap.

This particular aspect of policing is therefore closely connected to the wider interests and authority of the state. It is the state policies and practices in other sectors which provide the defining context for the police in the exercise of their substitutional authority. To take one example, the effectiveness of policing initiatives against drug-trafficking will depend on how they fit into the wider set of social and public health policies by political authorities towards the problem of drug abuse. In general, the police role has to be capable of reasonable coordination with other public services provided by or under the authority of the state.[2]

Can it be suggested that policing function and state interests are in fact inextricably intertwined, or is this assumption unwarranted? In the developing EC this question can be refined in two ways. First, if in the short and medium term, we assume a level of political and institutional integration falling short of that associated with the emergence of a state, can we nevertheless conceive of the development of robust EC–police institutions? Second, and in the longer term, if we turn the question on its head, is it possible to conceive of the emergence of a new West European 'superstate' possessing most of the attributes of a state, but without its own police force? Reduced to essentials, can we have either a police force without a state or a state without a police force?[3]

A police force without a state?

Some commentators have stressed the significance of the single market programme and the broader enterprise of European integration in creating the need for a Community-wide policing facility (Birch, 1989; van Reenen, 1989; Benyon *et al.*, 1990; Walker 1991, 1992, 1993; den Boer and Walker, 1993). The increasing propensity of terrorists, drug traffickers and other more or less organised criminal networks to disregard national boundaries will, it is argued, receive additional stimulus from a free market in goods, people, capital and services, and from the deeper process of social integration which the move towards a common European citizenship will bring. This argument has been inadequately scrutinised and the rhetorical justifications for increased cooperation have received insufficient critical attention (McLaughlin, 1992; see also chs 9 and 10 in the present volume), but the case for enhanced police cooperation remains persuasive. Leaving on one side the normative question whether or not new forms of police cooperation *should* develop, and concentrating upon why they are developing and what further changes lie in store, a tentative explanation can be provided from within the tradition of general European integration theory.

As Anderson (present volume) has argued, while the debate in its current form rarely reaches sophisticated heights, the case for a new policing facility may be underpinned by a neo-functionalist analysis, change flowing from the demands of increased social and economic integration as filtered through political parties, politicians, ministries and law enforcement agencies into a new agenda for cooperation. As against this, however, Anderson argues, a more venerable realist/pluralist tradition would hold that entrenched notions of national sovereignty are likely to act as a 'veto in the background' on the operation of a neo-functionalist dynamic in the policing domain. Therefore, the overall prognosis available by reference to general themes in the 'pre-theory' – as Haas (1971) characterised the debate on European integration – is a mixed one, which we must investigate below.

Recent trends in European police cooperation

The Luxembourg and Maastricht summits of 1991 in which the delibera-tions of the IGC on political union were moulded into a new draft treaty witnessed the first stirrings of institutional recognition of the Europol idea. The decisions endorsed could be said to signal the end of the beginning of the debate on police cooperation within the EC. Since 1976 the Trevi group has provided the anchor of an intergovernmental approach to policing matters, and internal security policy more generally; viewed against this modest development, the incorporation of an embryonic Europol in the new Treaty on European Union endorsed at Maastricht represents a significant departure. However, its precise meaning and import remains deeply ambiguous.

On the one hand, Europol may provide the foundations for a system of 'vertical integration' (van Reenen, 1989: 48–49) in the form of a genuinely supranational police facility with the power to operate throughout the EC area. In its legal and organisational *form* the new institution is in some respects supranational rather than intergovernmental. Its source of authority lies within the EC treaty framework rather than a separate international agreement, and it has a distinct organisational identity rather than simply being a mechanism for coordinating the separate endeavours of member states.

The *substantive measures* to which the member states have committed themselves in the development of Europol and within the arena of police cooperation more generally, involve significant initiatives in operational support and general policing strategy as well as in more modest forms of cooperation (Walker, 1991: 28). As regards operational support, the foundational provision in the Maastricht Treaty envisages development of a system of information exchange to deal with terrorism, drug-trafficking and other serious crimes, which may involve customs authorities as well as police officers (Art. K.1. (9)). The associated Political Declaration commits its signatories to explore the possibility of providing coordination of national investigation and search operations with an international dimension, of creating new data-bases for exchange of information, and of providing a facility for central analysis of information to aid the planning of operational investigations. The Trevi Ministers decided that the first step in the development of Europol should be a Europol Drugs Unit (EDU), building upon an earlier Trevi blueprint for a European Drugs Intelligence Unit, and involving the central analysis of operational intelligence foreshadowed by the Maastricht Political Declaration (Trevi, 1991). This commitment has since bore fruit. A special Trevi *ad hoc* group on Europol was appointed to prepare for the establishment of the new organisation, and, in turn, this spawned a Europol project team, instituted at Strasbourg in September 1992, to work on the practicalities of the EDU (Fode, 1993). Eventually, a formal Ministerial Agreement setting out the working remit for the EDU was signed at the Trevi ministerial meeting in Copenhagen in June 1993, so paving the way for a pioneering unit.[4] On broader strategy questions, the Maastricht Political Declaration announced a commitment on the part of member states to explore supranational initiatives in respect of crime prevention policy, while a similar commitment was made to joint endeavours in training, research, forensic science and criminal records. Since then, numerous projects along these lines have been pursued in a variety of Trevi Working Groups operating under the earlier, but similar, remit of the Trevi Action Programme which had been established at the Dublin meeting of the European Council in 1990.

The *broader regulatory context* is also in some respects favourable to the Europol initiative. The Maastricht Treaty brings the whole area of justice and home affairs cooperation closer to the mainstream framework of the EC. Member states are also committed to regard as 'common interest' policies on immigration, asylum and external borders, and strategies to combat international fraud and drug addiction, as well as matters falling under the rubric of judicial cooperation in civil and criminal matters, and customs cooperation (Art. K.1–K.8). Policy on visas for third country nationals is brought explicitly within the legislative competence of the Community (Art. 100C), while provision is made for the adoption of joint positions and international conventions across the range of justice and home affairs policy (Art. K.3). This will facilitate for more systematic regulation in an area with unratified agreements on asylum and external frontiers policy (HM Government, 1992). The detailed work programme on harmonisation of asylum and immigration policy which was submitted by the immigration ministers and approved at the Maastricht European Council will be implemented over the next few years (*Ad Hoc* Group on Immigration, 1991), and this, too, will be expedited by the more secure legal framework provided in the new treaty. Finally, the expanding remit is also acknowledged at the wider institutional level. The authority of the Council of Ministers is now recognised in this field (Art. K.3), and it will be aided at senior official level by a new Coordinating Committee of permanent representatives (Art. K.4). Indeed, a K4 Committee has already been established in anticipation of the post-Maastricht body,[5] and three steering groups will be established under its auspices, dealing with customs and policing, immigration and judicial cooperation respectively (Woodward, 1993).

There is also a more general backdrop of laws, conventions and institutional developments particular to or inclusive of the EC states in the area of criminal justice cooperation (Home Affairs Committee, 1990). As regards terrorism, drugs and fraud, a network of institutions will provide for policy consultation; at the legal level, there are various international agreements under the United Nations and the Council of Europe for mutual recognition and assistance in police and criminal justice policy

(Hondius, 1993), and an increasing range of pan-Community preventive measures enshrined within EC law.[6] These provide an important supplement to Maastricht; for example, the relationship between the 1991 Directive on Money Laundering (Gilmore, 1991) and the proposal that money laundering and associated organised crime should provide the second phase of the sectoral development of Europol (Trevi, 1991), supports the expansion of the new central policing capacity.

However, in each of these formal, substantive and contextual dimensions of police cooperation, there are other, less positive indicators. Although Europol and policing more generally are accorded recognition within the amended EC Treaty framework, they are not yet fully integrated within the constitutional structure of the Community. Community institutions still lack both legislative and judicial competence in this area.[7] The achievements of Maastricht in strategic and operational matters are limited, as conveyed by the inclusion of a saving provision which guarantees the retention by member states of their existing responsibilities for law and order and internal security (Art. K.2 (2)). The indecisiveness of the Treaty is reflected in the uneven pace of post-Maastricht progress. For example, the Ministerial Agreement on the EDU was delayed beyond the Edinburgh summit in December 1992 because of the disagreement over the site of the new organisation, and this most basic question remained unresolved when the agreement was signed in June 1993. The decision to draft the Convention providing a legal basis for a fully developed Europol was delayed until the Lisbon European Council of June 1992, and the projected completion data for this Convention continued to be measured in years rather than months (Fode, 1993).

The Community legal order remains characterised by a 'pillar' structure, Justice and Home Affairs joining the Common Foreign and Security Policy (CFSP) as an outside column of activity distinct from the Community's main policy sphere. The continuing absence on the part of the Community of direct *legislative* competence in the area of internal security is particularly significant. This is because policing, unlike foreign affairs, is traditionally associated with the attainment of general order in accordance with uniform criteria, and so requires strong underpinning by the universal, authoritative standards typically associated with law. It is, therefore, difficult to envisage any significant police operational role in the absence of an appropriate legal framework at EC level.[8] Substantive criminal law itself, has so far remained entirely outside the competence of the EC (Schutte, 1991; Sevenster, 1992). We must look to the alternative track of bi-lateral and multi-lateral agreements in international law for progress towards criminal law harmonisation. However, despite modest advances (Gilmore, 1992; Hondius, 1993), international law has not yet provided a key medium for reform at this more exalted level.

Another important negative factor is the tendency of the various emergent international policing and criminal justice systems and arrangements to compete with one another (van Reenen, 1989: 49–50; Johnston, 1992: 202). The Interpol and Schengen systems are not necessarily compatible with the Europol idea (den Boer and Walker, 1993; Walker, 1993).[9]

Programmes may be pursued which, at best, are imperfectly coordinated, and at worst, hinder the realisation of each other's full institutional potential.

The present pattern of police cooperation in Europe, therefore, reveals a highly ambiguous message, and it would be premature to draw any firm conclusions as to what level of common police organisation can be sustained by a political entity falling short of a state. However, if we examine the evidence which is available in the light of the hypotheses developed in the previous section, a clearer picture of the limits to growth emerges.

Interpreting the trends

It is a central irony of police cooperation that many areas in which demand for collaboration is greatest are also those which bear most intimately upon state-specific interests. Terrorism is the most obvious example. The organisational sophistication, contact network and scope of activities of many terrorist organisations, whether 'international' or 'transnational',[10] is such that international cooperation is required if they are to be effectively combated. However, these organisations offer such direct and profound threats to state interests that targeted states will jealously guard the right to mount operations and to determine the security context within which such operations take place (Riley, 1991: 9). It is instructive that although the need for cooperation in terrorist matters supplied the initial impetus for the development of Trevi and although anti-terrorism remains a priority in the Maastricht Treaty, it has not figured in early plans to develop Europol.

Public order problems raise a similar, if less acute, dilemma. The Trevi Ministers recently agreed to establish national contact points for public order matters (HC Debs, 20 December 1991, col. 352 (WA)), largely stimulated by football hooliganism (Home Affairs Committee, 1990), although other public order flashpoints exist. Holiday hooliganism and cross-border 'spillover' disorder may be joined by a more calculating strain of international disorder in the form of increased coordination across the EC of fascist fringe groups agitating to stem the flow of immigration from the South and East (Woolacott, 1991). Indeed, in the wake of a spate of attacks on Turkish communities in Germany and France in May 1993, the Trevi ministerial meeting at Copenhagen in June decided to initiate an investigation into the possibility of transnational orchestration of racist violence.[11] Nevertheless, public disorder poses a threat to the security of the individual state, which is perceived to be all the more acute when disorder has political roots. In these circumstances, despite a functional imperative for collaboration, it is difficult to envisage a state ceding authority in its own territory to an external police agency.

Are there similar impediments to the development of operational competence for Europol in the wider dimension of police activity concerned with general order? On the face of it, it would seem not, since the demand for public tranquillity and the prevention and detection of certain common categories of crime transcends boundaries. While there are no immediate prospects of criminal law harmonisation in the EC, there is nevertheless a remarkable similarity between European states in their specification of the main categories of crime.[12] However, three problems associated with supranational competence in the domain of general order remain, corresponding to the general qualifications referred to earlier in discussion of the idea of general order as a neutral standard across states.

First, there is the impossibility of cordoning off questions of general order from those of special order. Even with crimes which have a strong international dimension, but whose treatment has no direct bearing upon the specific order of a particular state, such as road traffic offences (Home Affairs Committee, 1990: x), or car crime and art thefts (Gregory and Collier, 1992; HC. Debs, 10 Dec. 1991, col. 352), the general order to which their suppression contributes is a precondition for securing the specific order of a state. Thus, although there may be no conflict of interests between states, the pooling of operational authority is unlikely unless and until national authorities are persuaded of the competence of any supranational entity.[13]

Second, there are more specific connections. As a crime of considerable common concern to member states, drug-trafficking was chosen as the initial focus for Europol (Trevi, 1991). However, beneath a broad consensus there exists disagreement over the scope of the trafficking problem and the best methods of containing it, which reflects differing national attitudes to the appropriate balance between permissiveness and control. Indeed, the fact that anti-drugs policy strays into the domain of specific order has contributed to the uncertain progress of the EDU. Disagreement over the location of Europol is partly due to the opposition to The Hague by the French government, showing its disapproval of the Dutch policy of licensing the sale of soft drugs.[14]

The tentacles of the networks and syndicates involved in drug trafficking reach across the general order/specific order divide. In order to maximise effectiveness, police strategies in this area may, accordingly, concentrate on the criminal rather than the crime (Dorn et al., 1992: ch. 3), but this may lead law enforcement efforts into sensitive territory. One example is the close relationship between drug trafficking and money laundering, recognised in various international law initiatives (Gilmore, 1991; 1992) and in the provisional agreement of the Trevi Ministers to extend Europol in its next stage to the sphere of money laundering (Trevi, 1991). But as Levi argues, there are too many potential conflicts between national interests for the idea of an 'international Police State' (Levi, 1991: 299) to take root easily in this domain. Money laundering is one of the 'crimes of the powerful' (Pearce, 1976). In a market economy, its regulation demands difficult choices between the circulation of capital, on the one hand, and the intrusion of monitoring devices to trace illicit sources and destinations, on the other. Ultimately, these choices remain questions of specific order.

As recent initiatives of Trevi in the area of organised crime more generally indicate,[15] as international coordination of criminal activity intensifies, the more varied it becomes and the more likely to challenge both specific order and general order. The idea of 'narco-terrorism' (Anderson, 1989: 28) denotes one such bridging activity. Indeed, the links between terrorism and wider criminal activity and organisation are generally very strong within the EC. Examples include the relationship between Mafia groupings and terrorist movements in Italy, and the extensive involvement of the IRA in smuggling, extortion, armed robbery and commercial and construction industry frauds (Fijnaut, 1991: 109–110; Northern Ireland Office, 1993). Insofar as such activities assume international dimensions, difficult questions arise as to how a supranational policing response may be effective without encroaching on states' conceptions of their particular security interests.

The third and final problem with conferring authority on a supranational unit within the domain of general order has to do with the capacity of the police to exercise residual authority across a range of policy sectors. If, as is suggested, there are strong reasons why such authority should be exercised at the same level as the original authority (the individual state level), then this militates against the assumption by a supranational body of the generic policing capacity required to exercise such a role.

The implications of these are not to dismiss the feasibility or deny the legitimacy of a supranational police capacity within the EC as presently constituted, but rather to set limits on such an enterprise. The role of a supranational police agency within the domain of specific order would seem to be strictly limited. Within the domain of general order, too, the jurisdiction of a supranational body may be circumscribed by various factors. Because general order always has some bearing upon the specific order of constituent states, participants in any supranational venture are likely to insist upon high general standards of efficiency and security. Where issues of general order shade into matters of specific order, the competence of a supranational unit may be strictly demarcated and national responsibilities jealously guarded. Finally, the overall profile of any new organisation may be monitored so that it does not reach the point of critical mass distinguishing an agency which is merely the sum of its specialist parts from one which can assume a generic policing role. As the brief history of Europol indicates, the appropriate model is one of incremental rather than exponential expansion, providing an umbrella for particular functions rather than a source of general policing capacity.

A state without a police force?

While there may be limits to the development of the policing remit of the EC in its present form, the picture may alter considerably in the next few years. Following the period of stagnation in the 1970s, from the mid-1980s onwards the Community developed renewed institutional momentum through initiatives such as the 1992 programme, the Single European Act and the Intergovernmental Conferences which preceded the Maastricht Treaty (Keohane and Hoffmann, 1991; Weiler, 1991; Nugent, 1992). If this 'logic of deepening' (Nugent, 1992: 313) is sustained to the beginning of the new millennium, the Community may evolve into an entity with many state-like characteristics. In such circumstances, would the impediments discussed above disappear, and would the EC become the primary authority for the policing of its territories?

A post-Hobbesian state?

It is arguable that even in the most strongly integrationist scenario for long-term change, the EC, as 'a novel form of political domination' (Bryant, 1991: 204), will have a rather different profile from that of the traditional state, and that monopoly control over internal security is particularly vulnerable to exclusion from this new profile. Schmitter has recently depicted the developing Community structure as a prototype 'post-Hobbesian state', or 'European supranational nonstate' (Schmitter, 1990 [discussed in Bryant, 1991]; Streeck and Schmitter, 1991: 152). The distinctive precondition of such an entity is 'the absence of military insecurity as the overriding motive/excuse for the exercise of political authority'. The state in the Hobbesian world order, although not necessarily born of military struggle, typically emerges 'when the accumulation and concentration of coercive means grow together' (Tilly, 1990: 19). This necessarily implies security against threats and disruptions from both within and outside the new entity. The post-Hobbesian state, by contrast, emerges in a context of incremental political development where loyalty to the state as supreme political authority remains, and where, in the absence of conditions which formed the Hobbesian order of nation states, it is difficult to envisage how an 'authority-legitimacy transfer' (Haas, 1971; Anderson, present volume) could take place. Schmitter forecasts that the post-integration Europe will lie 'somewhere between sovereign units each with an unambiguous monopoly on violence ... and diffuse networks based upon multiple voluntary exchanges' (quoted in Bryant, 1991: 204).

Schmitter's approach, while highly suggestive, tends to become trapped by the very terms of the discourse he seeks to reject. Given the novelty of the EC, it may be understandable that those attempting to understand it should have recourse to concepts developed in the analysis of the conventional type of state, but this has unfortunate consequences.[16] It can encourage a negative form of analysis, an emphasis upon what the Community is *not* rather than a positive attempt to identify and understand its unique qualities. Rejection of the state model need not mean that certain institutions and relations associated with the idea of the state cannot also be identified as salient characteristics of the new model. In short, the 'the nation state–European entity' dichotomy does not adequately acknowledge the complexity of the political form emerging in the new Europe and fails to capture its uniqueness in blending some of the qualities of the conventional state into an entity with a novel structure and a distinctive dynamic of growth.

Uneven development

The EC defies easy classification in terms of old oppositions such as federation/confederation and state/non-state. Rather, it provides a striking case of uneven development in terms of the main indices of structural cohesion. There is a major imbalance between, on the one hand, its limited 'political supranationalism' and, on the other hand, its mature 'juridical supranationalism' (Hartley, 1989: 47) and sophistication as an economic organisation. In the political sphere, even after Maastricht the two major supranational organs, the Commission and European Parliament, lack the strength of the central tier of a traditional federal state, while there also remain strong centrifugal tendencies within the Council of Ministers and the European Council. In the juridical sphere, however, the doctrine of direct effect of Community legislation in member states, the supremacy of Community law over national law, and the ever-widening jurisdiction and increasingly intensive activity of the Community in legislative matters, provide a significant development.

The implications for police institution-building of this diverse and inconsistent set of trends are mixed, in both the long and short terms. First, many of the emerging areas of regulation will require their own sanctioning system in order to enforce Community-wide norms. There are early signs of an EC capacity in the domain of 'administrative policing' (van Reenen, 1989: 47; Johnston, 1992: ch. 6 and 202) in the enforcement of competition law (Lavoie, 1992) and in the work of UCLAF since 1989 in coordinating efforts to combat fraud against the Community budget (Reinke, 1991; Clarke, 1993). In time this might extend to cover matters such as environmental protection, health and safety at work and nuclear safety. The development of administrative policing may, of course, be hampered by the absence of general jurisdiction in criminal law. This disqualifies the EC from imposing penal sanctions but the Commission can impose administrative fines and other civil sanctions in certain areas, notably competition law, and EC law can also oblige national authorities to impose suitable penalties. Similarly, although the Commission has no general investigative competence, exceptions in the sphere of competition law and VAT give scope for future development (Sevenster, 1992: 32–35).

Second, there is the growing perception of a 'security deficit' within the Community (Bigo, present volume). The immediate catalyst for this is the 1992 programme which has encouraged the view that vigilance at external border controls must be extended to compensate for the loss of internal border controls (den Boer and Walker, 1993; den Boer, present volume). As Bigo argues, this line of thought has stimulated the creation of an 'internal security field', a domain of practices and ideas which presupposes a single 'security continuum' along which the issues of immigration and asylum are linked to concerns with organised crime, terrorism and drugs. As well as encouraging the growth of Schengen and Europol and the development of coordinated immigration policy, the new internal security ideology has also spawned proposals for the creation of a unit dedicated to the policing of external borders against illegal immigrants (van Reenen,

1989: 48) and emphasised the threat posed by criminal syndicates from Eastern Europe and beyond.[17] The ideology of internal security, which involves a sharp focus upon the specific order of the Community and its differentiation from the specific interests of other territorial regions, also encourages the development of an administrative class with a strict duty of allegiance to the Community. Indications of such a development are found in recent Commission proposals for an official secrecy law applicable to Community information and to public servants handling such information,[18] and in the insistence of the Council of Ministers that categories of classified information should be identified to which the new European Ombudsman envisaged under the Maastricht Treaty should be denied access.[19] If this trend towards the creation of a new ethos of secrecy, confidentiality and exclusive loyalty within the administrative apparatus of the Community continues, this may encourage the institution of a security service to police the enforcement of the new security régime.

Two other trends associated with the internal security field may enhance the law enforcement capacity of the Community in the longer term. The developing legislative and social policy profile of the EC increases the likelihood of public order protests with 'a real European character' (van Reenen, 1989: 46) – directed against European institutions and policies. Apart from the increasing incidence of EC-wide anti-immigrant protests, other potential flashpoints include coordinated protest against CAP, and, with emergent common energy and employment policies, anti-nuclear protests and strategies of industrial action.

The other trend associated with the specific order of the Community concerns threats by terrorist organisations made directly against Community institutions and interests. Again, these may be an internal response to the Community's developing public policy programme. For example, the Marxist Revolutionary November 17 Group, based in Greece, attacked the local EC offices in December 1990 in protest against austerity measures which it claimed demeaned Greek sovereignty (Riley, 1991: 23–24). The French group, Action Directe, or a successor, may re-emerge in conjunction with a variety of other indigenous European groups to challenge the implementation of the single European market (O'Ballance, 1989: 120). Alternatively, ideologically motivated threats to the Community may emanate from beyond its frontiers. Notwithstanding Schmitter's prognostication, the new CFSP Chapter in the Maastricht Agreement indicates a shift toward Community competence in foreign affairs, and so towards incorporation of the second pillar of the Hobbesian state, namely external coercive potential. This may involve the Community in challenges to its internal security, through both espionage and terrorism, by external hostile powers. For the first time, therefore, terrorism and strategic intelligence associated with 'state security' may become bound up with the specific order of the EC, rather than its member states.

Finally, the cumulative effect of institutional integration is bound to produce ever greater social and cultural integration including the growth of intra-Community travel, friendship and commercial ties across state boundaries, and common language skills and commodity preferences. In turn, the encouragement of these benchmarks of a European civil society may accelerate the internationalisation of the traditional forms of national crime.

However, none of these incipient trends declares the inevitability of a strong central policing capacity in the longer term. So diverse and specialist are the matters involved, that the growing demand for administrative policing may be met through a series of specific agencies rather than through a unified service with the capability to develop generic police functions. Further, in the flagship area of fraud against the Community, the inability of UCLAF to develop an effective strategy has attracted mounting criticism from the European Parliament and elsewhere; this centres upon the tendency of member states to treat fraud against the Community as less serious than defrauding the state, a clear case of the specific order of the nation state retaining top priority (Clarke, 1993).[20]

The existence of a common threat at the external borders does not entail a common solution. Indeed, failure by the EC states to meet the 1993 deadline for dismantling internal controls and the abandonment by the Schengen countries of their plan to remove airport controls by the end of 1993, signal a continuing reluctance to rest internal security primarily upon the maintenance of an external frontier for which there is shared responsibility.[21] As to the growing internal public order and terrorist threats, where the uniform law and policy against which these are directed are a product of mere legislative sovereignty at the centre with no concomitant political authority, then member states may persist in defining the Community's policy profile in terms of their own specific orders and continue to treat any common problems by intergovernmental means. For its part, a common anti-terrorist capacity directed against external threats depends upon a contingency – the development of a strong Community identity in international security and military matters – which, as the failure to develop a robust coordinated response to war in the Balkans indicates (Hoffman, 1993), is as uncertain in the 'post-Hobbesian' world as the central policing capacity itself. Finally, the incremental growth of cultural ties within the Community is as likely to prompt an extension of existing forms of intergovernmental liaison as to generate demand for a new European police force.

Despite fissiparous trends in the EC, it is arguable that the whole may prove greater than its parts, and the cumulative effect of various factors may provide the conditions for a gradual transformation of the authoritative basis for European policing. The propensity of the governing structure of the Community to develop into new areas despite the absence of strong popular or political initiatives from constituent states should not be dismissed (Bulmer, 1993), but the major obstacle to supranational policing in each key area is the absence of the preconditions of the 'authority-legitimacy' transfer which would vest in Brussels the right to defend its own conception of specific order. As this is the pervasive problem, unless and until it is overcome, there seems little prospect of the Community developing an autonomous policing capacity, whether by incremental development or wholesale innovation.

Transfer of legitimacy

What then are the preconditions of the requisite authority-legitimacy transfer, and what are the prospects of these being met? By depicting the conventional Hobbesian state as an entity which emerged in the context of a general struggle over security, writers such as Schmitter and Tilly alert us to the fact that the legitimacy of policing within such a state is closely linked with its basic *raison d'être*. To understand how the post-Hobbesian state might acquire policing authority, we must appreciate the conditions under which the Community emerged and sustains itself. The defining context for the Community has been the history of post-war Western European democracy. Originally charged to pursue the economic benefits of free competition in a common market, the Community has assumed a wider range of social and welfare objectives. It has pursued these against a background of widespread expectations that important decisions which distribute key resources and influence life-chances must be controlled by a range of representatives and participatory democratic institutions.

Unlike the Hobbesian state, therefore, the link between the integrity of the political entity and the policing function is not a direct one. Nevertheless, can sufficient indirect links be forged to legitimate the policing function? One possibility concerns the functional link between policing and economic prosperity. The Community's modest advances in the field of administrative policing are attributable to the fact that this contributes to a system of fiscal regulation through which the Community's economic objectives are pursued. The potency of the appeal to the threat from external populations as a justification for an increased policing capacity is partly due to the perception that the material prosperity of insiders might otherwise be undermined. However, a rationale which is purely economic, and which is seen in 'top-down' terms, as an objective imposed from above, is insufficient in itself. As Meehan has argued in her discussion of citizenship in the European Community, the legitimacy of the European order rests upon an indivisible 'cluster of meanings' (Meehan, 1993: 177). As the Community originated as a series of voluntary agreements between states, each of whose political orders was premised upon a framework of individual rights and obligations, the legitimacy of the Community has also come to depend upon its regulation of the economic, social and political domains being couched in terms of individual rights and obligations.[22] As Meehan puts it, in a revision of Marshall's analysis of citizenship (Marshall, 1950), by the time of the creation and development of the EC it was broadly accepted that there was a strong connection across the broad range of civil rights (and associated economic freedoms), political rights and, to a more limited extent, social rights of the citizen. Such a holistic treatment of EC citizenship rights may be gradually developed and extended; this may in time persuade the citizens of the legitimacy of accepting a set of obligations from the same political authority, together with the institutions, *including policing institutions*, required to enforce such rights and obligations.

This argument is not intended to support the complacent conclusion that the population of Europe will only legitimate the transfer of policing functions to the EC in return for a full set of citizenship rights. But without significant expansion of the range of citizenship rights to supplement the functional economic arguments cited above, such a shift will not be easily accepted. Civil and economic rights have always been closely bound up with the purposes of the EC; and both the completion of the 1992 programme and the reception of fundamental rights into Community jurisprudence culminating in recognition of the ECHR in the Treaty of Maastricht (Art. F.2), have consolidated this (Coppel and O'Neill, 1992). In the social field, again the Treaty of Maastricht has embraced a broad vision of entitlements in employment and social security. It has also extended political rights through the establishment of the new status of citizenship of the Union (Closa, 1992).

Despite these advances, European citizenship remains a limited conception. The UK has refused to accept the terms of the Social Chapter, which, in any case, does not embrace a comprehensive range of welfare provision and is concerned with Community powers rather than individual entitlements. More generally, the unevenness of economic development across the Community militates against uniform welfare standards (Majone, 1993: 167–168). The new political rights, too, are limited. They provide no general entitlement to participate in national general elections. Nor do they address the fundamental democratic deficit of the Community, namely the denial of an effective legislative role for the only directly elected European institution, the European Parliament.

Two alternative conclusions may be drawn. On the one hand, the conception of citizenship advanced at Community level may be insufficiently robust to legitimate the reciprocal development of European policing institutions. Legitimate authority in Western Europe may depend upon the development of a rounded conception of citizenship, but that does not mean that all rights and duties need to be articulated at one level. Meehan has argued that there is developing instead 'a kind of three-dimensional framework for the exercise of the rights, loyalties and duties of citizenship' (1993: 173), with the regional, national and supranational levels each legitimate within its own sphere. In such a scenario, there is no compelling reason why powerful policing institutions should be appropriate and acceptable at the supranational level rather than at the two other levels where they have traditionally been located.

It is not, however, easy to predict the level of citizenship rights required before a European police authority would be politically acceptable. The growing persuasiveness of the wider economic functionalist argument as a secondary rationale for institutional growth in 'the internal security field' may lower the acceptability threshold in terms of the provision of citizenship rights. Furthermore, if the citizenship base remains narrowly state-derivative, then in a context where the theme of the external threat is central to the purpose, and also, presumably, the practices of new European police institutions, those 'denizens' and 'margizens' (Martiniello, 1993) whose interests may be most directly challenged by an exclusionary security policy will be deprived of the very framework of rights upon which the legitimacy of such police institutions primarily rests.

Conclusion

Our analysis of possible developments in policing in the post-1992 Community reveals a complex relationship between police institutions and the socio-political environment within which they are located. Police institutions are not simply epiphenomena, to be 'read off' from the social and political framework , whether this takes the form of a state or some more novel political arrangement. However, policing institutions remain linked to these wider political forms, which both encourage and set limits to developments in the policing domain. Policing, therefore, is aptly described as a 'semi-autonomous field' (Falk Moore, 1973: 720; Goldsmith, 1990: 93), to which the contrasting policy orientations of structural fatalism and naive separatism are equally inappropriate. Instead, what is required in the effort to build effective and legitimate police institutions in the new Europe is a framework of analysis which both remains aware of the influence exerted and restrictions imposed by the macro-political context, and also addresses matters of intrinsic relevance to the policing sector.

The difficulties involved in such an exercise should not be under-estimated. For example, I have argued elsewhere that the choices available in the structural design of a set of policing institutions for the Community can be mapped onto a continuum, with one pole representing a *highly integrated* set of arrangements and the other a *loosely structured* set of arrangements (Walker, 1993). On the one hand, such a choice has sector-specific implications for police effectiveness and efficiency, involving considerations such as cultural harmony, good communications, avoidance of functional overlap, and optimal use of expertise. On the other hand, organisational structure also has a bearing upon effective accountability arrangements, which in turn connects with the macro-political question of legitimacy. Accountability and legitimacy involve consideration of issues such as dispersal of power, transparency, and vested professional interests. Clearly, both the sector-specific and the macro-political agendas are complex in themselves. The fact that they overlap when particular policy choices, such as structural design, are being considered, compounds this complexity. However, we have no choice but to acknowledge this and to develop both internal and external perspectives when engaging seriously with issues of police reform. The present chapter has sought to contribute to this process by deepening our external perspective through consideration of how the semi-autonomous field of policing interacts with the rapidly changing environment of the European Community.

Notes

1 The difficulty in specifying truth-conditions for claims concerning the essential nature of the police function and its relationship to the wider political order helps to explain the durability of debates between those who favour public-order and

crime-fighting conceptions of the police role respectively; see the review symposium on Reiner (1985) in *British Journal of Criminology*, 1986, 26, 94–105. See also the defence of a theory of 'minimal policing', concerned mainly with crime-fighting, against wider public order models, in particular that of the American criminologists Wilson and Kelling (1982), in Kinsey *et al.*, (1986), esp. chs. 4 and 9.

2 The fact that police are located within the state does not guarantee that they will perform their substitutional role in a manner which meets with the agreement of other social agencies or their clients (Kinsey *et al.*, 1986: ch. 6; cf. Punch, 1979). However, the dangers of divergence from the general approach of other state agencies by the police would seem to be greater where a police organisation does not owe exclusive loyalty to a particular state.

3 For a briefer attempt to address these two questions, see den Boer and Walker (1993).

4 *The Guardian*, 3 June 1993.

5 *The Guardian*, 2 February 1993.

6 For example, in 1991 EC Directives were enacted in the areas of money laundering (91/308/EEC) and the acquisition and possession of weapons (91/477/EEC).

7 Whereas a procedure is set out whereby the Community may acquire legislative competence in certain areas of justice and home affairs, this does not apply to police cooperation, or, indeed, to judicial cooperation in criminal matters or customs cooperation (Art. K.9). As regards the Court of Justice, the Treaty leaves open the question whether it may acquire jurisdiction over any or all areas of justice and home affairs in the future (Art. K.3 (2)).

8 Although see note 12 below.

9 Note, for example, the public criticism of the Europol idea as premature by Raymond Kendall, the Secretary General of Interpol, immediately after the conclusion of the draft agreement on the Maastricht Treaty (*Agence Europe*, 22 January 1992). As for Schengen, delays in the dismantling of internal borders post-1992 may mean that assumptions that it would be superseded by the wider security arrangements involving Europol and the other Article K.1 institutions have been premature. Indeed, the resilience of Schengen is signified by the fact that its Secretariat is engaged in active negotiations over future arrangements with various candidate states who will not join the Community until 1995 at the earliest (Interview with Jan Ohlander, Ministry of Foreign Affairs, Stockholm, 18 May 1993).

10 International terrorism involves activities directed by a sovereign state, while transnational terrorism involves activities executed by autonomous terrorist groups across state boundaries. Thus, in the EC context, the external threat is from international terrorist groups, while the internal threat is from transnational groups, whether operating singly or in combination. See Riley (1991: 12.)

11 *The Guardian*, 2 June 1993.

12 If this were not so, the law of extradition, which requires broad agreement between requesting and requested state as to the definition of criminal conduct, could not operate as it has done between all EC states since the ratification of the Council of Europe Convention on Extradition in 1990; nor would it be possible to envisage any role for Europol in the area of operational policing prior to harmonisation, yet just such an option has attracted some support in Trevi and elsewhere (van Outrive, 1992a; *The Independent* 20 April 1992).

13 One the difficulties of generating trust and confidence between national police forces, see Walker (1992; 1993); Robertson (present volume).

14 *Financial Times*, 9 December 1992.

15 A Working Group on Organised Crime was set up in June 1992 following the murder of the anti-Mafia Italian judge, Giovanni Falcone (van Outrive, 1992b; 1992c).
16 Arguably, this tendency to be trapped within a conventional form of discourse even when attempting to transcend it, and thus to provide an essentially negative form of analysis, restricts the otherwise highly illuminating perspective offered in two recent works. See MacCormick's critique of the notion of sovereignty within the new Community legal order (1993), and Weiler's critique of the idea of Europe as Unity (1991; esp. 2478–2481).
17 An indication of the significance of this new perspective can be seen in the themes of addresses given by various senior police officers at a recent international crime conference at Bramshill Police College organised by the Office of International Criminal Justice. See *The Guardian*, 25 May 1993.
18 *Statewatch* (January–February, 1993) 3(1), 1.
19 *The Guardian*, 11 June 1993.
20 Ibid.
21 *The Guardian*, 2 June 1993.
22 Thus, although not set out explicitly in the original Treaty framework, the doctrine of the direct effect of Community law, which allows individuals to enforce Community rights against member states, was confirmed by the European Court of Justice in an early case. See *Van Gend en Loos*, Case 26/62 [1963] ECR 1. See also Meehan (1993: 178).

References

Ad Hoc Group on Immigration (1991), *Report from the Ministers Responsible for Immigration to the European Council Meeting in Maastricht on Immigration and Asylum Policy*, Brussels, 3 December.
Anderson, M. (1989), *Policing the World – Interpol and the Politics of European Police Cooperation*, Oxford, Clarendon Press.
Bentham, K. (1992), 'A European Police Council', in M. Anderson and M. den Boer (Eds.), European Police Cooperation: Proceedings of a Seminar, University of Edinburgh, 121–131.
Benyon, J., Davies, P. and Willis, P. (1990), *Police Cooperation in Europe: A Preliminary Report*, Centre for the Study of Public Order, University of Leicester.
Birch, R. (1989), *Policing Europe after 1992*, Address to the Royal Institute of International Affairs, 19 April.
Bittner, E. (1971), *The Functions of the Police in Modern Society*, Washington DC, US Government Printing Office.
Boer, M. den and Walker, N. (1993), 'European Policing after 1992', *Journal of Common Market Studies*, **31**, 1, 3–28.
Brodeur, J.P. (1983), 'High Policing and Low Policing: Remarks about the Policing of Political Activities', *Social Problems*, **30**, 507–520.
Brogden, M.E. (1990), 'The Origins of the South African Police – Institutional versus Structural Approaches', *Acta Juridica*, **6**, 1–20.
Bryant, C. (1991), 'Europe and the European Community', *Sociology*, **25**, 189–207.
Bulmer, S.J. (1993), *Community Governance and Regulatory Regimes*, European Community Studies Conference, Washington DC.
Clarke, M. (1993), 'EEC Fraud: A Suitable Case for Treatment', in F. Pearce and M. Woodiwiss (Eds.), *Global Crime Connections*, London, Macmillan.

Closa, C. (1992), 'The Concept of Citizenship in the Treaty on European Union', *Common Market Law Review*, **29**, 1137–1169.

Cohen, H. (1985), 'Authority: The Limits of Discretion', in F.A. Elliston and M. Feldberg (Eds.), *Moral Issues in Police Work*, New Jersey, Rowman & Allanheld, 27–42.

Coppel, J. and O'Neill, A. (1992), 'The European Court of Justice: Taking Rights Seriously?', *Legal Studies*, **12**, 227–245.

Dorn, N., Murji, S. and South, N. (1992), *Traffickers: Drug Markets and Law Enforcement*, London, Routledge.

Dunleavy, P. (1989), 'The Architecture of the British Central State', *Public Administration*, **67**, 249–276 and 391–418.

Falk Moore, S. (1978), *Law as Process: an Anthropological Approach*, London, Routledge and Kegan Paul.

Fijnaut, C. (1991), 'Police Cooperation within Western Europe', in F. Heidensohn and M. Farrell (Eds.), *Crime in Europe*, London and New York, Routledge.

Fode, H. (1993), *Europol*, Bern, Regional European Interpol Conference.

Gallie, W.B. (1956), 'Essentially Contested Concepts', *Proceedings of the Aristotelian Society*, **56**.

Giddens, A. (1987), *Social Theory and Modern Sociology*, Cambridge, Polity Press, 166–182.

Gilmore, W.C. (1991), *Going after the Money: Money Laundering, The Confiscation of the Assets of Crime and International Cooperation*, A System of European Police Cooperation after 1992, Working Paper VI, Edinburgh.

Gilmore, W.C. (1992), 'Introduction', in W.C. Gilmore (ed.), *International Efforts to Combat Money Laundering*, Cambridge International Document Series, 4, Cambridge, Grotius.

Goldsmith, A. (1990), 'Taking Police Culture Seriously: Police Discretion and the Limits of the Law', *Policing and Society*, **1**, 91–114.

Gregory, Frank, and Collier, Alan (1992), 'Cross Frontier Crime and International Crime – Problems, Achievements and Prospects with Reference to European Police Co-operation', in M. Anderson and M. den Boer (Eds.), *European Police Cooperation: Proceedings of a Seminar*, Edinburgh, University of Edinburgh, 71–90.

Haas, E.B. (1971), 'The Study of Regional Integration: Reflections on the Joy and Anguish of Pretheorizing', in L.N. Lindberg and S. Scheingold (Eds.), *Regional Integration: Theory and Research*, Cambridge, Mass., Harvard University Press.

Hall, J. and Ikenberry, G.J. (1989), *The State*, Milton Keynes, Oxford University Press.

Hartley, T.C. (1989), *The Foundations of European Community Law* (2nd edn), Oxford, Clarendon Press.

HM Government (1992), *Developments in the European Community: July to December*, Cm. 1857, London, HMSO.

Hoffmann, S. (1993), 'Goodbye to a United Europe?', *New York Review of Books* (27 May), **40**, 10, 27–31.

Home Affairs Committee (1990), *Practical Police Cooperation in the European Community*, 7th Report 1989–90, HC 363-I, London, HMSO.

Hondius, F. (1993), 'Mutual Assistance between Business Regulatory Bodies – Treaty Aspects', in W.C. Gilmore (Ed.), *Action against Transnational Criminality: Vol. 11*, London, Commonwealth Secretariat, 20–26.

Jessop, B. (1990), *State Theory: Putting Capitalist States in their Place*, Cambridge, Polity Press.

Johnston, L. (1992), *The Rebirth of Private Policing*, London and New York, Routledge.

Keohane, R.O. and Hoffmann, S. (1991), 'Institutional Change in Europe in the 1980s', in R.O. Keohane and S. Hoffmann (Eds.), *The New European Community*, San Francisco, Westview.

Kinsey, R., Lea, J. and Young, J. (1986), *Losing the Fight against Crime*, Oxford, Blackwell.

Klockars, C.J. (1985), *The Idea of Police*, Beverley Hills, Sage.

Lavoie, C. (1992), 'The Investigative Powers of the Commission with Respect to Business Secrets under Community Competition Rules', *European Law Review*, **12**, 20–40.

Levi, M. (1991), *Pecunia non olet*: Cleansing the Money-lenders from the Temple, *Crime, Law and Social Change*, **16**, 217–302.

Lindberg, L.N. (1963), *The Political Dynamics of European Integration*, Stanford, Stanford University Press.

MacCormick, N. (1993), 'Beyond the Sovereign State', *Modern Law Review*, **56**, 1–18.

McLaughlin, E. (1992), 'The Democratic Deficit: European Union and the Accountability of the British Police', *British Journal of Criminology*, **32**, 473–487.

Majone, G. (1993), 'The European Community between Social Policy and Social Regulation', *Journal of Common Market Studies*, **31**, 154–170.

Marenin, O. (1982), 'Parking Tickets and Class Repression: The Concept of Policing in Critical Theories of Criminal Justice', *Contemporary Crises*, **6**, 241–266.

Marshall, T.H. (1950), *Citizenship and Social Class and other Essays*, Cambridge, Cambridge University Press.

Martiniello, M. (1993), *European Citizenship and Migrants: Towards the Postnational?*, Leiden, ECPR Joint Sessions.

Meehan, E. (1993), 'Citizenship and the European Community', *Political Quarterly*, **64**, 172–186.

Northern Ireland Office (1993), 'Tackling Terrorist Finance', in W.C. Gilmore (Ed.), *Action against Transnational Criminality, Vol. 11*, London, Commonwealth Secretariat, 19–22.

Nugent, N. (1992), 'The Deepening and the Widening of the European Community: Recent Evolution, Maastricht and Beyond', *Journal of Common Market Studies*, **30**, 312–328.

O'Ballance, E. (1989), *Terrorism in the 1980s*, London, Pluto.

Outrive, L. van (1992a), *Europol*, Committee on Civil Liberties and Internal Affairs of the European Parliament.

Outrive, L. van (1992b), *Police Cooperation*, Committee on Civil Liberties and Internal Affairs of the European Parliament.

Outrive, L. van (1992c), *The Setting up of Europol*, Committee on Civil Liberties and Internal Affairs of the European Parliament.

Pearce, F. (1976), *Crimes of the Powerful: Marxism, Crime and Deviance*, London, Pluto.

Poggi, G. (1990), *The State: Its Nature, Development and Prospects*, Cambridge, Polity.

Punch, M. (1979), 'The Secret Social Service', in S. Holdaway (Ed.), *The British Police*, London, Edward Arnold.

Rawls, J. (1987), 'The Idea of Overlapping Consensus', *Oxford Journal of Legal Studies*, **9**, 1–25.

Reenen, P. van (1989), 'Policing Europe after 1992: Cooperation and Competition', *European Affairs*, **3**, 2, 45–53.

Reiner, R. (1985), *The Politics of the Police*, Brighton, Wheatsheaf.

Reiner, R. (1992), '*Fin de Siècle* Blues: The Police Face the Millennium', *Political Quarterly*, **63**, 37–49.

Reinke, S. (1992), 'The EC Commission's Anti-Fraud Activity', in M. Anderson and M. den Boer (Eds.), *European Police Cooperation: Proceedings of a Seminar*, Edinburgh, University of Edinburgh, 13–30.

Riley, L. (1991), *Counterterrorism in Western Europe: Mechanisms for International Cooperation*, MA Thesis, University of Essex.

Robinson, C.D. and Skaglion, R. (1987), 'The Origin and Evolution of the Police Function in Society', *Law and Society Review*, **21**, 109–153.

Schmitter, P.C. (1990), 'The European Community as an Emergent and Novel Form of Political Domination', draft article in progress.

Schutte, J. (1991), 'The European Market of 1993: Test for a Regional Model of Supranational Criminal Justice or of Interregional Cooperation in Criminal Law', *Criminal Law Forum*, **3**, 55–83.

Sevenster, H. (1992), 'Criminal Law and EC Law', *Common Market Law Review*, **29**, 29–70.

Streeck, W. and Schmitter, P.C., (1991), 'From National Corporatism to Transnational Pluralism: Organized Interests in the Single European Market', *Politics and Society*, **19**, 133–164.

Tilly, C. (1990), *Coercion, Capital and European States*, Cambridge, Polity Press.

Trevi (1991), *The Development of Europol*, Report from Trevi Ministers to the European Council in Maastricht.

Walker, N. (1991), *The UK Police and European Police Cooperation*, A System of European Police Cooperation after 1992, Working Paper III, University of Edinburgh.

Walker, N. (1992), 'The Dynamics of European Police Cooperation: The UK Perspective', *Commonwealth Law Bulletin*, **18**, 1509–1522.

Walker, N. (1993), 'The International Dimension', in R. Reiner and S. Spencer (Eds.), *Accountable Policing: Effectiveness, Empowerment and Equity*, London, Institute for Public Policy Research, 113–171.

Weber, M. (1948), 'Politics as a Vocation' in *Essays from Max Weber*, London, Routledge and Kegan Paul.

Weiler, J.H.H. (1991), 'The Transformation of Europe', *Yale Law Journal*, **100**, 2403–2483.

Wilson, J.Q. and Kelling, G. (1982), 'Broken Windows', *Atlantic Monthly*, March, 29–38.

Woodward, R. (1993), 'The Establishment of Europol: A Critique', *European Journal on Criminal Policy and Research* (forthcoming).

Woollacott, M. (1991), 'Cry of a Lost Community', *The Guardian*, 15 November.

3

UNDERSTANDING POLICE COOPERATION IN EUROPE: SETTING A FRAMEWORK FOR ANALYSIS

John Benyon, Lynne Turnbull, Andrew Willis and Rachel Woodward

Europe will not be made all at once or according to a single general plan. It will be built through concrete achievements, which first create a *de facto* solidarity.

(Robert Schuman, 1950)

This quotation from Robert Schuman is perhaps prescient of the ways in which cooperation between the police forces of the member states of the European Community (EC) has developed. European police cooperation has a long and uneven history, and to date the solidarity Schuman speaks of has only been established incrementally. Concrete achievements have been reached, certainly, but the development of cooperative working practices and policies has been slow and progress fitful. Such cooperation as exists between European police forces has largely arisen as a response to changes and developments in the political, economic and social context of the EC and the wider Europe.

Cooperation certainly exists, but the agreements for cooperation are complex. Such agreements have developed step-by-step and have evolved from a number of sources. There are formal structures, secret agreements, bi-lateral arrangements and informal networks all working to promote cross-national policing activity. There is, however, little coordination of policy in this area, and this renders its study difficult.

This chapter constitutes an initial step towards the development of a better understanding of the arrangements for cooperation between the law enforcement agencies which exist in the EC and Europe. The rapid development and expansion of police cooperation in Europe makes such a framework for understanding increasingly necessary. In this chapter, we set out a heuristic device for mapping out the structures, institutions and arrangements for European police cooperation. Given the expansion of academic study in European policing issues, the time seems right for some preliminary work towards an explanatory framework. This initial step involves viewing European police cooperation as operating at three levels, these being the micro level, the meso level and the macro level. We explain these levels with reference to the four main structures for cooperation that currently exist, and conclude by emphasising the need for further research and conceptualisation in this area.

A subject in need of research

The need for research into the subject of European police cooperation has long been recognised by police and academics alike. It seems evident that the formulation of effective procedures for police cooperation, at any level, should be based on a rational and careful examination of the issues involved. There are four basic issues which should be included here, these being the level of crime in Europe; the likely impact of changes in the system of border controls within the EC; the difficulties attendant to the policing of the EC given the diversity of policing organisations that exist within the member states; and the experiences of agencies for cooperation that are already operational. Sadly, policy formulation in this field has all too often been based on little more than a cursory examination of these issues. For example, there have to date been rare attempts by police organisations, governments, the EC or academic research institutions to collect and analyse crime statistics in a comprehensive fashion for the whole EC, and there remains amongst policing agencies much confusion about the roles and capabilities of existing cooperative agreements. This is not a promising basis for the development of an effective pan-European policing policy, and further research into the issues outlined above is greatly needed.

There seems to be a number of reasons for the lack of research into European crime and European police cooperation. First, sources of research funding still tend to be *nationally focused*, so it is difficult to obtain support in certain fields from national research funding institutions for research that clearly has a European perspective. But this is clearly not the whole answer. Funding has been forthcoming from national bodies for some trans-European research, for example, on some economic and political topics. It may be that the field has been overlooked; funding bodies tend to follow fashion, and the economic and political decision-making aspects of European integration have been more to the fore than European law enforcement and crime.

A second possible reason is that the topic is *politically contentious*. Law enforcement remains essentially a national concern and some proposals to foster international police action touch on sensitive questions of political sovereignty. This may explain why intergovernmental funding for research in this field has not been more forthcoming. Criminal justice is such a potent symbol of the body politic that many feel must remain the primary, if not the sole, responsibility of individual national governments.

A third reason for the absence of European-wide police research is the sheer *complexity* of the topic. The police forces of Europe themselves are quite different. There are differences within countries and differences between countries. Parts of the EC have single forces, organised nationally, for example, Denmark, Greece, Ireland and Luxembourg. Germany has a system in which responsibilities are divided between state and federal levels. Belgium has three forces, with conflicts over jurisdiction and competence. Portugal has several, whilst Italy has five separate, but mutually integrated, police organisations. France has two highly centralised forces, whilst Spain has two national ones. In the UK there are 52 semi-autonomous forces, and in the Netherlands a new system has recently been established of 25 regional forces and one new national force. There is no basic uniformity or pattern to the organisation of European police forces. There is also a frequent lack of knowledge of the structure and organisation of EC police forces and other structures for dealing with crime amongst the police forces themselves. The police forces operate within diverse criminal justice systems. There is also a variety of bi-lateral and multi-lateral agreements which have developed to promote cooperation which add to the complexity of the topic. Old institutions have developed over the years, such as Interpol, while newer ones, such as the agreements between police forces either side of the Channel Tunnel, are in the process of developing.

A fourth possible reason for the lack of adequate research in this field may be that the *crime issues* that require investigation, as a first step towards policy formulation, are also *complex*. Is such crime likely to increase as a result of the removal of internal borders within the EC? In answer to this question, studies to date (Benyon *et al.*, 1993) have suggested that policy has relied on two – often competing – ideas about crime in Europe. On the one hand, various politicians and police officers have argued that the relaxation of internal border controls will result in a massive upsurge in crime rates throughout the European Community. Drug traffickers, terrorists, traders in stolen goods and other criminals will be free to move across Europe without impediment (Imbert, 1989; Milland, 1990). However, on the other hand there are those who argue that serious crime has been international for many years and that the removal of internal border controls will have little effect on the activities of these criminals, as they have successfully evaded such controls in the past.

Unfortunately, because of the lack of any detailed studies, there is no 'hard' evidence. The short answer to questions about the extent of crime in Europe is 'we don't know' – there is a paucity of information on which to construct a view (Heidensohn and Farrell, 1991). It is remarkable how little appears to be known about cross-border crime in Europe, and in this respect, as in so many others, the European journey is a voyage into uncharted waters. This lack of hard data has not prevented some politicians and senior police officers from making extravagant predictions about the adverse effects that the removal of national borders will have on international crime.

One piece of evidence comes from Interpol which shows a significant rise in the flow of messages in the European Region of the Interpol Network, up from 500,000 in 1980 to nearly 900,000 in 1989. However, these are not crime statistics as such but rather messages on the Interpol system. The increase in European messages through Interpol may reflect various sorts of changes, such as greater confidence in – or efficiency by – Interpol, new procedural arrangements and, ironically, they may also be the product of increased police cooperation itself. Of course, Interpol messages are concerned with various police issues, such as missing persons, as well as suspected criminals. However, the figures have been interpreted by some as indicative of greater criminal mobility and as showing an upward trend in the need for European police cooperation.

There may be other explanations for the lack of research into policing and crime in Europe and the EC, but it is most probably explained in terms of a combination of the variables listed above. However, the central point remains that this absence of a detailed trans-European study of crime and police cooperation should be a cause for concern and this should surely be a priority area for research in the immediate future.

Levels of police cooperation

The problems facing the police forces of the EC in establishing effective procedures for cooperation should not be underestimated. Research undertaken by the Centre for the Study of Public Order at the University of Leicester into this area has indicated that a high level of effective cooperation is often difficult to achieve between forces operating in the same country, or even within the same force (Benyon, 1992: 21).

These difficulties are compounded in the EC with the large numbers of different law enforcement agencies, and problems include a lack of both information and communication of information about the various forces that exist, rivalries and jealousies between and within agencies, and different approaches and perceptions of what policing is and how a policing agency should function. It may be very much more difficult to secure cooperation between police agencies operating in different countries, with diverse cultures and traditions, incompatible communications and procedures and quite different legal systems and organisational structures. Within each EC member state there exist a large number of agencies, organisations and structures with an interest or input into the policing and criminal justice systems of that country. The study of these agencies has produced a large volume of data on police, crime and justice issues, which require ordering and structuring.

An initial approach adopted by the Leicester team has been to examine European policing with reference to three levels of European police cooperation. As a heuristic device it has proved useful for structuring and ordering the growing volume of information on the organisation of European policing (House of Commons, 1990: xvi). The *macro level* is concerned with constitutional and international legal agreements and the harmonisation of national laws and regulations. The *meso level* is concerned with the operational structures of the police and other law enforcement agencies and with cooperation over police practice, procedures and technology. The *micro level* is concerned with the prevention and detection of particular offences and crime problems (Benyon *et al.*, 1990; Benyon 1992).

It should be stressed that this is a typology of different levels of police cooperation, and as such the classification does not in itself have explanatory powers. Nor should the three levels be taken as an indication of priorities or necessarily of the rank of individuals involved at each of the levels. Rather, the three levels should be taken as an indication of points along a continuum of the degree of political agreement required for the establishment of strategies for police cooperation. It should also be emphasised that the levels are not mutually exclusive. As the discussion below indicates, many of the major structures which exist for promoting closer European police cooperation cross-cut the three levels. The levels are an organising device for mapping out the cooperation that exists between such structures, rather than a classification device for the structures themselves. Different questions about the nature of police cooperation are raised at each of the three levels.

It is worth considering in further detail how European police cooperation can be mapped out with reference to the three different levels, and how some of the major structures for European police cooperation can be seen to work at the different levels.

The macro level

This level is concerned primarily with constitutional questions and international legal agreements, and the harmonisation of national legislation and regulations. The macro level is the level of government and senior officials, at which fundamental issues are resolved and major, far-reaching, decisions are taken. This is the level at which political agreement and consensus has to be sought as a precondition for action. Macro-level agreements as they currently exist relate to two basic issues: the policing of entry and exit of third country nationals to and from the EC and the powers of police across the internal borders of the EC.

It is in the economic interests of all that Europe should have an internal open market. Economic interests have been, and will continue to be, the main catalyst for change in Europe. The Single European Act of 1987 enabled this with the establishment of the principle of freedom of movement for capital, goods, services and people. The removal of internal border controls, which the Act entails, led in turn to a considerable amount of speculation and comment about the potential impact on crime rates within the EC, and on the need to tighten controls at the external borders of the community in order to compensate for the lack of internal border checks. Despite the fact that an internal frontier-free EC with solid external borders has yet to materialise (and still seems some way distant), perceptions of the roles of the internal and external borders of the EC have been crucial influences on the arrangements for policing the EC. Agreements on border-related issues can be termed macro-level agreements.

Macro-level cooperation is that which requires agreement at the constitutional and legal levels. Legislation and arrangements for extradition, immigration and visa agreements, and asylum application procedures can all be viewed as being macro-level arrangements. They are fundamental issues relating to the abolition of internal border controls and the consequent tightening of controls at the so-called external border of the EC. Agreements at this level require conventions and treaties signed by national governments. Discussions can only take place at the highest intergovernmental level, for they involve issues of national sovereignty (den Boer and Walker, 1993). Whatever the spirit of goodwill and cooperation that exists between governments, issues relating to the establishment of controls of movement of people into and within the EC, are not settled on an interpersonal or inter-organisational basis but require a constitutional and legislative framework established at the macro level.

It should be noted, however, that in the past many of the major legislative agreements involving the free movement of persons in the EC have been agreed outside the competence of the EC institutions. Extradition, immigration, visas and asylum applications have been dealt with under the auspices of the Council of Europe, European Political Cooperation, *ad hoc* groups specifically established to deal with these issues, or by intergovernmental agreement. Of course, many agreements concerning workers' rights, rights of establishment, and other less controversial issues relating to the controls on the free movement of persons have been addressed in EC regulations, directives and decisions. Agreements relating to extradition, immigration, refugees and asylum seekers and visa requirements have generally been reached in extra-EC fora.

The first of such agreements, the 1957 European Convention on Extradition, is the mechanism used to bring offenders to justice when they have either escaped across a frontier or where their crime has been committed in another country. The Convention was agreed within the forum of the Council of Europe. Extradition is sought on the basis of a formal request made to the country holding the offender. It is not necessary to state a *prima facie* case against the person being sought for extradition. The effectiveness of the Convention is unfortunately severely limited by three loopholes in its provisions. First, the Convention contains a political offence exception which has permitted some suspected terrorists to avoid extradition by claiming that their actions were politically motivated. Second, the principle of double incrimination applies to offences for which extradition is sought, where an offence is pursuable under the laws of both countries involved. Finally, states may refuse to extradite their own nationals provided they try the offender under their own law, a provision which is obviously open to corruption.

Some further macro-level cooperation relating to extradition has taken place under Articles 59–60 of the Schengen Implementing Convention (Schengen is explained in detail below). These articles specify that they are intended supplement the provisions of the 1957 European Convention on

Extradition, not replace them. The articles deal with the use of the Schengen Information System as a method of requesting extradition and other informal means of extradition. The extradition provisions therein do seem to be unnecessary given what has already been permitted under the hot-pursuit provisions. Even recognition that extradition is an important enough area to be treated in the Schengen Implementing Convention has not meant that the problems of the European Convention have been ironed out. If anything they have probably been augmented.

As yet, there is no convention or agreement which deals solely with immigration matters. The External Frontiers Convention which deals with such issues has yet to be agreed and ratified having been continually delayed by the dispute between Spain and the UK over Gibraltar. Again, this is an agreement which has been drafted between government representatives outside the framework of the EC institutions, but at the macro level.

Other agreements have been reached within the *Ad Hoc* Group on Immigration. This group was responsible for drafting the 1990 Convention determining the states responsible for examining applications for asylum lodged in one of the member states of the EC, commonly referred to as the Dublin Convention. As an example of macro-level cooperation, on an issue which impinges on the sovereign rights of the states, the Dublin Convention is an extremely detailed example of what can be achieved through cooperation, although such comment should not be read as acceptance of the Convention provisions or the probable results on application of those provisions. Similar provisions were agreed within the Schengen group, but it has now been accepted that the provisions of the Dublin Convention will take precedence on this issue over those of the Schengen Convention when the Dublin Convention has received the necessary ratification.

Visa requirements are another area where cooperation has occurred at the macro level. In this case there is no specific convention treating the subject and agreements have largely been made within the Schengen forum, although it should be noted that those states outside the Schengen group have been party to agreements on visa requirements through other intergovernmental macro-level meetings. The Schengen group has agreed a list of countries the nationals of which require a visa before entry to Schengen territory can be permitted. Considerable criticism has been levelled at the Schengen group about this list, as it is claimed that only rich countries or those countries with a majority white population do not require visas. All the countries on the list are African, Asian, South or Central American, and most recently the countries of Eastern Europe have been added. Whilst an example of cooperation at the macro level, and proof that sovereignty issues do not present insurmountable difficulties, the agreements on common visa requirements are continuing to cause controversy.

This situation could be on the point of change given the terms of the Treaty on European Union (Maastricht Treaty). Article K.1, Title VI of the Maastricht Treaty sets out nine areas which are to be regarded as matters of 'common interest'. K.3 develops this further by requiring member states to 'inform and consult one another within the Council with a view to coordinating their action'. Finally, K.4 sets out details of a Coordinating Committee which will administer this. The terms of the treaty are somewhat ambiguous. They neither provide that such areas are to become matters falling within the competence of the EC, although this would be a reasonable interpretation of those terms, nor do they specifically retain the extra-EC character of these matters. The Council is given a role to play, and the Commission is accorded a lesser role (Article K.4 (2)). The European Parliament is noted in the Title and while its role is larger than it has been previously in these matters, the degree to which it will be involved still raises questions concerning the lack of democratic accountability.

A second major area of European policing where cooperation at a macro level can be identified is agreements and legislation granting police forces operational powers across borders. Primarily, this involves agreements on investigation, arrest, detention and interrogation. Any discussions on harmonisation, streamlining and compatibility in these areas can only take place at the highest level. The highly sensitive issue of national sovereignty cross-cuts all discussion in this area, and requires macro-level political agreements in contrast to cooperative arrangements at an interpersonal or sub-national organisational level.

For example, the powers of police for 'hot pursuit' across borders can only be decided at the macro level. This is an issue which impinges on sensitive questions of sovereignty and requires national legislation. Another example of macro-level cooperation is firearms control. The EC member states have historically had different policies, procedures and traditions on the carrying and use of firearms, and harmonisation in this area was not possible without high-level agreements. This macro-level agreement was reached in the form of the 1991 EC Directive on Firearms. Legislation on the transfer of police intelligence across national boundaries is also an example of macro-level cooperation. Again, this sort of police cooperation can only proceed with harmonisation of data-protection laws and agreement at ministerial level. To a certain extent this has been effected by the terms of the 1981 Council of Europe Data Protection Convention to which all the EC states have given their signature, although not all have given effect to its terms.

Much police cooperation enabled by the Schengen Agreement and the 1992 Treaty on European Union, and much already carried out under the Trevi umbrella, is cooperation at the macro level, and this is discussed in detail in the sections dealing with these organisations.

The meso level

Issues at this level are primarily concerned with the operational structures, practices and procedures of the police and other law enforcement agencies. This is the framework within which day-to-day operational policing occurs.

One important meso-level concern is communications between police forces. A number of issues arise under this heading, including police information systems, common data-bases and coordination and access to information such as criminal intelligence. The rapid growth in advanced information technology and the police use of computers make this area all the more important. Police cooperation at the meso level requires cooperation over the use of compatible communications systems.

A central feature in enhanced European police communications is language. Besides the obvious need to speak a common language, when necessary, there are also problems of technical language and terminologies which vary between countries. This directs attention to language training for police officers and others, such as customs officials, and also to further work on a 'Policespeak'language, currently being developed in the UK (Follain, 1989).

An important feature of meso-level cooperation is face-to-face contact between middle-ranking officers from different countries. A good example of this is the cooperation established between officers from Kent County Constabulary in England and their colleagues from the Pas-de-Calais area in northern France in preparation for policing the Channel Tunnel (Gallagher, 1992).

One major difficulty preventing close European police cooperation at the meso level is the sheer diversity amongst the law enforcement agencies within the EC. In terms of their histories, their organisational structures, their practices and procedures, there is great variety amongst police forces, and this is a majorproblem at the meso level. In fact, it is surprising that police cooperation in Europe proceeds as well as it does, given the diversity of agencies involved.

There is enormous variation, first, in defining what is meant by 'police' (Gregory, 1991: 146; Mawby, 1991). There is variation especially in relation to border policing and illegal immigration, customs, the policing of airports and ports, railway police, political police and forestry police. For example, in Portugal the Guarda Fiscal is essentially a customs and tax police service, whereas in the UK both these duties are performed by (separate) groups of civil servants and HM Customs and Excise. In contrast, the Guardia di Finanza in Italy has responsibilities for the prevention and investigation of smuggling, illegal immigration and tax evasion. In Spain, within the framework of two national police organisations, there is additional provision for the Policia Autonomica, but these have only so far been established in the autonomous regions of the Basque Country, Catalunya and Navarra. In Italy, there is a police force called the corps of foresters, responsible for the forests and the environment. Greece also has a forest police force.

Taking account of these broad definitions, we identified 80 separate police forces in Europe (Benyon et al., 1993). At one end of the spectrum, Denmark and Spain have national police forces; at the other end, the UK has 52 autonomous forces. Dividing the 80 principal forces by the 12 EC member states gives an average of nearly seven separate police forces for each member state. Even if the UK's 52 separate forces are excluded from the calculations, there is still an average of 2.5 police forces per member state.

There is also considerable variation in the numbers of police officers in each member state. The CSPO study has found there are over 1.2 million police officers in the 12 countries of the European Community (Ibid.). Given a total population of some 343 million, this means that there is one police officer for every 270 people. But there is also considerable variation between member states, with an estimated one police officer for every 191 citizens in Italy and only one officer for every 499 citizens in Denmark.

Other areas of variation include arrangements for public accountability, in pay and promotion prospects, in the quality of recruits and in the social status of policing as an occupation or profession, and in police standards of assessment, standards of service and codes of ethics. Research already undertaken in this area (Ibid.) suggests that greater research into, and understanding of, the different police forces within the EC is needed if meso-level cooperation is to succeed further.

The micro level

European police cooperation at the micro level is concerned with the investigation of specific offences and the prevention and control of particular forms of crime. Cooperation at this level mainly occurs in relation to specific crime issues, such as drugs trafficking, terrorism, organised crime and environmental crime.

To take one example, problems of public disorder tend to vary between different countries and regions in Europe. Distinctive cultures and traditions may give rise to different forms of behaviour, which need different forms of policing. Micro-level cooperation can be effective in certain circumstances as was seen, for example, during the World Cup in Italy in 1990 when police from different countries offered information and assistance to their Italian counterparts.

Liaison officers who are seconded from one country to work with their counterparts in another country, especially in the fields of terrorism, drugs and football hooliganism, are good examples of micro-level cooperation.

There are considerable opportunities for micro-level initiatives, and indeed many already occur through the various formal, and particularly the informal, police networks which exist between officers of different countries. But successful networks themselves tend to be established at the meso level, and indeed many micro-level instances of cooperation do depend on effective meso-level arrangements.

Arrangements for police cooperation in Europe

The three levels offer a model for mapping out and describing cooperation between European police forces in a more coherent manner. This section examines how the arrangements for police cooperation in Europe might be clarified using this typology, by examining how the work of Interpol, the Schengen Agreements, Trevi/K4 and Europol might be understood through their work at the three levels. It is important to remember that the organisations discussed below do not fit neatly within any one level; sometimes the boundaries are blurred and the categories are not mutually exclusive.

Interpol

The International Criminal Police Organisation, or Interpol, exists to provide a communications system for the exchange of information between the police forces of member countries. This is done by the transmission of information and requests for action in the form of 'international notices'. Interpol is based in Lyons, France and has 169 members. It is the oldest structure for assisting police cooperation, tracing its history back to the interwar period (Anderson, 1989).

The majority of Interpol's work is Europe-based, with around 80 per cent of messages originating in the National Central Bureaux (NCBs) of the Council of Europe countries. Of this, around 40 per cent of messages originate within the EC member states. A European Secretariat was established in 1986, and a European Regional Conference is held annually.

In the past many reservations have been expressed about Interpol, including allegations of inefficiency and complaints about unacceptably slow response times. Doubts about its security have also been raised, and some members have expressed suspicions about the policing policies and motives of other members. These are obviously serious allegations. It is interesting to note that many of the debates about the development of efficient European police cooperation in the 1970s arose in the first instance from discussions and criticisms of Interpol (Fijnaut, 1991).

Interpol has, however, changed considerably in recent years (Bressler, 1992). The General Secretariat has moved to Lyons and under the management of Raymond Kendall the efficiency of Interpol has improved. New computers have lowered response times for requests for information to 1.5 hours and better safeguards have been established to improve the security of information passing through the system. Criticisms continue to be made, however, and it will clearly take more time for Interpol's reputation for efficient and secure operations to improve amongst many police officers.

Interpol's role in enabling greater police cooperation in Europe is restricted. It is not an operational organisation, and exists essentially as a communications network and also increasingly as a forum for discussion and analysis of European crime trends. It does not enable police cooperation at the macro level. However, at the meso and micro levels it has a valuable role. The structure of Interpol potentially enables cooperation at the meso level, through the work of contact officers in each of the European NCBs. The function of these officers is to resolve problems specific to individual cases, and to provide a single contact point at each NCB. The basic bread-and-butter work of Interpol is to promote police cooperation at the micro level, involving collaboration and assistance in the investigation of specific cases.

The restriction of Interpol's role essentially to that of a communications system has raised questions about its ability to play a greater role in developing police cooperation in Europe. Benyon (1992: 29) argues that the capacity of Interpol to promote wider police cooperation in Europe is constrained by its international world role, on the grounds that its primary obligations are world-wide and that this is incompatible with taking on a greatly enhanced role in Europe. It does however appear to be the case, increasingly, that Interpol is developing its European role, in response to both internal demands and external recommendations for increased regionalisation. At the meso and micro levels it has established itself as a useful structure for increased European police cooperation, and current indications suggest that Interpol will develop its work further in this field. It is important to remember that whilst other communications systems suggested for Europe will rely solely on the exchange of information orginating in, and dispatched to, other European countries, Interpol's international role enables international police cooperation to develop, involving all parts of the world.

One important issue which is not covered by regulations governing Interpol are arrangements for political and public accountability. Whilst this is not really a problem at present, given Interpol's primary role as a means of communication, if Interpol were to assume a greater role in police cooperation in Europe much consideration would need to be given to the incorporation of structures to increase accountability and hence legitimacy and public consent.

The Schengen Agreement

The Schengen Agreement is the most ambitious attempt to date to formalise police cooperation in Europe. The contracting parties to the Schengen Agreement have proceeded in two stages. In 1985 five states – Belgium, France, Luxembourg, the Netherlands and Germany – signed the Schengen Agreement, the articles of which all relate to methods of speeding up frontier crossing, as a prelude to the gradual abolition of checks at common borders. In June 1990 these countries signed the Schengen Implementing Convention which includes measures on visa régime harmonisation, hot pursuit and the establishment of a computerised data exchange system known as the Schengen Information System (SIS). On 27 November 1990 Italy joined the Schengen arrangement. Portugal and Spain joined in June 1991 and Greece in November 1992. Denmark, Ireland and the UK have maintained that they will not join the group, citing concern about existing border agreements (Denmark) and an island geography (Ireland and the UK) as reasons.

The structure and operations of the Schengen group reflect a division into the levels suggested by the heuristic device presented above. At the top there is a Council of Ministers who meet bi-annually, providing the macro-level discussions and agreements. Below the Council is the Central Negotiating Group (CNG) which directs the practical work of the Schengen group, supervising the operations of the four working groups and four supplementary groups, and presenting the decisions of the working groups to the Council of Ministers. Both the CNG and the working groups fall within the meso-level category of cooperation. The CNG comprises senior officials from the member states, represented by both police and civil servants. The working groups are formed from police and professionals with expertise and responsibilities in the particular area with which the working group is involved. Micro-level cooperation will, of course, occur when the police officers in the countries cooperate in the investigation of specific cases.

European police cooperation is enabled at each of the three levels through the provisions of the Schengen Agreement. The development of a common visa policy and common asylum policy is required as part of the Schengen Implementing Convention which, as indicated above, is a macro-level aspect of police cooperation which can only be decided at a ministerial and intergovernmental level, that is, in the Council of Ministers. At the macro level, cooperation is also facilitated through agreements to allow police officers to operate outside the territory of their 'home' nation state, specifically through granting police powers of 'hot pursuit' up to 10km from internal borders. This agreement excludes France, while in the case of Germany there is no limit on the extent of hot pursuit. Agreement on the use of firearms has also been reached, although this has been largely superseded by the 1991 EC Council Directive on the control of the acquisition and possession of weapons. These are issues which entail some loss of sovereignty, as expressed through a nation state's right to police its own territory. This is, therefore, best described as cooperation at the macro level because it involves fundamental constitutional questions which require consideration at the highest level. Schengen is an important indicator of the level of commitment made by some member states towards enhanced European police cooperation.

Other provisions of the Schengen Implementing Convention allow for cooperation to be enhanced at the meso level. For example, the development of the communications system can also be seen as meso-level cooperation. The Schengen Information System (SIS) will take some years to bring to full fruition. It will be a sophisticated system with a capacity of around 1 million personal records and information will be held on wanted criminals and suspects, aliens described as 'undesirable', missing persons, and people under surveillance. Inevitably, the information to be held on the SIS raises issues of accountability, civil liberties and human rights.

The Schengen Implementing Convention is a comprehensive attempt by nine member states of the EC to facilitate transborder cooperation in policing and law enforcement. It is intended to operate at macro, meso and micro levels. Crucially, it is the first step towards allowing cross-border operations. Many commentators suggest that its provisions will be superseded by future arrangements, as has already occurred in relation to procedures for asylum seekers, firearms and money laundering and as may occur with the development of Europol in the future. It remains the first attempt to provide for European police cooperation at all three levels through its provisions on legislative harmonisation, communications and liaison, and operational matters. In this respect it has been described as a prototype for future cooperative arrangements.

The Schengen Agreement fails to meet the standards for the ideal prototype in the arrangements for democratic accountability. Each of the levels of administration is directly responsible to that immediately superior to it and at the top the ministers are responsible to their own national parliaments. However, there is no provision for public account-ability or redress for citizens of Schengen countries, or for persons from outside Schengen countries. The only provision for the resolution of disputes is the Executive Committee (Title VII). The Executive Committee is in fact the Council of Ministers and is not therefore an appro-priate forum for the resolution of individual cases of complaint. No recourse may be had to either the European Court of Justice, or the European Court of Human Rights, since neither is appointed with juris-diction to consider such cases. In addition to the lack of a judicial remedy, the accountability of the Executive Committee to the national parliaments is also severely limited. Article 132 provides that the Committee may decide its own rules of procedure and set up any working groups it wishes.

Given the foreseeable effects of the Schengen Implementing Convention it is extremely likely that, at least in relation to the asylum provisions, there will be cases of dispute. The lack of judicial control of the actions of the Executive Committee can only be described as a fundamental flaw in the descriptions of the Schengen Convention as a prototype for future cooperative arrangements.

The Trevi group

The Trevi group is probably best described as a forum rather than an organisation. The decision to establish Trevi was taken in December 1975 by the Council of Ministers and the first meeting was held in Luxembourg in June 1976. Trevi is structured in three tiers. At the top is the group known as the Trevi Ministers, basically the ministers for home and interior affairs from each member state. The ministers are serviced by a group of senior officials, who form the middle tier. This group of senior civil servants and police officers undertake much of the groundwork in preparation for the meetings of Trevi Ministers, and in particular receive reports on the work undertaken by the three (previously four) working groups. The working groups form the bottom level and consist of police officers, civil servants and other experts in specific areas where required.

Working Group I was established in May 1977 to coordinate activity against terrorism, exchange information and ideas and undertake threat assessments. Working Group II was also established at that time to exchange information on training, equipment, public order and private security issues. Until 1985 Trevi remained essentially a forum for the discussion of terrorism and associated issues, but in the June of that year Working Group II was given additional responsibility for coordinating the exchange of information and ideas on best practice on football hooliganism, in the wake of the Heysel Stadium tragedy. A third Working

Group was also established to deal with the exchange of information on serious crime. Its remit has grown, and various groups meet under the Working Group III umbrella to discuss drugs trafficking and organised crime, computer crime, environmental crime, car crime, trafficking in stolen antiques and works of art, and money laundering. A fourth Working Group on 1992 existed between December 1988 and December 1992 to examine the policing and national security consequences of the reduction or abolition of border controls within the EC.

Trevi is an important forum for police cooperation in Europe. All 12 member states are represented within it and, in addition, a further seven 'friends of Trevi' are associated with its work and attend meetings, these countries being Norway, Sweden, Austria, Switzerland, Morocco, USA and Canada. It provides a forum to promote cooperation on a number of issues and at a number of levels. It should be noted, however, that Trevi's predilection for secrecy at times precludes a fully informed assessment of its work.

The three levels of cooperation identified earlier in this chapter are again useful in mapping out the extent of Trevi's functions. At the macro level, police cooperation is fostered through the meetings of the Trevi Ministers. In practice, there is little evidence to suggest that Trevi has itself promoted or provided for legislative or constitutional changes, and nor has it in the past promoted discussion on the harmonisation of national laws. However, through the provisions of Article K.4 of the Maastricht Treaty on European Union, the role of what are now Trevi Senior Officials is enhanced through the creation of a Coordinating Committee to develop arrangements for cooperative practices amongst police forces. It is likely that the development of conventions and treaties, for example on European external borders, will be a K.4 responsibility, thus granting this group responsibilities for cooperation at the macro level.

Cooperation between police forces is enhanced through Trevi's meso-level functions. For example, it was through the recommendations of Working Group III that the network of Drugs Liaison Officers both outside and within theEC was established. There is also evidence that on an extremely informal level cooperation is enhanced through the mere fact of Trevi meetings and discussions which bring together representatives from different police forces. Through the development of personal relationships cooperation is in fact enhanced even though it is not provided for formally.

An important micro-level function is the development of cooperation over specific issues and offences, and it is here that the working groups have made a substantial contribution. Although with regard to the work of Working Group I no information is available, research undertaken at the CSPO suggests that the exchange of information between representatives from member states under the umbrellas of groups II and III has been useful in the development of a common – and cooperative – approach to the policing of specific types of crime. There is little to suggest that at this level specific cases are discussed, but certainly specific offences are, such as certain types of environmental crime and football hooliganism.

The serious criticism levelled at Trevi about the secrecy of its meetings and their outcomes, leads to fundamental doubts about the democratic accountability of the group, and related to this its political legitimacy. The working groups report to the senior officials group who in turn report to the ministers. This is where the accountability structure appears to stop. The Trevi Ministers are really responsible to no one but themselves and their own governments. There is no requirement even for them to report to their national parliaments about decisions and discussions occurring within the groups. As what has been an extra-EC forum, there have been no procedures for reporting to the Commission or the European Parliament. There are serious questions to be raised over the control and accountability of the activities of the Trevi groups. Whether this will change as a result of the Maastricht Treaty on European Union is doubtful, at least in the short to mid-term.

Europol

The Maastricht Treaty on European Union, signed on 7 February 1992, establishes under its so-called 'third pillar' on Justice and Home Affairs, a number of areas where European police cooperation might proceed, including provisions for the establishment of a 'Union-wide system for exchanging information within a European Police Office (Europol)' (Article K.1). Europol will start initially by limiting its activities to the exchange of information about drugs-related crime. Indeed, it will be known in the first instance as the EDU/Europol Drugs Unit (EDU).

In the first instance the EDU will act as an agency for the bi-lateral exchange of information about drugs-related crime. The EDU will also provide analyses of drugs-related crime in Europe, in order to provide a broader picture of the nature of the drugs threat and identify investigative approaches. By mid-1993 no further areas of activity or the location of the EDU had been agreed. However, following the signing and ratification of a convention for the establishment of Europol, it is likely that this agency will develop into a fully fledged European police office or agency (Woodward, 1993).

It is not as yet possible to assess the functions of EDU/Europol in relation to the three levels outlined above. However, it is possible to speculate on this. It appears that EDU/Europol will promote effective cooperation at all three levels. At the macro level, agreements will have to be signed and ratified allowing for the exchange of information between member states, and this in turn will require some further thought on the harmonisation of data-protection standards. Meso-level cooperation will be permitted through the work of liaison officers based at EDU/Europol headquarters and at the national criminal intelligence services to be established in each member state. Potentially, micro-level cooperation may be given legislative recognition in the distant future if EDU/Europol is granted an operational and executive function for the investigation of specific offences. However, this is not being planned for currently, and the eventual realisation of this lies some way in the future, because again such cooperation raises a number of issues relating to sovereignty which would have to be negotiated and agreed at the macro level. The exchange of information will, however, promote some micro-level cooperation.

The accountability of EDU/Europol must be questioned. As an adjunct of the Trevi group, which, as already noted, has no procedures for democratic accountability, Europol must be open to the same criticism. Concern has already been expressed by members of the European Parliament over the lack of control or possibility for assessing the worth of Europol (Marshall, 1993). If and when the K4 Committee assumes the work of the Trevi group it may be that procedures for accountability and democratic control will be incorporated in its terms of reference, but it is as yet unclear what functions the K4 Committee is to have and therefore difficult to speculate on the future position of either the K4 Committee or Europol.

Other structures for police cooperation

In addition to Interpol, the Schengen Agreement, the Trevi group and the nascent Europol, there is a large number of smaller and less formal arrangements for promoting police cooperation in Europe. Together they form a complex interconnecting mesh of formal structures and informal arrangements, serviced by a range of information systems (which are often incompatible). These arrangements are most usefully viewed as meso areas of cooperation, although they may receive sanction at the macro level. Under the umbrella of these meso-level arrangements, micro-level activities on specific investigations occur.

These formal and semi-formal networks include the Police Working Group on Terrorism (PWGOT), the network of European Drugs Liaison Officers and National Drugs Intelligence Units, the Football Hooligan Intelligence Network, and the European Traffic Policing Meeting. There are also networks in fields such as technical and forensic matters, port and airport policing, and railway policing, and formal and informal bi-lateral arrangements which facilitate cooperation between adjacent forces, such as the Garda Siochana and the Royal Ulster Constabulary, at the Irish/UK border, or the Police de l'Air et des Frontières and the Guardia di Pubblica Sicurezza, at the Italian/French border. Cooperation between customs officers occurs through the Customs Cooperation Council of the United Nations and through the European Mutual Assistance Group 1992 (MAG '92) and the EC Matthaeus initiative. Cooperation is often also facilitated through professional groups and organisations, such as the International Federation of Police Unions (Union Internationale des Syndicats de Police or UISP) or the European Network for Policewomen (ENP).

These meso-level agreements are both beneficial and problematic. They are beneficial because they can produce achievements in particular crime areas, and promote cooperation over particular issues. However, there is a possible danger of an over-proliferation of these meso and micro-level structures, and the implications of a lack of overall coherence for the development of policing policy requires due consideration at the appropriate levels. There is considerable risk of (and indeed evidence of) duplication of effort and confusion with a number of networks claiming similar areas of responsibility. Furthermore, many of the bi-lateral, or tri-lateral, arrangements are relatively informal, and these informal arrangements also do little to secure accountability or legitimacy. Well-intentioned activities may lead to legal or constitutional difficulties if officers from different countries cooperate at the micro and meso level without official approval.

Conclusion

This chapter has taken a preliminary step towards providing a device through which the various structures and agreements which promote European police cooperation can be mapped out. The macro, meso and micro levels, are helpful in ordering the mass of organisations and factors integral to the subject of European police cooperation, have been outlined. Interpol, the Schengen Agreement, the Trevi group and the EDU/Europol have been examined with reference to these three levels. It is worth stressing again that the three levels constitute a heuristic and preliminary device for directing understanding of police cooperation, and do not provide an explanation in themselves.

A fruitful next step in the development of a system for mapping out the structures and agreements for European police cooperation may be a conceptualisation along the lines developed by Rhodes and Marsh (1992). This would take the exercise beyond the rather basic heuristic offered here. Network theory has been useful in mapping out policy areas at a sub-national governmental level. In particular, it has been successfully employed to order material within specific policy areas such as health education and agricultural policy in such a way as to raise questions about membership of policy networks, levels of integration, the distribution of resources and the balance of power. It remains to be seen whether the application of network theory might shed more light on the organisational structure of the networks which formulate European policing policy. Such an exercise might constitute a useful development on the preliminary conceptualisation developed here.

Indeed, the experience of the CSPO research project to date suggests that European police cooperation comprises a set of issues to do with policing, crime and justice in the EC which are urgently in need of continued and thorough research and monitoring. It is still the case that insufficient research into these areas has been undertaken, and it will always be necessary to monitor developments continuously. This is, after all, a constantly changing field.

Research is necessary not only because so little is known about this field. In addition, there is a strong argument that future European policing policies *have* to be constructed on the basis of detailed information. It is apparent that ill-thought out policies and overlapping networks and strategies exist in this area. This is potentially harmful to the development of efficient, workable cooperative strategies. Coherent strategies need to be developed and these cannot be formulated without a full awareness of the basic issues involved and the mechanisms which already exist for promoting police cooperation.

One final point must be emphasised in conclusion. Throughout this chapter attention has been drawn to the lack of procedures for account-ability of the various structures which exist to promote European police cooperation. It is surely essential that suitable mechanisms should be developed to ensure proper accountability of these structures. Police cooperation in Europe has developed at a number of levels, and through-out these there appears to have been a widespread neglect of mechanisms to ensure political and public accountability. Politicians, civil servants and police officers all seem to have underestimated the importance of such mechanisms, yet they are most necessary in order to secure the legitimacy and public consent which are vital for the effective policing of the liberal democracies of the EC (Benyon and Bourn, 1986). Without public support and consent, based on legitimacy which comes from accountability, effective law enforcement and the identification and prosecution of criminals cannot occur. Effective police cooperation in Europe ultimately depends on information and assistance received from members of the public. The fight against crime must be waged by both the police *and* the citizens of Europe.

References

Anderson, M. (1989), *Policing the World. Interpol and the Politics of International Police Cooperation*, Oxford, Clarendon Press.

Benyon, J. (1992), *Issues in European Police Co-operation*, Discussion Papers in Politics, No. P 92/11, Leicester, CSPO.

Benyon, J. and Bourn, C. (Eds) (1986), *The Police: Powers, Procedures and Proprieties*, Oxford, Pergamon Press.

Benyon, J., Davies, P. and Willis, A. (1990), 'Police Co-operation, Security and Public Order Management and Crime Prevention in Europe', in House of Commons, *Practical Police Co-operation in the European Community: Seventh Report from the Home Affairs Committee*, Session 1989–90, Volume II, Memoranda of Evidence, HC 363-II, London, HMSO, 181–185.

Benyon, J., Turnbull, L., Willis, A. and Woodward, R. (1993), *Police Co-operation in Europe: An Investigation*, Leicester, CSPO.

Boer , M. den, and Walker, N. (1993), 'European Policing after 1992', *Journal of Common Market Studies*, **31**, 3–28.

Bressler, F. (1992), *Interpol*, London, Sinclair Stevenson.

Fijnaut, C. (1991), 'Police Co-operation within Western Europe', in Heidensohn and Farrell, 1991: 103–120.

Follain, M. (1989), 'On the Trail of a Simple International Language', *Financial Times*, 28 June.

Gallagher, F. (1992), 'Kent County Constabulary: Its European Perspective', *Police Requirements Support Unit Bulletin*, **42**, 18–24.

Gregory, F. (1991), 'Police Co-operation and Integration in the EC: Proposals, Problems and Prospects', *Terrorism*, **14**, 145–255.

Heidensohn, F. and Farrell, M. (Eds.) (1991), *Crime in Europe*, London, Routledge and Kegan Paul.

House of Commons (1990), *Practical Police Co-operation in the European Community: Seventh Report from the Home Affairs Committee*, Session 1989–90, Volume I, Report and Proceedings of the Committee, HC 363-I, London, HMSO.

Imbert, Sir P. (1989) 'Crimes without Frontiers', *Police Review*, **97**, 5015 (9 June), 1174–1175.

Marshall, A. (1993), 'Drug Squad to be Part of "Fortress Europe" Strategy', *The Independent*, 3 June.

Mawby, R. (1991), *Comparative Police Systems: Searching for a Continental Model*, Paper presented to British Criminology Conference, York.

Milland, J. (1990), 'Transnational Criminality', in J. Alderson and W. Tupman (Eds.), *Policing Europe After 1992*, Exeter, University of Exeter Press.

Rhodes, R. and Marsh, D. (1992), 'New Directions in the Study of Policy Networks', *European Journal of Political Research*, **21**, 181–205.

Schuman, Robert (1990), *Europe: a Fresh Start. The Schuman Declaration 1950–1990*, Luxembourg, Office for Official Publications of the European Communities.

Woodward, R. (1993), *The Establishment of Europol: A Critique*, Paper presented to the Cyprus Police Academy, Nicosia, April.

ISSUES AND PROBLEMS

4

POLICING REFUGEES AND ASYLUM-SEEKERS IN 'GREATER EUROPE': TOWARDS A RECONCEPTUALISATION OF CONTROL

Mike King

The main aims of this chapter are, first, to propose and explore some concepts towards theorising processes of control of refugees and asylum-seekers in contemporary Europe, with particular reference to Western, Central and Eastern European states. Second, we consider the position of the Visegrád group, namely the Czech Republic, Hungary, Poland and Slovakia, within those processes, suggesting that they are increasingly becoming a *de facto* buffer-zone between what we will call 'greater-inner' and 'outer' Europe. The primary concepts with which we will be concerned are those of 'Europeanisation' and what we shall term 'Fortification'. We will also examine some realities of contemporary East–West refugee migration in critique of the dominant political discourse.

Superficially, it would seem as though the socio-political and economic structures and alliances in 'greater Europe' are converging. In other words, it appears that such alliances and structures are subject to processes of blanket and all-encompassing incorporation, harmonisation and Euro-peanisation. However, on closer examination, and especially so with regard to (and to some extent even determined by) border controls concerning refugees and asylum-seekers, we see that it is not simply a case of increasing convergence or Europeanisation *per se*. Rather, what is emerging, we suggest, is a system of definite and distinct 'Europes', from the 'inner' to the 'greater-inner' to the 'outer', culturally, socially, economically and politically protected by a series of buffer-zones. Further, to the extent that the concept of Europeanisation needs some refinement or qualification, on this basis so too, we argue, does the notion of 'Fortress Europe'. Rather than a simple exclusionary process, as implied in the Fortress analogy, what we are witnessing in contemporary Europe is more a process of 'Fortification' in which such exclusion is layered, again from the centre to the periphery. However, an important effect of contemporary harmonisation in the institution of restrictive policies by inner-Europe is that it is causing a ripple of corresponding controls to the borders of outer-Europe.

Europeanisation I

Elsewhere, we have applied the concept of Europeanisation specifically to trends for European policing system change (King, 1993a; 1993b). However, it is our suggestion here that such a concept equally applies to changing policies, alliances and other structures in Europe generally, that these are undergoing certain processes of incorporation. Although similarly applying this to policing systems, Fijnaut has argued that Europeanisation is a process entailing a linear progression, or evolution, from cooperation, involving multi-lateral and Community dimensions, to harmonisation to integration (1990: 20–21). We would suggest, additionally, that Europeanisation incorporates in its early stages a movement from the informal to the formal. Both the Benelux and Schengen Treaties contain prime examples of this process of formalisation of informal bi- and multi-lateral policing cooperation practices. Even further than this, however, the concept of Europeanisation that we employ as distinct from Fijnaut's, nominally at least moves beyond the European Community boundary restriction, nor do we suggest that the separate 'stages' are either unilinear or uniform. Moreover, we feel, that Fijnaut's category of integration can be further elaborated by importing van Reenen's (1989) distinction between Horizontal and Vertical Integration. Van Reenen has suggested that European policing systems are undergoing a process of Internationalisation involving three distinct modes. The first of these modes is Cooperation, which is loosely similar to Fijnaut's general Cooperation category. The second mode is Horizontal Integration, which, in terms of policing practice exists where police officers 'obtain the authorisation to operate in another country or [where] government officials from a country get authority over the police or parts of the police of another country' (van Reenen, 1989: 48). This we suggest could apply more on an intergovernmental basis, again in some circumstances under Schengen, such as 'hot pursuit' or even potentially within the European Drugs Intelligence Unit, set up under the Treaty on European Union (TEU) as the forerunner of Europol. Finally, van Reenen's third mode, that of Vertical Integration, involves supranational authorities, in van Reenen's terms being where 'a police organisation is being created that can operate within the area of the EC. . . . [presupposing] a central authority on which it depends, probably a central political power at EC level' (1989: 48–49). It is of course possible, on this basis, that vertically integrated structures may follow an initial incrementalist development of horizontal structures. Examples of the distinction here in respect of refugee controls would perhaps not only be the harmonisation of restrictive policies, but the right of cross-border enforcement (on the basis of an intergovernmental treaty or structure), to such competence passing to supranational authorities.

Fortification I

The question regarding the adequacy of the notion of 'Fortress Europe' is, again, raised by us elsewhere (King, 1992). We suggest that what is happening in respect of exclusionary border policies in contemporary Europe is not simply the creation of a situation of 'insiders' and 'outsiders'. Indeed, by the very nature of the fortress walls that are currently being constructed, even some of those inside are not in a superior position, in terms of freedom of movement within the internal area for example, than those on the outside. Another important limitation to the notion of fortress is again the multi-layered nature of exclusionary measures emanating from the centre outwards. We shall elaborate on this later, when picking up the the problematic mentioned earlier of different Europes, involving different levels of control. Rather than 'Fortress Europe', we employ here a concept of Fortification, suggesting that this is perhaps more sensitive to the process of fortress construction in Europe as being dynamically encompassing, particularly with regard to Readmission Agreements between some Western states and the Visegrád group, for example. What we are depicting is, then, analogous to Gramsci's notion of the state being a relatively defenceless 'outer ditch' without its 'fortresses and earthworks' (1971: 238).[1] In other words, the perimeter walls of the fortress are expanding and incorporating those on the margins. Again more detailed reference will be made to this later regarding, for example, the development of the European Economic Area (EEA).

Migration trends and policies

Garson (1992) suggests that there are currently three main types of migration trends, namely, acceleration, globalisation and regionalisation. Globalisation not only entails migratory movements affecting all continents, but also an increase in migrant nationalities and a convergence of the multi-various forms. Regionalisation, on the other hand, involves especially migrant-worker flows between bi- and multi-national economic partners. We shall refer to some of these arrangements later, such as those on the basis of association agreements between the EC and members of the Visegrád group, and that of the EEA. However, in this chapter we are particularly concerned with the third type of trend, namely acceleration. This type of migratory movement involves 'permanent migrants and asylum-seekers and refugees ... [and is] explained in essence by the political changes in the countries of Central and Eastern Europe ... and the continuing demographic and economic imbalances between North and South' (Garson, 1992: 18). Cohen similarly argues that within East–West migration specifically, a distinct pattern of three main categories of migrant was emerging, which we suggest conform well with the above acceleration trend, namely 'co-ethnic returnees to their homelands, co-ethnic migrants to communities abroad ... and those ... seeking to escape from political and economic hardship' (1991: 20). The first of these categories is especially important when considering *Aussiedler* and the contemporary situation of Germany as we shall later, however, it also involves the potential exodus of ethnic Greek Pontians from Albania and Kazakhstan, Turks from Bulgaria, Jews to Israel and Hungarians from Transylvania and Romania.

The categories or types of migrants that we have referred to here are especially important for our later discussion of the distinction between those that fall within the confines of the 1951 Geneva Convention, and those who are excluded from this but may be termed *de facto* refugees. This is a crucial distinction and particularly relevant for an understanding of contemporary 'inner' Europe exclusionary policies. It is worthwhile, there-fore, briefly to consider the UN Convention in its historical context. Coles (1990) argues that in the post-Second World War period, there were three discernible refugee movement periods. Given the changes in the East–West dimension since he wrote this, however, we would suggest that there have been four. The first period, from the late 1940s until the late 1950s, Coles suggests, saw the Western powers, on the one hand composing a majority within the United Nations and, on the other hand primarily being concerned with an ongoing problem of refugees from Europe. As opposed to utilising the definition of refugee as applied to the Palestinians in 1949, namely 'someone who, as a result of the conflict in Palestine in 1948, had lost his [or her] home ... [through] in part ... armed conflict' (Coles, 1990: 375), however, the UN Convention relating to the status of refugee defines this as being a person who is unwilling or unable to return to his or her country 'owing to well-founded fear of being persecuted for reasons of race, religion, nationality, membership of a particular social group or political opinion' (1951: Article 1A (2)). This restriction in terms of 'persecution' was, Coles argues, specifically adopted because it was seen as constituting the essential characteristic of the new refugee, in the belief that this would satisfactorily define European asylum-seekers, the majority of whom were from Eastern Europe. This would thereby, in the Cold War climate, stigmatise communist régimes from those states as 'persecutors' (Coles, 1990: 374–375). The second period of migration was from the early 1960s until the late 1970s, and characterised by its primarily intra-South nature. The third period, until the late 1980s, still involved East–West and intra-South movements, but that from South to North has been taken as especially prominent due to the concern placed on it by those 'with the economic and political power to control or influence international approaches to the problem of refugees, i.e. the Northern (or Western) countries' (Coles, 1990: 373). We suggest that the contemporary fourth period would indicate a shift of concentration, concern and political discourse, given a changed socio-political and economic situation, and that it is posed within a different problematic from that of the first period.

This would appear to confirm Cohen's argument that the distinction between refugees and asylum-seekers on the one hand and migrants on the other, or even between those with refugee status under the 1951 UN Convention and *de facto* refugees including 'economic migrants', 'often rests largely on the definitions accorded to the movement by the host state' (1991: 16) or, even further, we would add, definitions by the excluding state. The distinction becomes even more blurred with Giorgi *et al.*'s assertion that 'the underlying eliciting forces for migration in the case of Eastern Europe can be traced to the social, political, economic and psychological context of societies in transition' (1992: 32). Such a consideration certainly brings into question a recent suggestion by Lord Mackay of Ardbrecknish, during a debate of the Asylum and Immigration Appeals Bill (referred to later) in the House of Lords that:

When granting political asylum we must try to distinguish between those people who, if they stayed in their country of origin, would be persecuted for their political views and others who would not. I believe that we should treat the former sympathetically and speedily. However, those people who want to come here as economic migrants are, I am afraid, quite a different kettle of fish (*Hansard Weekly*, 1993: 1164).

It must be remembered, however, that the UN Convention is not the only definer of refugee status. Many states have incorporated wider categories in their statutes. Sweden, for example, currently (although this is now subject to review in line with other greater-inner European states) grants asylum on three counts, namely under the UN Convention, on the basis of *de facto* refugee status and on humanitarian grounds (*Migration News Sheet (MNS)*, January 1993: 7). There are regional 'solutions' too. For example, Article 1 (2) of the Organisation of African Unity Convention on Refugee Problems in Africa, 1969 provides that:

The term refugee shall . . . apply to every person who, owing to external aggression, occupation, foreign domination or events seriously disturbing public order in either part or the whole of his [or her] country of origin or nationality, is compelled to leave his [or her] place of habitual residence in order to seek refuge in another place outside his [or her] country of origin or nationality (Okojie, 1992: 23).

The UNHCR also makes the recommendation that Western governments at least provide 'temporary refuge' to those refugees fleeing from civil war or disaster (Loescher, 1990: 26). In fact, this is what many states bordering on what used to be Yugoslavia, for example, are forced to do, and of course, in respect of establishing so-called 'safe-havens', what many Western states would be relieved to see happen. The distinction between the numbers of asylum-seekers in Hungary, for example, between 1990 and 1991 give some indication of the scale of the problem. During 1990 there were 18,283 persons registered as asylum-seekers, their country of origin being Romania 95 per cent, (ex-)USSR 2.7 per cent and others 2.3 per cent, compared with 1991 in which 54,693 registered as asylum-seekers, their country of origin being (ex-)Yugoslavia 87 per cent, Romania 10 per cent, (ex-)USSR 2 per cent and other 1 per cent (Tóth, 1992: 17).

Germany

By far the largest proportion of those fleeing the 'Yugoslav' crisis to the West have been taken in by Germany. The UNHCR estimated that by August 1992 approximately 2 million refugees and 'displaced persons' had been created by the conflict in former Yugoslavia. About two-thirds of these were still located in the various republics (*MNS*, September 1992: 4). Currently it is estimated that almost 1 million Bosnian Muslims and Croats have fled. Of these, approximately 500,000 are now located in Croatia, 250,000 in Germany, 80,000 in Sweden, 73,000 in Austria and 40,000 in Hungary (Block, 1993). Further, Germany during 1992 received the highest number of asylum-seekers in the EC, namely 79 per cent of the total compared with 4.4 per cent for the UK (Carvel, 1993). Also, between 1977 and 1991, the number of asylum-seekers in Germany rose from 16,410 to 256,110 (Bundeszentrale für politische Bildung, 1992: 32). In 1992, this figure had increased to 438,191 applicants, being from: former Yugoslavs 122,666; Romanians 103,787; Bulgarians 31,540; Turks 28,327; Vietnamese 12,258; citizens of the former USSR 10,833; Nigerians 10,486 and Zaireans 8,305 (*MNS*, January 1993: 6). Giorgi *et al.* suggest that the high number of asylum-seekers from Romania in 1992 may largely have been due to a displacement effect caused by the success of restrictions imposed by Hungary and Austria (1992: 29). More than 90 per cent of all asylum-seekers arrive in Germany from its common borders with Austria, the Czech Republic, Poland and Switzerland (*MNS*, January 1993: 5) and it is this that Germany now seeks to plug by its change to the constitution.

Article 16 (2) ii of the 1949 constitution provides that 'Persons persecuted on political grounds shall enjoy the right of asylum' (*Basic Law for the Federal Republic of Germany*, 1969), however, the new Article 16A, effective from 1 July 1993, excludes from this 'right' those entering through what is decided to be a 'safe' third country, namely a fellow signatory of the Geneva Convention. Further, asylum-seekers are excluded where their claim to asylum is being or has been considered elsewhere. This incorporates both Schengen and EC exclusionary practices proposed (and in some states already in operation) concerning 'safe' countries, and also the 'first chance only rule' under the Dublin Convention. We refer to these later when considering the question of harmonisation of controls. Accordingly, the provisions of the new Article 16A are as follows:

Paragraph 1 Politically persecuted people enjoy the right of asylum.

Paragraph 2 Paragraph 1 does not apply to those entering from a member state of the European Communities or from a third state in which the application of the treaty concerning the legal position of refugees and the convention for the protection of human rights and basic liberties is guaranteed. Those states outside the European Communities to which sentence 1 applies are to be determined by law requiring the consent of the Bundesrat. In the cases of sentence 1 measures to terminate stays can be carried out regardless whether appeals have been lodged.

Paragraph 3 It will be determined by law which states may be defined, with the consent of the Bundesrat, on the basis of the legal situation, the legal application and the general political circumstances, as appearing to guarantee that neither political persecution nor inhuman or humiliating acts of punishment or treatment is taking place. A foreigner from such a state is not regarded as politically persecuted, except in the case where he presents evidence from which can be derived the contrary.

Paragraph 4 The carrying out of measures terminating stays may only be suspended by court in the cases of Paragraph 3 and in other cases, which are manifestly unfounded or are regarded as manifestly unfounded, where serious doubts exist concerning the lawfulness of the measure; [however] the extent of [such] review can be restricted and belated pleading can be left unconsidered. Further details are to be determined by law.

Paragraph 5 Paragraphs 1 to 4 are not contrary to treaties concerning law of nations of member states of the European Communities amongst each other and with third states, which, subject to obligations resulting from the treaty concerning the legal position of refugees and the convention for the protection of human rights and basic liberties, the application of which has to be guaranteed, decide on regulations concerning competence for the review of asylum applications, including the mutual recognition of asylum decisions (*Frankfurter Allgemeine Zeitung* (1993), author's translation).

On this basis, it would already appear that those passing through any of Germany's neighbouring states will have no right of application for asylum. Further, it is proposed that Slovakia be added to the list of safe countries, and also that Bulgaria, Gambia, Ghana, Romania and Senegal be 'safe countries of origin' (*MNS*, May 1993: 5). These exclusions are reinforced in respect of illegal migrants through Readmission Agreements, again something to which we refer later. We should mention, however, that it is likely that Germany will provide 'temporary asylum' in situations of *de facto* refugees fleeing from civil wars (*MNS*, January 1993: 6).

East–West realities

The situation regarding Germany, and also refugees into Western Europe generally needs to be put into wider context. For example, Europe receives only 5 per cent of the world's population of refugees (CEC, 1992: 4). Further, many of the 'pressures' on Germany specifically have been through its policy of automatic admission and citizenship for ethnic Germans, or *Aussiedler*, enshrined in Article 116 of the Constitution, which provides:

(1) Unless otherwise provided by law, a German within the meaning of this Basic Law is a person who possesses German citizenship or who has been admitted to the territory of the German Reich within the frontiers of 31 December 1937 as a refugee or expellee of German stock (*Volkszugehörigkeit*) or as the spouse or descendant of such person.

(2) Former German citizens who, between 30 January 1933 and 8 May 1945, were deprived of their citizenship on political, racial, or religious grounds, and their descendants, shall be re-granted German citizenship on application. They shall be considered as not having been deprived of their German citizenship if they have established their domicile (*Wohnsitz*) in Germany after 8 May 1945 and have not expressed a contrary intention (*Basic Law for the Federal Republic of Germany*, 1969).

There would seem to be no moves towards amending this 'right', although there are now proposals to limit the annual intake of persons on this basis to 220,000 (*MNS*, January 1993: 6).

There is a danger of over-dramatising the potential migratory forces from Eastern Europe with the effect of legitimising exclusionary controls against refugees generally. Zimmermann and Straubhaar have argued that 'Projections of East–West permanent or temporary migration during 1991–2000 range from serious academic estimates of some 5 to 15 million (some 3–4 per cent of Eastern Europe's current population) to speculative estimates by newspapers and politicians of some 20 to 40 million' (1992: 30). Okojie has similarly suggested that 'arguments about floodgates dominate the debate about refugees. The refugee is presented as the modern social plague' (1992: 13). Two examples, from the many instances of this creation of a 'moral panic' in Britain, that we give here are first, banner front-page headlines in the *Evening Standard* newspaper proclaiming 'Immigration: This Threat to Society' (Reiss, 1992) and, more recently a statement by Douglas Hurd, the British Foreign Secretary, that 'Germany is already coping with a wave of new immigration from the East. If we do not take action, the wave could turn into a tidal wave with dramatic consequences for the whole of Europe' (Gow, 1993).

Giorgi *et al.* in contrast to the above, make the point that neither Hungarians, Czechs nor Slovaks emigrated in large numbers following the 1989 reforms in their states. Further, although migration from Poland did peak during 1981 following the introduction of martial law, it has since 'remained at stable and containable levels'. Also, although 'migration from the CIS is viewed as a political threat, till now, however, migration within the former republics of the Soviet Union has by far exceeded migration to the West' (1992: 32). The 'threat' concerning 'economic migrants' is also put somewhat more into perspective by the results of a 'unique survey' conducted during February 1991 in Czechoslovakia, Hungary, Lithuania, Poland and Russia on a 'stratified random sample' of respondents which yielded 41,269 interviewees aged 15+, analysed by Brym (1992).The survey omits potential 'sponsored emigrant' respondents, those referred to earlier under Cohen's (1991) categories of co-ethnic returnees and co-ethnic migrants.

The survey results indicate that, if given the opportunity, most citizens of the former 'Communist World' would not 'pack up and leave', even given the disastrous economic situation and unstable political climate of the region' (Brym, 1992: 389). One could however, Brym suggests, 'state with 95% certainty that of the 216.1 million people in the 5 countries surveyed ... between 10.2 and 16.7 million wanted to settle permanently in the West' (1992: 390). However it is important to qualify this finding by stressing that the results constitute only a single 'snapshot' of a particular conjuncture, and as Brym argues, the general conclusions drawn from the analysed data suggest 'that political motives are rather more important than economic motives in prompting people to express the desire to settle in the West ... [i.e. it] has more to do with political freedom than material advantage' (1992: 393).

Europeanisation II

As part of the generally cooperative basis of Europeanisation, there now exists (and increasingly so) a multiplicity of bi- and multi-national fora and agreements, ranging from economic, to policing, to military security. Indeed, what is happening is something that Cohen has graphically described as 'a process of herding and sorting [that] is taking place as sheep are separating from goats,outsiders from insiders, the excluded from the included' (1992: 336). Certainly, as we have already indicated, we would suggest that this process is not simply one of all-encompassing incorporation or even convergence. The structures that are emerging are layered, perhaps similar to a series of concentric circles, from the centre or core to the periphery. Accordingly, the inclusionary elements of Europeanisation entail Fortification and a layered exclusion, which we argue moves roughly from an inner-Europe of Schengen member states to a greater inner-Europe of the EEA to a periphery eastwards, at least with the Visegrád group, and an outer-Europe from their external borders. Of course, as implied in Cohen's quote, the process is dynamic, changing over time according to relationships of economics and power among many other factors. However, with some consideration of historical development it is possible to indicate some trends or directions within the process. We do not propose to dwell here on the content or structure of the different fora or agreements, but more refer to their nation-state membership, in order to give some indication of such development.

First, we have suggested that inner-Europe is composed of the Schengen group. This, in turn, was a development from the Benelux Economic Union. There are now nine Schengen member states, being the original signatories (Benelux, France, and Germany) plus Greece, Italy, Spain and Portugal. Schengen's central coordination group is currently discussing the possibility of Austria, Finland and Sweden joining (*MNS*, March 1993: 1). In principle, at least, Schengen members must also be member states of the EC and these three countries are, similarly, being considered for this too.

The 12 formal members of the EC include the Schengen 'nine', plus Denmark, Ireland and the UK, although not only are the three countries mentioned above currently being considered for membership, but so is Norway since April 1993 (CEC, 1993d), and the EC has an additional membership of Associate and Cooperative Member states. Associate membership is based on a European Agreement between the EC and the respective signatory. The main objective of the Agreement is to achieve accession to the Community, however, probably the longest standing Associate Member (since 1963) and one with little chance of full membership to date is Turkey. Malta signed an Agreement in 1971[2] and more recently, since December 1991, the Visegrád group have been Associate Members. In February 1993 an Agreement was signed with Romania and with Bulgaria in March 1993 (*MNS*, April 1993: 11). The EC have recently announced that such agreements will be 'extended progressively' to all Central and Eastern European states, although 'eligibility will depend on their progress in establishing democratic political systems and free-market based economies giving full respect to human rights' (CEC, 1993b: 2). Further, eventual accession to the EC will be conditional on the following (ibid.):

- the capacity of the country concerned to assume the obligations of membership (the '*acquis communautaire*');
- the stability of institutions in the candidate country guaranteeing democracy, the rule of law, human rights and respect for minorities;
- the existence of a functioning market economy;
- the candidate's endorsement of the objectives of political, economic and monetary union;
- its capacity to cope with competitive pressure and market forces within the European Union;
- the Community's capacity to absorb new members while maintaining the momentum of European integration.[3]

The EC have, further, signed Cooperation Agreements with Algeria, Morocco and Tunisia, all entailing cooperation 'in the field of labour' (Guild, 1992: 12). Another agreement signed by the EC is with six members of EFTA (i.e. Austria, Finland, Iceland, Liechtenstein, Norway and Sweden, excluding Switzerland although it will have 'observer status', towards the establishment of the European Economic Area (CEC, 1993c)). Further associations exist between the members of the Visegrád group and also for purposes other than economic trade and internal 'freedom of movement', such fora as the proposed Budapest group on Immigration (*MNS*, March 1993: 4), the Council of Europe 26 or the Conference on Security and Co-operation in Europe 52 (including North America) or even the Western European [Security] Union. Finally, the EC is currently considering the establishment of a European Confederal Cooperation System providing 'a framework for associating partner countries with the work of the Community and the European Union. These could include common foreign, security policy and internal and justice affairs' (CEC, 1993b: 5). A problem with this, however, is that it may well firmly marginalise Association and Cooperation Agreement members to the periphery of greater-inner Europe and beyond, and for non-members, of course, even further.

Fortification II

At the beginning of this chapter we suggested, following Fijnaut and van Reenen, that harmonisation and integration were primary characteristics of Europeanisation. We refer to them here under Fortification, however, because of their essentially exclusionary form. Macey argues that 'over the last two decades or so, increasingly stringent controls have been implemented at the external borders of Western European countries. . . . This is not due to the establishment of the EC, but is, rather, a function of changing labour market demands' (1992: 145). Such 'stringent controls' we suggest include the harmonisation of visa and border policies, asylum legislation and even the creation of *de facto* buffer-zones on the borders of greater-inner Europe through a policy of Readmission Agreements, those with the Visegrád group being a prime instance of this. The *Ad Hoc* Group on Immigration, composed of the 12 EC Ministers of the Interior, at its meeting in London in November/December 1992 passed a 'resolution on manifestly unfounded applications for asylum'. This resolution, we suggest, stands as a classic example of harmonisation of restrictions. It provides for a 'fast track' approach to those applications which are deemed to be manifestly unfounded on the grounds of 'satisfactory protection for the applicant in another country' or where there is 'clearly no substance to the applicant's claim to fear persecution' (Carvel, 1992) and also where there has been 'deliberate deception or abuse of asylum procedures' including where the applicant has (*MNS*, December 1992: 5):

– had ample earlier opportunity to submit an asylum application, submitted the application in order to forestall an impending expulsion measure;

– flagrantly failed to comply with substantive obligations imposed by national rules relating to asylum procedures; and

– submitted an application in one of the member states, having had his application previously rejected in another country following an examination comprising adequate procedural guarantees and in accordance with the Geneva Convention on the Status of Refugees.

Such provisions are now being incorporated into respective member state legislation, as can be seen from the amendment to Article 16 of the German constitution, for example, and also in the UK's Asylum and Immigration Appeals Bill. The latter not only makes the fingerprinting of all asylum-seekers compulsory,[4] but extends provisions under the Immigration (Carriers' Liability) Act 1987 to include visa restrictions for transit passengers.[5] At present, transit visas are required by the UK for nationals of Iran, Iraq, Lebanon, Lybia, Somalia, Sri Lanka and Turkey (*MNS*, November 1992: 8).

Harmonisation of visa policies is another important restrictive practice. Currently, a common list between Schengen member states contains 120 countries (*MNS*, January1993: 2).[6] Such harmonisation is also taking place on wider levels than Schengen, however. In June 1992, for example, at their meeting in Lisbon the *Ad Hoc* Group on Immigration agreed the addition of 12 states from the ex-Soviet Union to the EC's compulsory visa list (Drüke, 1992: 17). Indeed it would seem that a common list of countries whose nationals require visas together with the uniform format for a EC visa, are the 'only two [immigration] matters [to be] brought within the Community competence' under the Maastricht Treaty on European Union and not subject to intergovernmental democratic deficit (*Hansard*, 1993: 472).

Not surprisingly, given such controls within inner- and greater-inner Europe, these are impacting on those states on the periphery. At a meeting in Prague in March 1993, the Ministers of the Interior of Austria, the Czech Republic, Hungary, Poland, Slovakia and Slovenia agreed to 'work towards harmonising their immigration regulations ... [and] strengthen ... [their] border controls' (Bridge, 1993). This 'strengthening' will, of course, be eastwards, and is due in part also to bi- and multi-lateral Readmission Agreements between East and West. These Agreements generally provide for the return of illegal immigrants from inner- and greater-inner European states to the peripheral countries of origin or transit. Poland signed a Readmission Agreement with all the Schengen states in March 1991 (*MNS*, October 1991: 8) and since then Austria has signed such agreements with both Hungary and Romania (*MNS*, April 1992: 3). Germany now has agreements also with Bulgaria (November 1992) on the offer of DM28 million (*Platform Fortress Europe*, December 1992/January 1993: 3) and with Romania (September 1992, which took effect from November 1992) on payment of DM30 million for 'resettlement costs' (*The Guardian*, 1992). This latter agreement is already operational, with over 6,000 Romanians being returned by Germany since January 1993 from Schönefeld airport alone (*MNS*, April 1993: 3). Further, on 7 May 1993 Germany signed a bi-lateral Readmission Agreement with Poland, after agreeing a payment of DM120 million (*The Guardian*, 1993). In March 1993 the Prime Minister of Slovakia, V. Meciar, stated that his country would 'reinforce controls at its eastern borders [by tripling the number of border guards there] as well as strengthening its border with the Czech Republic in order to prevent people from travelling on to Germany to apply for asylum' (*MNS*, April 1993: 5). The Budapest Group, referred to earlier, may well shortly be considering whether the multi-lateral Readmission Agreement between the Schengen group and Poland should be enlarged 'to include many more states' or whether it would be better simply to establish more bi-lateral agreements. Membership of the group is likely to be those states assuming the presidency of the Schengen group, the EC and EFTA, the Czech Republic, Hungary, Poland, and Slovakia (*MNS*, March 1993: 4). This, we feel, certainly gives some indication of the expansionist developmental trend within the process of Fortification, but also the important situation of the Visegrád four as an exclusionary buffer-zone between East and West within that process. The question is, of course, how transitional that buffer-zone is likely to be even given the Association Agreements mentioned earlier.

The combination of Readmission Agreements regarding illegal immigrants, plus the proposed return of manifestly unfounded asylum applicants to 'safe' third countries is, as we have already indicated, having the effect in Central Europe of moving the outer ditch of the fortress eastwards. Similarly, Mather (1993) has argued that 'on the other side of Europe's new fault line are Romania, Bulgaria, Ukraine, Lithuania, Belarus and . . . Russia'. However, Russia too is a 'safe' country from May 1993, it acceding to the Geneva Convention (*MNS*, March 1993: 7). A further dimension to this is of course that Readmission Agreements are not restricted between West and East. France is currently negotiating for a multi-lateral Readmission Agreement with member states of the Mediterranean zone (*MNS*, January 1993: 3) and an agreement was signed between Portugal and Spain in February 1993 (*MNS*, March 1993: 5).

Conclusion

Although our primary concerns in this chapter have been with the Western, Central and Eastern European dimension of the refugee and asylum problem, and with the situation of the Visegrád group in particular, this is not to deny similar situations in the South–North context, indeed we have touched on some of these. Part of our focus on the East–West dimension has been to question some aspects of the dominant Western political discourse regarding the refugee 'threat' from the East, especially the notion of economic migration *per se*. Further we have proposed that concepts of Europeanisation and Fortification may be utilised in a consideration of processes of control of refugees and asylum-seekers in Europe. Such concepts, we feel, potentially provide more understanding to the dynamic nature of those processes. However, both concepts themselves need refinement to take account of the progressive layering of controls and treaties as well as powers and buffer-zones within the many Europes. We have examined some of these here, from Schengen to the European Confederal Cooperation System or even the Budapest group for example, suggesting a developmental trend towards both general and particular incorporation. We have also considered controls in respect of visa and asylum harmonisation and the development of expulsion practices to 'safe' third countries and the practice and effect of Readmission Agreements. The layering of Europe, we suggest, is taking place primarily from the inner Schengen group, to the greater-inner European Economic Area, to the Eastern periphery Visegrád group, to the outer.

Notes

1 Although to some extent this may be more meaningful for our analogy if the state were the fortress and the defences its outer ditches.
2 A formal Commission opinion concerning Malta's and Cyprus's applications to join the EC should be forthcoming sometime later in 1993, but indications are that they 'are unlikely to be members . . . this century, if at all' (Walker, 1993).
3 The Commission has recently announced that it is considering a joint review together with respective Eastern and Central European Associates of the situation regarding 'progress . . . towards satisfying [these] conditions for eventual membership . . . mid-way through the decade' (CEC, 1993d).
4 This would seem to be moving towards a Europe-wide harmonisation of such practice and the possible development of a 'European Information System based on the fingerprints of asylum-seekers'. There are even suggestions that Australia and Canada are interested in joining such a system (Bundesamt für Flüchtlinge, 1992: 5, 50).
5 'Carrier Sanctions' themselves are another example of harmonisation of exclusionary controls and an obligation for all Schengen member states under Article 26 of the Supplementary Agreement (1990). Further, a comprehensive introduction of Carrier Sanctions was agreed at a meeting of the Berlin/Budapest Group of Immigration Ministers from 33 countries in Budapest in February 1993 (*Statewatch*, 1993: 4).
6 Three more African States are likely to be added to this list shortly, namely: Burkina Fasso, Niger and Togo, their now being included in Benelux restrictions (*MNS*, April 1993: 1).

References

Asylum and Immigration Appeals Bill (1993) [HL Bill 56], HMSO.
Basic Law for the Federal Republic of Germany (1969), Bonn, Press and Information Office of the German Federal Government.
Block, R. (1993), 'Doors Shut on Fleeing Muslims', *The Independent*, 8 March.
Bridge, A. (1993), 'Poles and Czechs Move to Halt Flow of Immigrants', *The Independent*, 20 March.
Brym, R. (1992), 'The Emigration Potential of Czechoslovakia, Hungary, Lithuania, Poland and Russia: Recent Survey Results', *International Sociology* (December), **7**, 4, 387–395.
Bundesamt für Flüchtlinge, Eidgenössisches Justiz- und Polizeidepartement [Switzerland] (1992), *Eurasyl: Feasibility Study on a European Information System Based on the Fingerprints of Asylum Seekers*, 3 June, Berne.
Bundeszentrale für politische Bildung (1992), *Informationen zur politischen Bildung: Ausländer*, No. 237, 4. Quartal.
Carvel, J. (1992), 'New EC Policy Likely to Oust Thousands', *The Guardian*, 25 November.
Carvel, J. (1993), 'Changing Face of EC Refugees', *The Guardian*, 1 June.
Cohen, R. (1991), 'East–West & European Migration in a Global Context', *New Community* (October), **18**, 1, 9–26.
Cohen, R. (1992), 'Migrants in Europe: Processes of Exclusion and Inclusion', review article *New Community* (January), **18**, 2, 332–336.

Coles, G. (1990), 'Approaching the Refugee Problem Today', in G. Loescher and L. Monahan, (Eds.), *Refugees and International Relations*, Oxford, Clarendon Press, 373–410.

Commission of the European Communities (CEC) (1992), *Immigration and Asylum Background Report* (Press Briefing 10 March, ISEC/B6/92).

Commission of the European Communities (CEC) (1993a), Press Release 4 February, WE/5/93.

Commission of the European Communities (CEC) (1993b), *Towards a Closer Association with the Countries of Central and Eastern Europe*, Press Briefing 17 February, ISEC/B6/93.

Commission of the European Communities (CEC) (1993c), Press Release 18 March, WE/11/93.

Commission of the European Communities (CEC) (1993d), Press Release 25 March, WE/12/93.

Convention Applying the Schengen Agreement of June 1985 Between the Governments of the States of the Benelux Economic Union, the Federal Republic of Germany and the French Republic, on the Gradual Abolition of Checks at their Common Borders, 19 June 1990.

Drüke, L. (1992), 'Asylum Policies in a European Community Without Internal Borders', CCME Briefing Paper no. 9, Brussels.

Fijnaut, C. (1990), 'Europeanisation or Americanisation of the Police in Europe', in Nederlandse Politie Academie, *The 2nd Police Summer-Course*, 19–27.

Frankfurter Allgemeine Zeitung (1993), 'Der neue Artikel 16a: Das Asylrecht', 22 January.

Garson, J.-P. (1992), 'International Migration: Facts, Figures, Policies', *OECD Observer* (June/July), **176**, 18–24.

Giorgi, L., Pohoryles, R., Pohoryles-Drexel, S., and Schmid, G. (1992), 'The Internal Logic and Contradictions of Migration Control: An Excursion into Theory and Practice in Relation to East–West Migration', *Innovation in Social Sciences Research*, **5**, 3, 25–37.

Gow, D. (1993), 'Hurd offers Yeltsin Trade Package Lifeline', *The Guardian*, 30 March, 12.

Gramsci, A. (1971), *Selections from the Prison Notebooks* (edited by Q. Hoare and G. Smith), London, Lawrence & Wishart.

The Guardian (1992), 'Berlin Asylum-Seekers Will Fight Repatriation', 30 September.

The Guardian (1993), 'Bonn Tightens Eastern Border', 8 May.

Guild, E. (1992), 'Protecting Migrants' Rights: Application of EC Agreements with Third Countries', *Churches Committee for Migrants in Europe*, CCME Briefing Paper no. 10, Brussels.

Hansard (1993), House of Lords, Migration Policy: ECC Report, 8 February.

Hansard Weekly (1993), House of Lords, Asylum and Immigration Appeals Bill, 26 January, **1552**, cols. 1147–1225.

King, M. (1992), 'The Impact of EC Border Policies on the Policing of Refugees in Eastern and Central Europe', *Innovation in Social Sciences Research*, **5**, 3, 7–24.

King, M. (1993a), *Towards Federalism? Policing the Borders of a 'New' Europe*, Discussion Paper in Federal Studies, Centre for Federal Studies, University of Leicester.

King, M. (1993b), *Europol: A Model for Convergence of Policing Systems*, Paper presented to the SIULP Conference on Europol – Project for an International Bureau, Bolzano, Italy, 13 March.

Loescher, G. (1990), 'Introduction: Refugee Issues in International Relations', in G. Loescher and L. Monahan (Eds.), *Refugees and International Relations*, Oxford, Clarendon Press, 1–33.

Macey, M. (1992), 'Greater Europe: Integration or Ethnic Exclusion', in C. Crouch and D. Marquand (Eds.), *Towards Greater Europe? A Continent Without an Iron Curtain*, London, Blackwell, 139–153.

Mather, I. (1993): 'Refugees Face Iron Curtain', *The European*, 18–21 March.

Migration News Sheet (MNS) various from October 1991 to May 1993, Brussels: CCME.

Okojie, P. (1992), 'The March of the Invaders: Racism and Refugee Policies in Europe', *Race Relations Abstracts*, **17**, 1, 5–29.

Platform Fortress Europe (December 1992/January 1993), Circular Letter no. 11, Falun, Sweden.

Reenen, P. van (1989), 'Policing Europe after 1992: Cooperation and Competition,' *European Affairs* (Summer), **3**, 2, 45–53.

Reiss, C. (1992), 'Immigration: This Threat to Society', *Evening Standard* 11 May, 1.

Statewatch (1993) (March–April), **3**, 2.

Tóth, J. (1992), *National Report – Hungary*, Conference of the Trier Academy of European Law, Comparative Law of Asylum and Immigration in Europe, 12–13 March, unpublished paper.

United Nations (1951), *Convention Relating to the Status of Refugees*, 28 July.

Walker, L. (1993), 'EC Likely to Block Malta and Cyprus', *The European*, 6–9 May.

Zimmermann, K.F. and Straubhaar, T. (1992), 'Towards a European Migration Policy', *CEPR Bulletin*, **50/51**, 29–43.

5

UNPRECEDENTED PARTNERSHIPS IN CRIME CONTROL: LAW ENFORCEMENT ISSUES AND LINKAGES BETWEEN EASTERN AND WESTERN EUROPE SINCE 1989

Frank Gregory

The literature on the evolution of police systems in developed states has, first, recorded and evaluated their history in relation to the rise of urbanised, industrialised societies and, second, examined how those systems meet the challenges of societies that have become characterised by sharper, ethnic and social divisions.[1]

In all of the communist states the pre-1989–91 police systems were, in Chapman's terms (1970), the most powerful repressive agents of the state with the principal task of maintaining the rule of a particular political élite by suppressing dissent. The tight controls in the USSR and in the Eastern European states of borders, economic activity, property, consumer goods production and the movement and lives of citizens left limited opportunities for the everyday form of crime, common in Western Europe and North America. Although, of course, criminal activities did occur both for universal reasons, such as the French category of *crime passionnel* and through official corruption.

Now there exists a very significant combination of challenges for these states *and* their neighbours. How, with very scarce resources, do you transform police systems from oppressors of the population to protectors of the population? If, indeed, that is a real option in all the cases because post-communist authoritarian political systems may yet arise. Can the pace of development of the police system match the pace of development of criminal activities? A range of reports from the Russian republics and the Eastern European states suggests that the police systems are already under severe pressure. Related to this is the question of how do neighbouring states in Western Europe cope with the crime problems resulting from the newly permeable borders.

Carter (1992: 62) has

hypothesised that organised crime groups from Eastern Europe will aggressively spread into Western Europe during the present decade. Their involvement will be in drug trafficking, information-related crimes, technological crimes and 'black marketeering'. In the latter case the groups will be involved in the distribution of both counterfeit merchandise and stolen property. This is a product of the opening of previously closed trade markets and the desire of people, notably in Eastern Europe, to obtain western merchandise. The counterfeit goods will fill this 'property desire' very rapidly and at a low price. For those persons wanting original goods, the stolen property will provide the black marketeers the most lucrative profit margin.

Two recent crime examples can illustrate the reality of elements of Carter's hypothesis. The BBC2 *Assignment* programme ran an edition called 'Blood on the Icons' (27 April 1993) which examined the evidence for widespread theft of icons from Russian churches and the growth of thefts from state and private art collections. The programme revealed that many items were apparently 'stolen to order' for clients in the West. Linked to these crimes was related evidence of official corruption and the use of violent means, including firearms, to gain possession of the desired items.

In early 1993 two men from Chechina, a small region in the northern foothills of the Caucasus mountains claiming independent status from the Russian Federation, were murdered in London. The two men were negotiating the minting of currency for Chechina with the Bank of England. However, there is information to suggest that Chechina, headed by former Soviet Air Force General, Dzokhar Dadaev, is under the influence of Chechan crime groups who returned to the region from Moscow after the August 1991 coup in the region. So great is the penetration of the economic life of that region by crime groups (mafia in Russian parlance) that *The Times* (13 May 1993) ran a story on the crime under the heading: 'The Land the Mafia Stole'.

This chapter seeks to address some of these issues by looking at police systems and general reform issues, case studies of the Czech Republic, the Slovak Republic, Poland and Hungary, crime problems in Eastern Europe and the Commonwealth of Independent States, and the processes and prospects for cooperation.

Police systems and general reform issues

Academic analysts studying events in Eastern Europe and the Russian republics must try and identify non-transitory features in the field of study in order to have some definitive basis against which the rapid changes can be evaluated. There are three points of departure for analysis which do seem to be capable of being used as a relatively fixed base. These are: the adaptation of the police system within one of the familiar general typologies; the desire of many of the police managers to sever all links to the 'political policing' and to become police professionals in terms of the broad Western model; and the evidence of strategies to forge international cooperative links for both crime control and police service development purposes.

Terrill (1989: 18) suggests that, 'with regard to the organisation and administration of law enforcement agencies in the world today, there have emerged essentially two basic models. One model is a fragmented system found in only a few countries . . . (cf. USA and UK) . . . The other model is a nationally centralised police system whose style is found in both democratic and non-democratic countries'. This latter mode is normally called the 'Roman model' and as Terrill amplifies, 'It necessitates the central government creating a police force and imposing it on the community.' Moreover, in Russia to which this model clearly applied, 'the legacy of police control was confirmed rather than expunged by the Bolshevik revolution and the civil war that followed' (Shelley, 1990: 41 citing Bayley).

The Soviet communist version of the Roman model was also common to the communist régimes of post-Second World War Eastern Europe. But in these countries the communist police system was built upon pre-war centralised police systems. The key feature of the communist police system was a hierarchy of two police agencies: the state security police, ranking first (e.g. KGB) and, ranking second, the 'ordinary' or criminal police (e.g. Militia) with the latter's primary function being to act in support of the state security police in maintaining the rule of the Communist party. An associated feature of communist police systems was the existence of large riot control and border security forces.

In addition to these two, rather simple police system models, Hunter (1990: 119–124) reminds us that a third model can be identified, namely the 'integrated' system with a mixture of local and nationally organised police agencies. This model may well be particularly suitable to the political fragmentation process that is a very visible feature of the current situation on the former USSR and in Eastern Europe. An example of this process is the recent formal division of Czechoslovakia into the separate states of the Czech Republic and the Slovak Republic.

It can reasonably be assumed that the Eastern European states and new Russian republics will continue to have at least partly centralised national police systems. However, the position inside the former territory of the USSR is slightly different in that the 'all-Union' police agencies, KGB and Militia, will either have to be decentralised to new centralised structures in the new Republics or new police agencies created by the Republics. The Russian Federation, at present, seems to be an example of the first option. Data on the other republics is sparse but the creation of new police agencies is the more likely line of development. Though it has been suggested that the former MVD troops will be devolved, by ethnic origin, to the new Republics as the nucleus of 'National Guards'.[2] Depending upon how the Commonwealth of Independent States (CIS) evolves these units could either form part of the armed forces of the new Republics or continue as border guards and provide an order maintenance capability.

Police professionalism, as understood in Western Europe and North America, can also be expected to develop. One of Gorbachev's contributions, to the new relationships between police forces on both sides of the former 'iron curtain', was, through *perestroika*, to stimulate critical discussion of the Militia's performance (Shelley, 1990: 44) and to stimulate the development of the ordinary policing functions of the KGB.[3]

In fact, even pre-Gorbachev, corruption scandals prompted open criticism of the Militia. In January 1983 USSR Procurator General A.M. Rekunkov in *Pravda* '. . . accused the regular police not only of being ineffective in bribery speculation and theft but also of deliberately covering up these crimes' (Knight, 1990: 92, see also von Burke, 1990; Markovitz, 1989). Also under the protection of *glasnost* the rivalry between the KGB and the MVD was openly spoken of. Amy Knight quotes from former Ukrainian dissident, Valentya Moroz: 'There is also an irreconcilable conflict between the KGB and the Militia . . . The driving force here is ordinary envy. The Militia does a lot of work, dirty and dangerous work (in view of alcoholism, hooliganism andthieving in the Soviet Union) but militia pay and privileges are far less than what the KGB receives' (Knight, 1990: 191–192).

In Eastern Europe there were similar early signs of efforts to reform the police systems, for example, in Autumn 1990 Major General Barna – the chief of police in Budapest – dismissed six senior officers whom he described as 'total dilettantes'[4] and in Sofia in 1990, when 3,000 police demonstrated against their senior officers a proclamation was read calling for the resignation of incompetent commanders and for a politically independent police force. Their demand for a politically independent police force was accepted by the Bulgarian Parliament in late 1990.[5]

Evidence is also becoming available relating to the scarcity of the simple crime prevention and detection equipment taken for granted by Western police forces. Octavian Pop, the Deputy Police Chief of Romania said that his force (*not* the old Securitate, but the ordinary police) had 'hardly any cars and only about one police officer per 2,000 of the population'.[6] In Albania, the forensic wing of the police academy was equipped with 'one worn and battered camera'.[7] When Krzystof Kozlowki was appointed as Solidarity's new Interior Minister in Poland, he reported that 'We have inherited generous supplies from the communists including 8,500 machine guns from the riot police, tonnes of tear gas and riot shields, but until the other day we did not have a single fax machine in the interior ministry.'[8] British police advisory teams, sent out under the FCO auspices through the 'Know How' fund, have provided detailed confirmation of the dire conditions facing the police in post-communist societies. Two of the following case studies, those of the Czech Republic, the Slovak Republic and Poland, are based upon interviews with members of the British police teams. The terms of reference of the Polish team are reproduced in the appendix. Both teams focused on the problems of developing democratically accountable police systems and the associated training needs.

The former Czech and Slovak Federal Republic (CSFR) – Case Study I

Because of the requirement to assess real needs and plan responses, some Western European police forces' aid teams have now built up quite detailed pictures of the political, social, organisational, legal and crime problems in parts of Eastern Europe. Contacts with the former Soviet Union have been of a more superficial nature to date. Whilst there will be obvious individual variations between the Eastern European states and between the new states in the former USSR the general picture is probably fairly typical.

However, it must be said that the situation in what was the CSFR was complicated by the initial determination of the two regions to maintain separate institutions and ministries. This policy included those which were responsible for policing. The policy produced problems for federal institutions, including the small sized Federal Police, which was trying to work on the territories of the two regions. Now the two separated states have to work out the consequences of political 'divorce'. In this section the policing problems in the territorial area of Czechoslovakia will first be examined for the period of the post-communist CSFR and, second, the problems of the 'divorced' republics will be considered.

In the CSFR the two key problems were the low calibre of the majority of the police personnel, in terms of training, attitude and ability and the extreme lack of 'normal' effective resources, patrol cars, communications equipment and criminal investigation aids. These problems were further complicated by the views of some political and police officials who saw large inputs of modern technology as providing a 'quick-fix' solution to the development of a modern, democratically accountable police service. The British police team spent much time on efforts to persuade the CSFR representatives that without an investment in 'people', first, they would not obtain the police service they desired.

A few examples will serve to illustrate the very real problems which face those states. Three Ministries of the Interior and confusions over legal powers and jurisdictions made even finding a base-line for development difficult. For example, an acknowledged crime problem is the smuggling of illicit drugs coming from Turkey and passing through CSFR territory. However, the police do not have the powers to stop and search a lorry en route from Turkey.

Communications equipment dated from the 1950s and 1960s and the Federal Police only had 22 radio-equipped patrol cars. The patrol cars that were available were low-performance cars like Skodas and Ladas and the drivers have had no specialist pursuit driving training; now they are facing criminals driving high-performance cars like BMWs and Mercedes. There was also evidence of inter-force rivalries in the competition for new, scarce equipment. The republics complained about the Federal Police wanting priority over the allocation of new computer equipment, claiming that the Federal Police only handled some 2 per cent of police work in terms of volume.

Among the personnel problems experienced are: poor rates of pay and difficulties of recruitment. Following the 'velvet revolution' there was widespread use of 'people's committees' to vet the probable loyalty and suitability of members of the senior ranks of the police to serve a post-communist political system. The vast majority of the upper ranks were dismissed. Linked to this process was a priority policy of eradicating both the 'VB' (political security police) role, personnel and insignia.

In the Czech Republic the ratio of police to public is about 1:900 and the police role includes a high general administration load. Simple image changing moves such as new uniforms are problematic because of the costs involved. By contrast Western businesses, like Pinkerton and Group 4 Security are supplying elaborately equipped, locally recruited, security guards to private enterprises in the CSFR that are able to afford them. Not surprisingly, because of the past record of the police as the key repressive agency of the communist régime, even small pay rises have not helped recruiting, and anyone in reasonable physical condition had to be accepted. A common conclusion from the British police team, was of the gap between the aspirations and abilities of many senior police commanders and the situation on the streets of aimless, ineffective and unsupervised patrolling.

The evidence concerning crime in the CSFR needs to be examined from two perspectives: the difficulties facing the police agencies in providing a prevention and protective service to the public and the 'spill-over' crime problems that may arise for other states which will necessitate the development of inter-state police cooperation. The advantage of being able to consult British police sources on CSFR crime problems is that it is possible to provide some data to put the CSFR crime problems into a comparative perspective.

In general, the British police team found the CSFR crime rates were 'low' by British standards. A measure of this difference can be shown by reference to the fact that in 1990 the CSFR 'Scenes of Crime Officers' (SOCOS) were handling 142 cases/head/year whereas the British SOCOS had a load of 800 cases/head/year. One factor, in the initial crime rate rise was the action by Vaclav Havel to release large numbers of prisoners, many of whom could have been classed as 'ordinary' criminals. Because the British team visited the CSFR at the beginning and end of 1991, it is possible to provide some comparisons between 1990 and 1991. In 1990 very high rates of crime, especially all forms of stealing were being recorded, of the order of a 70 per cent –100+ per cent rise. Moreover, clear-up rates were falling dramatically from over 80 per cent pre 1990 to around 30 per cent – 40 per cent in 1990. However, by the end of 1991 the rate of increase of all forms of stealing was down to about 50 per cent and clear up rates were rising to over 40 per cent.

Overall, the domestic crime patterns are very much what one might expect from a society facing unprecedented freedoms, economic and employment crises and general social instability, such as evidence of more stealing from people, buildings and movable property; increased violence, including murder and more juvenile crime. Some of the 'new' crimes are not surprising, such as the counterfeiting of 'hard' currencies – American dollars, German Deutschmarks and Dutch guilders. There is a fear of 'terrorism' because of the fragility of the internal political situation, however, there is currently little hard evidence for this fear. Although the police, in some areas, have responded by deploying relatively well-equipped SWAT units. An interesting rationale for developing counter-terrorism units was a linkage made to the fact of the CSFR now being a democracy and terrorism being a common problem facing democracies!

Evidence of inter-state related criminal activities is strongest in respect of illicit drugs trafficking. Three forms of 'drugs route' pass through the CSFR: first, lorries from Turkey bringing mainly cannabis and heroin into Western Europe, 'Yugoslav' criminal groups running drugs to Scandinavia and South American drugs groups running cocaine to Western Europe, especially Britain. Crime 'gangs' from Poland and 'Yugoslavia' are known to be operating in the CSFR and there are fears of 'Russian' 'mafia' gangs also coming into the CSFR. Another, newly visible, form of inter-state crime is the sudden rise in the 'white slave trafficking' of young girls from the CSFR by foreign criminals. A visible sign of reaction by Western European states is that Austria has started to create frontier barriers where none previously existed on its side of the border.

The Czech Republic

This new republic's police faces two organisational challenges, first, absorbing a large number of the members of the former Federal Police and their functions, second, the probable reorganisation of police areas. Tackling the first problem will require an increase in the crime investigation capability and the provision of specialist services such as VIP and Embassy protection. The police command areas may be reorganised so as to coincide with the 16–18 proposed new local authority areas.

In summary, it appears as if policing in the Czech Republic will evolve as a nationally controlled system but with substantial devolution of powers and functions to police territorial command areas. In addition, some centrally provided police services will remain or need to be created whilst at local levels supplementary police services will be available from separate municipal police forces. During this transition period, which may take quite a few years, private security firms of varying quality are likely to flourish.

Among the many continuing shortages in the Czech criminal justice system two particular shortages are likely to exacerbate adjustments in relations between the population and the criminal justice authorities. Disposing of apprehended offenders may be considerably delayed by shortages of judges and procuracy staff. Creating new police community relations will be impeded by the continuing shortages of the new, post-communist, police uniforms.

The Slovak Republic

In the Slovak Republic there are similar problems of absorbing Federal Police functions and police command area reorganisations. Although in the latter case the police appear to favour larger command areas than simply paralleling Slovak local authority areas. The police are also concerned about the range of tasks they continue to be required to carry out. These include the issuing of driving licences and the carrying out of fire safety inspections.

Police officials are concerned with the continuing problem of inadequate laws in relation to new crime problems such as drug trafficking. There are no laws to allow confiscation of drug trafficking profits and still no powers exist to carry out random checks on TIR vehicles using the Balkan drug routes into the country (Mates, 1993: 55–58). As in the Czech Republic there are still inadequate resources available for new style police uniforms and new police vehicles. The vehicle problem is made more difficult by the lack of resources for basics such as fuel and driver training.

The Slovak police identify 'organised' crime as a problem and the definition and scope of this problem clearly needs monitoring. The Slovak Republic and its police also face some sensitive problems in relation to the neighbouring state of Hungary. There is the presence of a Hungarian ethnic minority in the Slovak Republic and the concern of Hungary over the Gabcikovo–Ngymaros dam project on the Danube.

Poland – case study II

In May 1990 the Polish government passed a new Police Act which gave the police service several months to set up a new police structure. A national police service has been retained, but with the old Militia title being replaced by 'Policia' and the 'security police' (SB) sections being separated out, although both forces come under the same Ministry of Interior. The Polish police have their national headquarters in Warsaw and 49 police commands roughly equivalent to English county regions. Military ranks have been replaced by civilian ranks, e.g. Inspector and Commissioner. Criminal investigation is handled by 'CID' officers who work in two separate sections, one section essentially handles pre-arrest work, such as surveillance and use of informers and the other takes on the heavy administrative load of the post-arrest period. In the latter work the 'CID' works under a procuracy system responsible to the Ministry of Justice. Entry to the various levels of the Polish police is determined partly by educational qualifications or previous military service. A graduate can enter as an 'aspirant' or officer cadet.

Although, as was found to be the case in the former CSFR, the initial Polish police reform planning centred on the use of technology for 'quick-fixes', it was soon realised that the investment of time and resources in people was a prerequisite of building a police force capable of serving a democracy. Apart from uniform and name changes the initial stages included a process of 'verification' to check whether an officer's background was suitable to service in post-communist Poland. The system was particularly vigorous for former Communist party members. However, the Polish police have retained their armed status and continue to have a wide range of riot control equipment available and one form of national service can still be done in the Polish equivalent of the CRS. As in the former CSFR political uncertainties still have their effects on the police, for example, there have been three heads of the national police in under two years.

The crime patterns are similar to those found in the former CSFR with particular problems relating to high-value car theft, drug trafficking and economic crime. An interesting criminal law deficit relating to a non-problem area for communist régimes, is that there is *no* Polish firearms legislation, so AK-47s etc. can be bought quite openly. The Polish police make frequent references to 'organised crime' and Russian criminal 'mafias'. However, the terms are used, as in Russia, rather loosely. A wave of burglaries can be seen as 'organised crime' if such events were previously a rarity. As in the former CSFR the equipment and services available to the police are rather outdated or scarce, the only forensic science laboratory is in Warsaw, so all fingerprint matching has to take place there and communications equipment is very outdated and ineffective. Some upgrading of patrol car types has, however, been started.

An interesting and important feature of the approach of the British police team response to the Polish request for training help is its emphasis on guided *self-help*. The idea is to help the Polish police feel an 'ownership' of the new training packages being developed. These packages, which will be introduced at various levels in the Polish police, are aimed not only at changing attitudes but also at promoting student-centred learning and more selectively focused skills packages. As with the CSFR case all this has to be undertaken with very limited resources, but at least there has been a move away from the situation under communist rule where well over three-quarters of the 'police' budget went on political (SB) work.

Hungary – case study III

In January 1991 Hungary's new political leaders embarked on the process of separating the state's national police force from both the state security apparatus and the direct control of the Minister of Interior. The national police chief was given operational charge of the police and the Interior Minister's powers were confined to a general supervisory role. At local level, representatives of local government became involved in the selection of senior officers. Unfortunately, since 1990, efforts to provide a new basic law for the police to reflect its role in a democratic society have yet to proceed beyond the draft stage. Consequently, the police operate under amended regulations from the communist era. Oltay (1993: 51) comments that opposition deputies in the Parliament feel that the draft laws still allow the police to 'remain a centralised and hierarchical organisation'.

As was found to be the case in Poland, the Czech Republic and the Slovak Republic, finding new and untainted police personnel has proved to be difficult. The ordinary police in Hungary number approximately 26,000 (about the size of the Metropolitan Police in England) but of that number up to 10,000 perform various administrative duties. The lack of suitable applicants, owing to poor pay and lack of status, meant that in the autumn of 1992 there were about 1,200 unfilled posts. The government hopes to increase police personnel by some 20 per cent in the period from 1993–96 and put the majority of the new personnel on to patrol duties. The government is also encouraging an increase in the formation of local or municipal police units. They hope to have 400 more by 1995 with one in each community of more than 2,000 people.

Like their Czech, Slovak and Polish counterparts, the Hungarian police have found themselves to be less well equipped than some of the new organised crime groups. However, Hungary has benefited from cooperative ventures with the Austrian police, in terms of training, and the police are acquiring modern Western cars and new communications and data processing equipment. As in the other countries, a police 'élite' unit has emerged. This is the 'police regiment' which has some similar functions to the former Hungarian communist police 'revolutionary police regiment'. It provides a public order reserve force capability, an anti-terrorist capability and a VIP protection function. It has also been used to patrol the border with Yugoslavia. An important distinction from the communist period is, as Oltay notes (1993: 53), that the internal affairs minister only 'supervises the unit but cannot assign it concrete tasks, only the national police chief and his deputy are authorised to order the regiment's deployment'.

There is the same evidence from Hungary, as was found in the other three countries, of a growth in private security firms, often staffed by policemen from the former régime. However, Hungary does appear to differ from the others in the growth of local neighbourhood watch schemes. These groups sometimes call themselves 'self-defence' groups or 'civil guards'. A National Federation of Civil Guards was set up in April 1991 and some 600 local areas now have such groups. The Internal Affairs Minister has supported cooperation between these groups and the regular police.

The crime pattern in Hungary is similar to that found in the other states studied. In the early 1990s there was a big rise in *recorded* property crimes, evidence of organised crime groups specialising in gambling, smuggling, prostitution and drug trafficking. The Hungarian police have also had to cope with violence from minority political groups and violence against ethnic minorities.

Conclusions from the case studies

There appears to be an emerging division between those countries, namely Poland, Hungary, the Czech Republic and the Slovak Republic, where there is evidence of sustained efforts to produce police systems which are compatible with democratic processes and those, in the CIS, where there is continuing evidence that the police system is still at the mercy of political power struggles with former communist apparatchiks. Moreover, in the case of the Russian Federation, Boris Yeltsin is clearly playing the role of the rather traditional Russian figure of the 'strong leader', ruling with wide-ranging personal powers. In this situation the police may still be a source of influence and power in any political realignment process. For example, May Day in Moscow in 1993, was marked by running battles between the police and pro-communist and extreme nationalist demonstrators. The demonstrators called for the removal of Yeltsin from office or his death. After the riot, the Moscow riot police (Special Purpose Militia Team) claimed that they had been inadequately equipped at the time. Major Vitaly Keiko said, 'If only we'd been authorised to use tear gas like they do in civilised countries we would have been able to beat them back like dogs.' The militia seem prepared, on this occasion, to increase their ability to defend Boris Yeltsin because, according to militia captain Pyotr Stoyanov, 'Yeltsin' is a strong leader. That's why we like him.'[9]

General crime problems – Eastern Europe and 'Russia'

Because of the unreliability or even absence of crime statistics under the communist régimes, the figures, now being quoted, of rising crime are best understood as reflecting greater openness, people more willing to report crime and enhanced opportunities for criminal activities as was found to be the case in the former CSFR. One common thread in reports from the former USSR and the Eastern European states is the references to criminal 'mafias'. However, as a report in *The Times* (8 December 1990) noted, 'The Russians employ the word mafia rather loosely . . .' and in part use it to describe: corrupt political élites (nepotism), corrupt *and* criminal political élites and criminal gangs. In the former USSR the criminal mafia are also distinguished by their ethnic or regional origins and, in some cases, by being made up partly of ex-KGB or MVD personnel.[10] Organised criminal groups have also been reported as active in Poland[11] including groups from Russia.[12] In 1992, the Russian Interior Ministry published statistics which referred to 2,600 'highly organised criminal groups in Russia, at least 200 of which operate beyond their home base, sometimes abroad'.[13]

The two basic causes of these crime rate 'rises' are well recorded in a 1990 *Times* report on crime in Poland.[14] The report quotes Polish sociologists' views 'that the crime wave has its roots in the problems of transition between systems: the impoverishment of society, unemployment (edging towards the million mark), and the lack of control on black marketeering'. These can be considered as the domestic causes. Second, the current minimal frontier controls have produced a steep rise in cross-border smuggling: arms, works or art and antiques and gold, motor vehicles and drugs.

The available reports provide two forms of indicator: the volume of crime and the most visible categories of crime. In the spring of 1990 the then Soviet Interior Ministry was reporting a 30 per cent plus rise in reported crimes.[15] Just prior to the break up of the Soviet Union a 27.5 per cent rise in the number of reported crimes was recorded for the period January to June 1991 as compared with the same six months in 1990.[16] Russian justice ministry statistics for the period January–February 1992 have recorded a 31 per cent rise in reported crime over the same period in 1991.[17] From across the border, the Finnish police have reported the arrest of 745 citizens of the former USSR in 1991, compared with only 32 similar arrests in 1989.[18] Polish figures for 1990 recorded a 117 per cent rise in thefts from private property and a 182 per cent rise in thefts from state property.[19]

Alarm signals are even being given in Britain. *The Times* (25 May 1993) reported that Metropolitan Police organised crime experts, including Deputy Commissioner David Veness, told a Bramshill (Police Staff College) conference that, 'Mafia gangsters from Eastern Europe and the former Soviet Union will become the biggest suppliers of guns and drugs to Britain's inner cities within five years.' Also from the law enforcement perspective in the 1990–91 period it was reported that the Soviet Interior Ministry was planning, over 1990–92, to deploy 40,000 more police vehicles, eight times the previous annual figures for police vehicles.[20]

The crime categories that are most visible from the press reports are crimes of violence, intimidation and protection rackets, vice related; thefts from people and of property, and smuggling. Two particular types of cross-border crime are confirmed by discussions with Western police and customs officials, the traffic in illicit drugs and stolen motor vehicles, the former running East to West, the latter running West to East. Heroin is known to be reaching the West from the Middle East via Turkey and the Balkans through Hungary and Czechoslovakia. The route is thought to be providing 70 per cent of the heroin reaching Western Europe. Some of this heroin is being produced from the opium poppy fields found in parts of the former USSR.[21] Also South American drugs gangs are routing cocaine into Western Europe via Eastern European entry points and borders.[22]

Going the other way a *Times* report (1 December 1991) spoke of a 'criminal epidemic ... [which] ... turned Poland into the world's leading clearing house for stolen luxury cars. The raising of the iron curtain has given birth to a seemingly insatiable demand for Western cars in the former Eastern bloc. To the dismay of police forces across Europe, gaps in the market are being plugged not by capitalist producers, but by highly skilled mafia gangs.' German police estimates of car theft totals have risen from 17,000 in 1989 to 40,000 in 1991. Official Polish police figures for 1991 estimated 20,000 stolen cars in the country but an expert (ex-police) private investigator, specialising in tracing stolen cars, gave an estimate of 60,000 stolen cars in the country.

A politically and socially disturbing feature of the new criminal activities is the rise of extreme nationalist or neo-fascist groups, often with a relatively young membership. These groups make vicious attacks on foreigners, often people of different colour, and national ethnic minority groups. During 1991, in Hungary, there were between 60 and 80 attacks on Arab, Asian and African students. Lt Ivan Krupa, who headed a special unit of the Budapest police charged with the investigation of race-related crimes, estimated that there were about 450 'hard-core skinheads' with up to 1,000 sympathisers in Budapest. Anti-semitic literature is also available in Budapest and there is evidence of linkage between neo-nazi groups in Austria, Germany and Hungary.[23]

Another special feature of the new opportunities for crime, or corrupt practices is the existence of large arsenals of conventional and nuclear weapons which offer tempting opportunities for foreign purchasers and large hard-currency rewards to 'sellers' in Eastern Europe and the 'CIS'. By March 1992 11 cases of suspect attempts at illicit nuclear materials deals had been identified, with locations in seven different states including Austria, Italy and Switzerland.[24]

One of the difficulties in assessing the potential problem of illicit nuclear material sales is that some of the cases may well have been simple 'scams'. Other cases, detailed by the Oxford Research Group (1993: 39) clearly have involved nuclear materials. For example, in November 1991 the Swiss police found about 30 kilograms of depleted uranium in a car in Zurich and arrested seven people including two from Czechoslovakia. In March 1992, Russian criminals were filmed in Moscow offering to sell an Australian a kilogram of highly enriched uranium. More importantly, CIS military sources have suggested that the West may have underestimated the number of Soviet nuclear weapons; Western estimates of *circa* 28,000 may need upward revision to 34,000.[25]

Already several inter-state, weapons-sales related, criminal cases are pending. Germany had to send a frigate to the Mediterranean to escort home the German registered cargo ship *Godewind*.[26] The *Godewind* was in the process of exporting 16 CSFR T-72 tanks to Syria, having taken on the cargo in the Polish port of Szczecin. The German crime investigation related to the alleged failure of the ship owners to obtain a German arms export permit as its final departure port was Hamburg.

Even where there is the will to tackle a serious crime problem, with international links, lack of resources can be a severe handicap. Currently, the Warsaw public prosecution office is trying to unravel a loss of millions of pounds worth of Polish public funds by FOZZ, an organisation of the communist régime for servicing Polish debt. FOZZ managed to channel funds out of Poland via many routes, including British and Channel Islands banks and firms. However, the Polish procuracy service is running up large debts for other government departments, because the Justice Ministry is running out of money. Consequently, the few remaining, poorly paid prosecutors, equivalent to Procurators-Fiscal (Scotland), Examining Magistrates (France) or DA's (USA), are unable to conduct effective inquiries either at home or abroad.[27]

The processes and prospects for cooperation[28]

There are three basic reasons for the Western states to help develop the ordinary policing capacity of the Eastern European states and the new states in Russia. First, even limited moves to democracy require the democratisation of the states' coercive agencies, which include the police. Second, more effective crime control inside these states is necessary both for the protection of the population and in order to provide a more efficient and equitable availability of foodstuffs, medicines and the means for economic development, all of which may help to decrease the possibility of new entrenched authoritarian régimes. Thirdly, lawless régimes provide enhanced opportunities for criminals to work from both West to East and East to West by taking advantage of the minimally controlled borders for crime transit routes between states.

A particular feature of the border-controls problem that has worried the EC states, was the fear of a continuous flow of large numbers of 'economic refugees' flooding in from Russia and other East European states. This was of particular concern to Germany, where in 1992 the Interior Ministry estimated that about 100,000 illegal immigrants had entered the country. However, many of these people were not from Russia or Eastern Europe, but from Africa, India, Pakistan and China.[29] A German border guard officer on the River Neisse border with Poland noted: 'Last year, the Polish guards on the other side warned us of a huge movement from Russia on the way: but it hasn't happened yet.'[30] None theless, criminal groups in both East and West are clearly prospering as people smugglers with the added bonus of being able to blackmail some of the illegal entrants into participating in further crimes.

There are already in existence several fora for police cooperation that are open to and used by the East European states, though the situation with regard to the new states in the former USSR is less clear. Interpol membership now includes all the Eastern European states including Albania and the meetings of the Heads of Police of European capital cities are open to East European and Russian participation. These states are all members of the Interpol European Conference and, at the moment, Hungary is represented on the six-state Interpol European Committee together with Britain, Finland, France, Luxembourg and the Netherlands.

Under the aegis of the Interpol European Conference the European Committee is focusing on policy issues, especially relations with the European Community's Trevi system and the Schengen Treaty states. Thus an East European state is already participating in the development of pan-European police cooperation mechanisms. The same will, presumably, apply to meetings of Heads of Drugs Units in Europe. The April 1992 meeting in London of 'The Capital Policing Europe Conference 1992' focused on the styles of policing needed to meet the growing demands of policing capital cities. It included police delegations from the capital city police of Hungary, Poland, Czechoslovakia, Bulgaria, the Baltic States and from Moscow. In Britain, the Metropolitan Police headquarters services section has a range of contacts reflecting the realities of the political situation in the former communist-controlled states. They have made contact with the Chiefs of Police of all the capital cities of all the Eastern European states and of each Baltic state with the exception of Albania, the states of 'Yugoslavia', and the new states in the former USSR (although there was contact with the Chief of Police of Moscow).

Currently, the principal cooperative process is the establishment of bi-lateral links. This has been especially evident in those crime areas of most concern in the West, mainly drug trafficking. For example, 'Russian' customs officers have received specialist training in Britain and the CSFR received offers of help from Britain, Germany and the United States Drug Enforcement Administration. France has utilised its SCTIP framework, originally designed to help police development in former colonies, to provide a mechanism for responding to requests for help from Eastern Europe.

Britain's linkages may be taken as fairly typical of those of other Western European states with Eastern Europe. The links comprise three main elements: fact finding – essential to a properly planned programme of help; provision of some training support in either country; and guidance on meeting equipment needs.

Britain's response (Beatt, 1992: 2246–2248) is organised through the Joint Assistance Unit (JAU) of the Foreign and Commonwealth Office (FCO) and funded by the Know How fund, established by Britain in 1989. Britain's police aid teams now cover Poland, the Czech Republic, the Slovak Republic, Hungary, Bulgaria, Romania, Estonia, Latvia, Lithuania, Albania and the city of Moscow.

The JAU provides a police aid team, following a request from the relevant foreign national authority, by seeking help from the Inspectorate of Constabulary, who, in turn, consult ACPO. The typical team consists of four officers led by an ACPO-rank officer. If possible, one of the team will be fluent in the language of the country of operation. The JAU has also arranged for British police officers to visit Bulgaria. Patrick Jenkins of the JAU is quoted as saying (Beatt, 1992: 2246) that the basic part of a 'team's responsibility . . . is to try and change people's attitudes'. It is not the job of a team to sell items of equipment. Sometimes this takes the form of helping to arrange training programmes in Britain. As an example, in January 1992, 14 senior Polish police officers attended a special one-month course on 'Policing a Democratic Society' at the Police Staff College, Bramshill.

At the outset it was suggested that analyses must find some non-transitory bases for examining the problems identified. With regard to types of policing there is clear evidence, from some states, that police reform based upon one of the main general types of democratic state

police systems is a likely prospect. There seem to be no calls for neighbourhood volunteer police as an alternative to policing continuing to be
mainly a state function. However, it must be recognised that we are witnessing a rather unusual form of political, institutional and social evolution
or revolution. These states, generally, show many contradictory features,
like 'dual-economies' with some advanced and some very backward
sectors, 'third-world' type transportation and distribution systems and a
very large group of former Communist party or state payroll employees,
including many in the political police and internal order maintenance
police. Corruption has become an inescapable feature of personal survival
for many of the people in these states. The theft of Western supplies given
to Albania's mentally ill children was a stark example. All of these factors
may frustrate, to some degree, smooth progress by the reforming
police forces towards their now clearly articulated goals of becoming
democratically accountable, professional in the Western police sense and
participating more fully in international law enforcement systems and
processes.

It may even seem odd to discuss police reforms as a priority if people are
facing acute food, medical and fuel shortages. Yet how else are the 'weak'
to be protected against the 'strong'? In some post-conflict collapses of
political systems either an occupying army, as in the case of Germany or
Japan, can 'hold the ring' until new institutions emerge or else variations
of anarchy emerge as in present day Sudan, Ethiopia, parts of the CIS,
Cambodia and the former Yugoslavia. If political leaders give too low a
priority to the quality of their police system then they will end up issuing
'public health warnings' as the Mexican government has done concerning
the many unlawful activities of the Mexican police.

The Western states cannot ignore these problems on their doorsteps,
they have advocated the overthrow of communism and the introduction of
democracy, but what if these states are not helped on the road to
democracy? A rather chilling *Times* leader article (8 February 1992) was
headed 'Weimar Russia'. It quoted Boris Yeltsin – 'I can already feel the
breath on our necks of those who wear the black and brown shirts'. The
article continued:

The spectre of Weimar is haunting Russia. Civil order is breaking down. Inflation
races inexorably ahead. Crime is rising and the black market dominates daily life.
Anti-semitism is on the rise and anyone making money is denounced as a criminal
and exploiter of poverty ... the communist old guard, bitter at 'being stabbed in
the back', ferments unrest and plans its revenge. All the ingredients for a fascist
coup are in place.

However, because Western resources are finite, Western governments will
establish priorities for aid, including police system aid. A key determinant
is likely to be assessments of the varying capacities of countries to utilise
the aid effectively. In such circumstances it is probable that Poland,
Hungary, the Baltic States, the Czech Republic and the Slovak Republic
will receive top priority. Bulgaria and Romania may receive second

priority, and Albania third priority. Big question-marks will hang over considerations of help to fragmenting polities like the CIS and Yugoslavia.

The statement of the British Foreign Secretary, Douglas Hurd, that among the goals of the British Presidency of the EC Council of Ministers was moving closer towards the prospect of EC membership for Poland, Hungary and the former CSFR provides a planning horizon within which certain stages in East–West European law-enforcement cooperation can be identified. First, and already in place, is the membership of Interpol by these states. Second, these states would need to be able to become signatories to the Council of Europe's Conventions on Human Rights, Suppression of Terrorism, Extradition and Mutual Legal Assistance (MLA). The Polish legal authorities are, in fact, already studying the issues related to a prospective Polish accession to the MLA Convention. Thirdly, those states would need to be able to undertake all the law-enforcement related provisions of the Maastricht agreements (Provisions on Cooperation in the Spheres of Justice and Home Affairs, Title IV).

The European Community has, subsequently, articulated (ISEC/B15/93) a two-stage process for joining the Community. Actual applicant countries 'must satisfy three basic conditions of European identity, democratic status and respect of human rights. The applicant state must also accept the Community system and be able to implement it. The obligations of membership presuppose a functioning and competitive market economy and an adequate legal and administrative framework in the public and private sector.' For potential East European applicants the EC insists that an actual application 'must be preceded by a thorough preparation by means of the Europe agreements . . .' These 'Europe Agreements' already signed between the EC and Poland, Hungary, the Czech Republic and the Slovak Republic, have as a key objective, 'to consolidate democratic structures and to accelerate the development of full market economies'. Clearly the EC would expect that a reformed police system would be part of the consolidated democratic structures.

We are only seeing the very early stages of cooperation with these states and there are many uncertainties, particularly regarding political factors and the real ability to provide resources for training, equipment, skilled management and an integrated, modern and democratically accountable criminal justice system. However, one positive human relations factor is that Western police officers do seem to be able to make useful contacts with new police commanders in Eastern Europe. This very much reflects Anderson's pre 'iron-curtain' break-up comments:

contact between police forces of sovereign and independent states has been intensifying to the point where there is a qualitative shift in its nature. It has become routinised, and some senior policemen are participating in an international professional community on a regular and systematic basis (Anderson, 1989: 13).

Now these comments can clearly be applied to police links between Eastern and Western Europe.

On this more positive note, two interviews reported in the Russian press provide interesting commentaries both on how police officials in the CIS see the need for international cooperation and on how they are seeking to work towards Western approaches to law enforcement. In September 1991 Colonel-General of the Interior Troops V. Barannikov said (*Trud*, 17 September 1991):

Crime knows no borders. It may be committed in Tatarstan today and in Moscow tomorrow. The crime rate continues to grow. Over the past eight months more than 2 million crimes have been registered. It is therefore very important to establish and maintain contacts and work jointly.

In September 1991 the new Russian Federation Interior Minister, Andrei Dunayev, was asked about his use of language relating to policing not found in the Statute of Soviet Police. He answered (*Izvestia*, 29 September 1991):

The Policeman's oath was worded in the period of class struggle, when the interests of the state prevailed over civil rights. I like much better the ethical standards of law enforcement bodies in civilised countries. Just listen to them, my chief duty is to serve people, protect their lives and property, defend the innocent against deceit, the weak against intimidation, and the peaceable against violence.

But how long will it take for these high hopes for new policing systems to be realised?

Appendix: The British police mission to Poland

Introduction

Following a suggestion made by Lord Bethell in a letter to the Rt Hon. Douglas Hurd, Foreign Secretary, dated 15 September 1989, the possibility of providing some kind of police training assistance for Poland was mooted within the Home Office and the Foreign and Commonwealth Office. This led to a positive decision to identify a small police reconnaissance mission to visit Poland to assess the Polish police training needs. It was further agreed that, depending on the team's findings, the possibility of sending trainers to Poland could be considered. The team were also required to consider how British expertise could be utilised for meeting any Polish requests for training.

The project team, Mr R.O. West, QPM, Assistant to Her Majesty's Chief Inspector of Constabulary, Chief Superintendent W. Fenton, Deputy Director, Central Planning and Training Unit, with Inspector T. Dorannt, Metropolitan Police (Interpreter), visited Poland from 4 to 14 June 1990.

Whilst I asked to head this reconnaissance mission, the report is the product of our joint deliberations and I am most grateful to Mr Fenton for his deep knowledge, wide experience, and sound advice which have enabled conclusions and the formulation of recommendations. The assistance of Inspector Dorantt as a skilled interpreter was essential in communication. His Polish roots and his membership of the British Police Service considerably facilitated our work on this visit.

Terms of reference

The project was financed by the Foreign and Commonwealth Office Know How fund, with the following agreed terms of reference:

To undertake an overall assessment of Polish police training needs, to discuss with the Polish government the question of police accountability to the civil population following the government reorganisation, to visit differing policing environments in Poland; to focus on organisational aspects, including training needs of newly appointed senior police officers; to look at basic training and development needs, including training in criminal investigation techniques, to make recommendations how British expertise can be utilised to meet any Polish requests for training.

Notes

Because of the fast movement of events, reference has been made to press reports supplemented by issues of: 'The Worldbeat' section of *Police Review*; *Report on the USSR* (translations Novosti Press Office); *Report on Eastern Europe* (translations Novosti Press Office); and *Keesings Contemporary Archives*.

1 See for example: D.H. Bayley (1985), *Patterns of Policing. Comparative International Analysis*, Rutgers University Press; J. Cramer (1964), *The World's Police*, Cassel; H.K. Becker (1980), *Police Systems of Europe*, C. Thomas; R.E. Fosdick (1969), *European Police Systems*, Peterson Smith; J. Roach and J. Thomaneck (1985), *Police and Public Order in Europe* Croom Helm; R.J. Terrill (1984), *World Criminal Justice Systems*, Anderson Pub. Co.; and see the useful discussions in Dilip K. Das (1991), 'Comparative Police Studies: An Assessment', *Police Studies*, 14, 23–35.

2 *The Times*, 30 December 1991.

3 *Sunday Times Magazine*, 19 August 1990 and *The Times Saturday Review*, 30 November 1991.

4 *Police Review*, 28 September 1990.

5 *Police Review*, 2 November 1990.

6 *Police Review*, 16 March 1990.

7 *Police Review*, 4 December 1992.

8 *The Times*, 20 October 1990.

9 *The Sunday Times*, 9 May 1993.

10 *Sunday Times Magazine*, 19 August 1990.

11 *Police Review*, 1990.

12 *The Times*, 20 October 1990.

13 *Police Review*, 11 September 1992. An important discussion of the use of terms referring to 'organised crime' is to be found in Dwight C. Smith Jr. (1991), 'Wickensham to Sutherland to Katzenbach, Evolving an "official" definition for

organized crime', *Crime, Law and Social Change*, 16, 135–154, and see also *Drug Trafficking and Related Serious Crime*, 7th Report from the Home Affairs Committee, Session 1988–89, HC 370 I and II, London, HMSO.

14 *The Times*, 20 October 1990.
15 *Police Review*, 27 April 1990.
16 *Sunday Times*, 17 November 1991.
17 *Police Review*, 24 April 1992.
18 *Police Review*, 11 September 1992.
19 *The Times*, 20 October 1990.
20 *Police Review*, 27 April 1990.
21 *Sunday Times*, 23 February 1992.
22 *The Times*, 18 October 1991, and *Police Review*, 1991.
23 *The Times*, 30 January 1992.
24 *The Times*, 19 March 1992.
25 *Sunday Times*, 9 February 1992.
26 *The Times*, 31 January 1991.
27 *The Independent*, 5 February 1992.
28 For a discussion of recent police cooperation issues in Western Europe, see Frank Gregory (1991), 'Police Cooperation and Integration in the European Community: Proposals, Problems and Prospects', *Terrorism*, 14, 145–155.
29 *The Sunday Times*, 7 March 1993.
30 *The Times*, 5 January 1993.

Interviews (undertaken in January, February 1992)

Interpol NCB, New Scotland Yard   Det. Supt. Bill Wooding*
UK Polish Project Police Team   Det. Insp. Tom Dorantt*
UK CSFR Project Police Team   Supt. Mike Bowron*

Additional information was also provided by:

The International Unit, Metropolitan Police   Chief. Insp. Bill Lisle*
The Deputy Commandant,   The Police Staff College
Dep. Asst. Commissioner Peter Bramshill   Lewis, QPM*

* positions held at the time of interviews

Assistance in locating Russian and East European sources in Translation was provided by Dr Adrian Hyde-Price of the Politics Department, University of Southampton.

References

Anderson, M. (1989), *Policing the World. Interpol and the Politics of International Police Cooperation*, Oxford, Clarendon Press.
Beatt, A. (1992), 'Hands Across the Water', *Police Review*, December, 2246–2248.
Burke, A. von (1989), 'Der KGB unter Kontrolle', *Politische Studien*, 309: 11–22.
Carter, D.L. (1992), 'A Forecast of Growth in Organised Crime in Europe: New Challenges for Law Enforcement', *Police Studies*, **15**, 62–73.

Chapman, B. (1970), *The Police State*, London, MacMillan.

Hunter, R.D. (1990), 'Three Models of Policing', *Police Studies*, **13**, 119–124.

Knight, A.W. (1990), *The KGB Police and Politics in the Soviet Union*, London, Unwin Hyman.

Markovits, I. (1989), 'Law and Glasnost: Some Thoughts about the Future of Judicial Review under Socialism', *Law and Society Review*, **23**, 3, 399–447.

Mates, P. (1993), 'Drug Abuse and Trafficking in the Czech and Slovak Republics', *RFE/RL Research Report*, **2**, 4, 55–58.

Oltay, E. (1993), 'Hungary Reforms its Police Force', *RFE/RL Research Report*, **2**, 4, 50–54.

Oxford Research Group (1993), 'The Plutonium Legacy – Nuclear Proliferation Out of Control?', *Current Decisions Report*, **12**.

Shelley, L.I. (1990), 'The Soviet Militia: Agents of Political and Social Control', *Policing and Society*, **1**, 1, 39–56.

Terrill, R.J. (1989), 'Organization of Law Enforcement in the Soviet Union', *Police Studies*, **12**, 18–24.

6

PRACTICAL POLICE COOPERATION IN EUROPE: THE INTELLIGENCE DIMENSION

Kenneth G. Robertson

Increased law enforcement cooperation, including intelligence cooperation, is a major part of European Community (EC) efforts to relax frontier controls. However, most discussion of the issue has centred on the political, legal, and cultural obstacles to achieving such cooperation. This chapter identifies some of the practical difficulties which will be faced, particularly in achieving successful information sharing.[1]

In order to carry out such an assessment the concept of 'police intelligence' must be defined. It is impossible to assess whether intelligence cooperation is taking place without some concept of intelligence. However, in the case of police intelligence this task is made more difficult by the lack of literature on the subject, particularly literature of a conceptual or theoretical nature. Practitioners have not been inclined to put pen to paper, something which is only partly explained by a desire to preserve secrecy, and British writers have tended to treat the issue as either an ethical or historical problem (e.g. Hewiit, 1980; Allason, 1983; Campbell and Connor, 1986; Porter, 1987; 1989). There are a few North American authors who have discussed police intelligence, most notably Gary Marx and Dintino and Martens, but an analysis of the concept of intelligence is not a major objective in either case (Dintino and Martens, 1983; Marx, 1988).

The chapter seeks to identify the problems associated with 'intelligence cooperation'. The question will then be asked as to whether developments in European law enforcement cooperation offer credible solutions to these problems. Indications that intelligence cooperation is developing will provide valuable evidence concerning the reality of European integration.

The concept of intelligence

The vast majority of intelligence literature deals with the intelligence requirements of nations operating within a competitive international environment and is therefore concerned with military and political conflicts between states. Such literature provides a useful starting point to explore the concept.

Abram Shulsky (1991: 1), in his *Silent Warfare*, defines intelligence as:

information relevant to a government's formulating and implementing policy to further its national security interests and to deal with threats to those interests from actual or potential adversaries.

According to this definition businessmen cannot be engaged in intelligence and policemen can only be so engaged when the information with which they are dealing concerns the national security interests of the nation. The definition is 'functional' in that intelligence is defined as an activity which has a specific purpose, protecting national security. It is also clear that intelligence is an activity which takes place within a relationship of either potential or actual conflict. Intelligence is information which enables a nation to assess and respond to threats. This implies that 'special' organisations and activities are necessary because one is trying to get information about an adversary. Shulsky is clearly arguing that information-gathering is not 'intelligence', and he is also clearly arguing that only states, institutions with responsibility for national security, can be engaged in intelligence. Not all intelligence experts would accept this narrowing of the meaning of the concept. Roy Godson argues that intelligence is a type of activity which is useful to any organisation, whether business or government, that must make decisions.[2] Godson does not define intelligence in terms of a specific aim or purpose but in terms of a process or cycle which involves the elements of collection, analysis, counter-intelligence and covert action (Godson 1987: 4). In this view, it is the integration of these parts into a whole which defines intelligence. Raw information is not intelligence, it is only when information has been processed that it becomes intelligence. Intelligence is information which enables decisions to be taken, that is, intelligence is information which is useful to the policy-maker.

I have argued in a previous work (Robertson, 1987: 552–554) that intelligence is the secret collection of other's secrets and that it is also the secret processing and secret use of information. Secrecy is the 'unique' distinguishing mark of intelligence work. It is the need to collect other's secrets which creates secret services and intelligence divisions of police forces. Intelligence, in this sense, is an activity which can be performed by any organisation whether business, police or nation state. However, it does exclude most information-gathering. Information gathered from open sources, or which is communicated freely, is not intelligence although information from such sources can become part of intelligence. The process of analysis involves information from both open and closed sources and the final product is protected by secrecy so that its use is restricted to those with a 'need to know'. This approach highlights the adversarial context within which information is gathered and processed. Without the protection of secrecy, the adversary would quickly learn of one's discoveries and would act to deny one access. If an adversary does not react in such a manner then there is no need for any special units or special protection; no need for intelligence.

This brief review of the literature on intelligence has highlighted several issues which need to be kept in mind when analysing the concept of police intelligence. The first is that intelligence is not synonymous with information-gathering or processing but refers to a distinct form of activity. Although there are somewhat different bases for distinguishing between information and intelligence, all authors clearly seek to make such a distinction. It is also clear that intelligence does not refer to a single activity such as the collection of information; it describes a package of activities, a process. Finally it is clear that intelligence describes an information 'war,' that is, there is conflict between the parties which means that what one party is trying to uncover, another is trying to keep hidden.

The concept of police intelligence

As one former senior police officer has admitted, the police concept of intelligence often means nothing more than information produced by a covert source.[3] Intelligence may simply refer to information which has been gathered by clandestine means. Intelligence is a finite product, a 'piece' of information which results from a particular source such as an informant or telephone tap. One can then speak of having a 'lot of intelligence' meaning that one has a number of pieces of information which have been obtained in a clandestine manner. One can speak of collecting 'additional' intelligence which may refer to installing an additional source to produce more 'pieces' or it may refer to continuing with an existing source so as to increase the total quantity of information available. Such usages of the word intelligence are far from uncommon, in fact, they may be the dominant usage within UK police forces, but we need to be clear that such a usage is much narrower and more limited than any of the conceptions of intelligence referred to earlier. One reason why the police meaning of the term is narrower is because the police *use* of intelligence is often tactical, the aim being to use information to assist a particular investigation. This means that information is not subject to processing except in the sense that it is 'assessed' by the senior officers in charge of the specific investigation.[4] A second reason lies in the nature of police command and control structures. To use information in a strategic manner requires an organisation with the capability to manage resources in order to achieve long-term goals. Many studies have shown that police officers exercise considerable discretion and that senior police officers have a limited opportunity to manage either human or material resources.[5] There is little point in creating a sophisticated information processing system if an organisation cannot utilise the output of such a system because it does not have the necessary command and control capability. However, it is clear that in recent years there has been a dramatic increase in police 'information processing' capability. The most visible sign being the creation of agencies which often have the word 'intelligence' in their title. Prior to the centralisation of much of this activity in the National Criminal Intelligence Service (NCIS) there existed the National Drugs Intelligence Unit, the National Football Intelligence Unit, and the Animal Rights National Index.[6] In addition, each major police force has its own Special Branch whose task is to investigate those activities which constitute a threat to the security of the state. However, despite these recent developments it still remains the case that the processing and use of information as a part of an intelligence process is confined to certain rather limited types of crimes. Only those crimes carried out by organised groups are likely to be the targets of *strategic intelligence* activity. This is so for the good reasons that organisations develop patterns of activity, have long-term goals, and acquire resources. Such characteristics make the analysis of information practical and worthwhile.

It is obviously the case that 'international', or as I prefer 'transnational', crimes are more likely to be carried out by organised groups and that intelligence cooperation will, therefore, have considerable value. This is the positive aspect of EC police cooperation. It can target those criminals involved in drug trafficking, terrorism and serious organised crimes. In order to achieve such cooperation, however, certain problems, identified above, must be solved. The problems are:

– The police concept of intelligence as involving discrete, high-value, covertly obtained pieces of information.

– The under-development of analytical capacity in many police forces.

– The police system of command and control which creates problems in utilising the product of analysis.

– Variations in the degree to which crimes are susceptible to 'strategic' analysis.

Such problems generate a hypothesis which can be tested against the developing system of European police cooperation:

when the value of information is seen as lying in its short-term and tactical use, such as during an investigation, and when the capability to generate or exploit strategic analysis is limited, then the greater will be the reluctance of any 'information producing' agency to share information with any other.

The above claim requires elaboration. The sharing of information will be carried out most willingly when all parties clearly see the gains to be made from being able to create a clearer, broader, deeper, picture of the environment. However, where there is scepticism, there will be reluctance to share information. The hope of immediate benefit may far outweigh what is seen as the rather unlikely possibility of long-term strategic gains. Such reluctance may be based on scepticism that the strategic analysis of crime is possible. Many crimes are carried out by individuals who are opportunistic in selecting both method and victim and in such situations the number of potential outcomes may be so great that the analysis of past behaviour, previous patterns of activity, may generate little or no useful information as to what may happen in the future. Reluctance to share can also reflect anxieties over the use another force will make of the information. Covert collection requires a heavy investment of human and technical resources. For example, 12 officers on each shift are required for the effective surveillance of one individual. Given the scarcity of police resources any 'manager' is likely to seek a 'return' on their investment such as building a case against a criminal gang. 'Speculative' investments in acquiring information, those without an immediate and clear pay-off, are unlikely except when an agency is 'rich' in resources. Most collection is therefore tactical, geared to a specific investigation, and the risks in sharing such information are considerable. Once information has been shared no one retains a monopoly over its use and others may use the information to achieve their own purposes. Such purposes may not be the same as those which inspired the original effort in collection. There may even be conflict between the short-term and long-term goals and over which criminal is the most appropriate target. Putting the point simply, sharing information means a loss of control. Of course, this loss of control must be weighed against increased gains which may arise from greater effectiveness in combating certain types of crimes. The fight against organised groups such as drug-traffickers and terrorists will be enhanced by bringing together information from a wide variety of sources. However, the difficulty which police officers face is in making calculations in conditions of uncertainty. This is especially acute in a situation in which there is little or no previous record by which to judge the likely gains from sharing. Getting a central analytical unit off the ground is a major hurdle given all of the problems identified above. However, there are additional factors which complicate the calculation. One is the 'organisational distance' between the cooperating parties. The more elaborate is the chain of command the greater will be the difficulty in assessing what the centre requires and the greater will be the centre's difficulty in communicating its requirements. Overcoming this problem requires an effective and continuous dialogue between the centre and the network which feeds it. Mechanisms must be established to enable such understanding to develop. Such mechan-isms may include the holding of joint exercises, the exchange of personnel, shared training, regular seminars, and the communication of results achieved. Complications will also arise from differences in procedures. The point has been frequently made that differences in legal, judicial and policing procedures will make the development of cooperation difficult. There are also differences in the human and material resources available to the police forces in Europe. Such differences may mean that some forces are seen as less able to exploit information effectively.

The conclusion is that effective police cooperation is not a matter of simply recognising a need for cooperation but requires a common understanding of intelligence, the development of units capable of utilising intelligence, and the development of mechanisms designed to enable police officers to make better calculations on the costs and benefits of sharing information. The next section will examine various forms of cooperation to see how well they solve these problems.

Police cooperation

Before examining recent developments in Europe it is worthwhile examining previous analyses of police cooperation. The main such effort is that of Malcolm Anderson in his *Policing the World*. He offers an analytical scheme based upon the way in which communication between different police agencies is controlled. The main basis of the typology is the degree of control exercised by a central body over communications between police agencies of different countries. This produces the following threefold model (Anderson, 1989: 172–178):

- the *centralised state model* in which a single national body controls all communication with other parties, including the exchange of information.

- the *decentralised state model* in which all levels are allowed to communicate with all other parties, the flow of information being unregulated except by the judgment of individual officers.

- the *qualified decentralised model*, an intermediate form in which communication is normally controlled by a central body but with independent communication being allowed in special circumstances.

This classification allows Anderson to identify an important issue facing all forms of police cooperation; if all levels of the police force are allowed to communicate with all levels of their opposite number the centre may become marginalised and ignorant but, on the other hand, if all communication takes place only through the centre then communication may be slower and less effective. I would argue that an 'intelligence approach', the strategic analysis of information, requires that communication takes place through a single central body whilst allowing independent communication indicates that an 'investigative approach', the tactical, has priority. Although this is discussed later, it is important to recognise that different forms of criminal activity may require different approaches, some more strategic and others more tactical. This may mean that different crimes will create different forms of cooperation, some centralised and others decentralised, rather than there being a single national blueprint covering all forms of international police cooperation.

Another approach is to analyse the basis upon which a decision to communicate is made. Does a transfer of information occur only when a request is made or does communication take place whenever either party perceives the information may be of value to the other? The first type is the *request* model, which may be crudely expressed as 'you only get information when you ask for it'. The second is the *reciprocal* model which is based upon a shared understanding of needs so that information is transferred whenever it appears relevant.

It is obvious that the second type, reciprocity, requires what many police officers would call a 'high degree of trust.' However, the idea of trust is notoriously vague so that far from being an independent variable it simply becomes another way of expressing the very thing being explained. Where cooperation exists, there is trust and where there is trust, there is cooperation; a puppy is a young dog and a young dog is a puppy. To break out of the circle requires some criteria whereby 'trust' can be assessed independently of the degree of cooperation. Included in such criteria are: a shared definition of objectives, either general and specific or both; equivalence in the standard of professionalism which includes such matters as the level of skill and resources; and a shared perception of the problem such as the nature of 'organised crime'. Where such criteria are met then some of the conditions of the development of the reciprocal model exist. However, in the case of EC countries it is clear that not all such conditions are met. There are differences in the level of training, computerisation, definitions of organised crime, and in the job specification of police agencies. The development of 'trust' therefore requires the transfer of personal skills and material resources, particularly from northern to southern Europe. The creation of central agencies such as Europol does not create the conditions for reciprocity although it may provide a mechanism within which some of these differences can be resolved. The problem can be simply expressed; what will be the interaction between the creation of mechanisms of cooperation and the development of 'trust'? Will mechanisms build trust or is the lack of trust going to prevent the success of the mechanisms?

European police cooperation

The main forms of police cooperation between European countries are Interpol, Trevi, the Schengen System, and Europol.[7] Although Interpol is an important part of international cooperation it will not be discussed here. Interpol operates under very different constraints and limitations which makes comparison with the other forms of cooperation misleading.

Trevi

The Trevi group is an organisation of the Home (Justice and Interior) Ministers of the 12 EC nations although other nations such as the United States and Morocco enjoy the status of 'friends' of Trevi.[8] However, Trevi is not governed by Treaty and does not come under the authority of the EC Commission, rather, it is a form of intergovernmental cooperation. It began as a response to terrorism but it has since expanded to include working groups on other transnational issues. Each Trevi Working Group has a coordinator who is a senior official from a member state and meetings are held which are attended by both government officials and law enforcement practicioners. The main aim of Trevi is provide a forum for the exchange of information and experience and to expedite cooperation by a system of liaison officers, joint exercises and common training. It can be argued that Trevi has been successful because it operates only with the consent of all of those involved. However, there is also no doubt that the Maastricht Treaty has, to a degree, by-passed Trevi and that it is of declining importance. The main disadvantage of Trevi has been the lack of a central secretariat and a central data-base of information. Although it did have a secure means of communication, which provided a mechanism for the exchange of information, each country was expected to maintain its own independent data-base. The main type of information with which Trevi concerned itself was data on the movement of suspect goods or people. This provided an important 'alerting' function but did not provide a basis for coordinated action. Meetings were held which attempted to arrive at a common assessment of a problem, such as terrorism, but strategic analysis requires full and complete access to all data whether from open or covert sources. The Trevi procedure, discussion at a meeting, tends to create competition rather than shared analysis since each nation offers its own 'picture' and attempts to persuade others of its view. This provides some incentive to disclose high-grade information but only insofar as it is necessary to persuade one's competitors; it does not provide an incentive for continuous and complete sharing, the pooling of information in order to allow for a single, central, strategic assessment. However, Trevi does have one attribute of all successful strategic intelligence systems, the involvement of policy-makers and ministers. Setting priorities, what the military call tasking, is an essential element of any intelligence process. Tasking involves the making of choices over what information to collect and what to analyse. An efficient system must avoid having too much of the 'wrong' type of information. The more the consumer of the intelligence product is involved in the making of choices the more likely it is that their requirements will be met. Although senior police officers may often be the most obvious consumer it is also important that officials and ministers from appropriate government departments have an opportunity to express their views. Otherwise there is a danger that management may become self-tasking. To conclude, Trevi has the characteristics of an organisation designed to enhance the basically investigative, operational, basis of most police work. It is designed to make such work more effective rather than to build a genuine intelligence system.

The Schengen System

The Schengen system was originally formed by Germany, France, Belgium, the Netherlands and Luxembourg although they have since been joined by Greece, Italy, Spain and Portugal leaving only the 'island nations' outside of the system.[9] The Schengen system was designed to compensate for the relaxation of frontier controls and was not intended as some form of European police system. There are therefore limitations as to the type of information which it can handle, those who can gain access to the data, and the nature of operational cooperation such as the pursuit of criminals across frontiers.

For the purposes of this paper, the important part of the system is the information system. The language of the agreement is often tortuous but the main categories of information which can be held are: wanted persons; undesirable aliens; missing persons; information concerning the place of residence of those required as parties to legal proceedings; information concerning those under active surveillance and those likely to commit 'extremely serious crimes'; information concerning goods to be seized or used in criminal proceedings.[10] Data is to be stored and transmitted for 'the purposes of border checks and controls' and, in certain defined circumstances, for the issuing of visas and residence permits although the agreement also refers to 'other police and customs checks' which would seem to cover any and all circumstances.[11] 'Other checks' does not appear to be a sub-category of 'border checks' but a general enabling clause. However, only certain types of data about named individuals can be held within the system. The personal particulars which can be stored are: name; distinguishing marks; birth details; sex; nationality; whether armed or violent; reason for the report; action to be taken.[12] These categories all refer to 'hard' data except for the heading 'reason for the report', the 'reason for a report' being limited by the set of purposes outlined above. The only legitimate 'reasons for a report' being, for example, that a warrant has been issued for an arrest or that a person poses a serious and immediate danger to state security.

The Schengen System, as with Trevi, is designed to enhance operational effectiveness; it is not an intelligence system. There is no central analytical unit or department bringing together the data from open and covert sources. There is also no unit with overall responsibility for tasking collection agencies or setting requirements. There is no clearly defined hierarchy of access, indeed the Information System will only operate effectively if all 'relevant users' have equal and speedy access to all parts of the data-base. On inspection the system is actually a rather modest step. It enhances existing practices but it does not create new institutions or new approaches to dealing with transnational crime. For that, we must turn to Europol.

Europol

The proposal to create a European Central Criminal Investigation Office was formally agreed at the Maastricht summit in December 1991.[13] It is intended to provide a system of police information exchange on terrorism, drug trafficking, other serious transnational crimes.[14] It also includes certain aspects of customs cooperation. The Declaration on Police Cooperation also commits member states to explore other ways of exchanging information and experience covering such matters as support for investigations, analysing information, training and research. A report is to be considered by the end of 1994.[15] There is no doubt that the Maastricht Treaty places police cooperation on a new formal basis and opens up new dimensions of cooperation. However, the question arises of whether there are any signs that Europol will act as more than yet another data-base. One dramatic possibility would be the creation of a central investigative police unit for Europe, a form of European FBI, but the difficulties involved make this a remote and unlikely event.[16] More significant is the idea of developing a central analytical unit for the processing and dissemination of information, or an intelligence system. However, the success of any such plan will depend upon solving the problems identified earlier.

One such problem is the costs and benefits of transmitting information to and from the centre. Individual officers in each country are unlikely to have sufficient information to calculate the costs of keeping information under their control or passing it to the centre. The difficulties of making a rational calculation are going to be compounded by the organisational distance involved. Assessing the costs involved in losing control over information becomes more difficult as one moves from the team, to station, division, force, regional or national unit. Such difficulties are compounded when an extra layer, in the form of a European agency, is added. So great are such difficulties that the most likely pattern will be the central, national, unit of one country passing on information to the European central agency. In other words the pattern will follow Anderson's *centralised model.*

A second issue is the question of who will control the use made of the product of Europol. National units will not transmit information to Europol if they lose control over its use. Here, the solution is likely to be some system of joint control whereby Europol will be required to insist that no operational use is made of the information supplied by any other agency unless the original source of the information approves. That is, each national agency will have a veto over any use made of the information which it communicated to the centre. Failure to ensure some such constraint will mean that the national units will not transmit information which they believe is time sensitive and has a high operational value. For example, information about a drugs shipment will not be transmitted unless the original source can control the use made of it. Imagine a situation in which French customs have information about a drugs shipment which is coming by air from South America to Paris via London. The French decide to pass the information to Europol which then alerts the UK authorities. The UK decides that this information allows them to arrest a gang, which they believe has also been responsible for shipping drugs into the UK, by intercepting the shipment at Heathrow. The UK gets all of the publicity, all of the credit, whilst the French have achieved nothing. The outrage that this would generate would destroy the credibility of the system immediately.

There is also the problem of setting priorities. Information for which no one has a use risks creating information overload. Although a great deal of important information can be generated by what one may call everyday policing there is the question of who manages the scarce resources involved in collecting information by clandestine methods. If it is the operational units in each country then the centre will only get what each country thinks is worth collecting rather than what the analysts require. If, on the other hand, Europol can task each country to collect the information which it requires this will create competition for resources between Europol and national agencies. Finally, there is the problem of access or secrecy, that is, who will have access to what parts of the information system and how will the product of the system be distributed? Trevi and Schengen operate on different principles of access and distribution. The aim of Trevi being to provide a secure network for the exchange of sensitive data and to improve the level of analysis by requiring each to offer an intelligence assessment to all others. The aim of Schengen is to provide speedy and equal access to information to all users in order to improve operational effectiveness. Europol will not be an egalitarian system like Schengen but will operate on the basis of the need-to-know with the centre making judgments about what to distribute to whom. This will solve the problem of security but it will risk alienating the suppliers of raw data who will receive assessments from Europol only when Europol considers it necessary. It will take great skill to maximise the flow of information *to* the centre whilst restricting information *from* the centre. It is difficult to believe that Europol can be an effective intelligence system unless it does operate strict security procedures; but security measures will create tensions between countries as to how, when, and to whom, information will be distributed.

Conclusion

In conclusion, the different forms of European police cooperation have been examined as to how they share information and whether they are moving towards true intelligence systems. Several difficulties have been identified not the least being the nature of most police work, which tends towards short-term immediate goals such as arresting an offender, and the opportunistic nature of many crimes which makes the application of intelligence techniques difficult, if not impossible. However, the transnational nature of many major crimes in Europe, such as drug trafficking or dealing in stolen luxury cars, does provide an opportunity to go beyond simply increasing the amount of data available to an investigating officer. The challenge is to create an intelligence system, a central analytical agency which can take a strategic view of crime. But creating such an agency requires far more than recognition of common needs and the political will to act on them. The problem of managing an intelligence system creates requirements which will mean great change not only at the European level but in domestic policing. The trend towards creating ever-more powerful central units within each country will be intensified, but managing relationships between traditional policing and the new central forces will not be easy. The risk is clear; the traditional units will supply much of the data but will receive little in return. This will create alienation and resentment between the local forces and the national units and between the national units and the European agencies. Schengen avoids most of these problems but at the cost of being a relatively low-level information sharing agency. Europol has much higher aims but such aims have not only the opportunity of higher dividends but also greater risks. The conspiracy theorists of European policing are wrong when they see a vast surveillance state, for the reality is that a true intelligence system is not an easy monster to produce but is one of the rarest of creatures.

Notes

1 For other discussions of this issue see: Geysels, 1990; Gregory 1990, 1991.
2 There is a series of books edited by Roy Godson: *Elements of Intelligence*; *Analysis and Estimates*; *Counter-intelligence*; *Covert Action*; and *Clandestine Collection* (these five published by the National Strategy Information Centre, Washington DC and distributed by Transaction Books) and *Domestic Intelligence*; and *Intelligence and Policy* (these published by Lexington Books).
3 Mr Barry Price, who was the first Coordinator of the National Drugs Intelligence Unit and a former Chief of Police, admits: 'From various sources such as surveillance and informants, we collected information about these individuals' activities . . . we labelled it intelligence – and that was where our ignorance began . . . What we were actually engaged in was information collection' (Price 1991: 131–132).
4 'This data, which was more often kept within a small circle of operational detectives, was subject to an unsophisticated interpretation process, by which I mean that the operational commander and his immediate support staff would discuss the implications of the information gleaned. Past experience and bias were the most powerful factors in this interpretation process' (Price, 1991: 132).
5 Excellent studies of this aspect of policing are Horton and Smith, 1988; Chatterton and Rogers, 1989.
6 These units are listed in the Home Affairs Committee Seventh Report, *Practical Police Co-operation in the European Community*, House of Commons, Session 1989–90, HMSO, London, 1990: xiv.
7 I have discussed the general issues associated with such plans in earlier works; see Robertson, 1989; 1991a; 1991b.
8 This section draws upon the discussion of Trevi in The Home Affairs Committee Report, *Practical Police Co-operation*: xx–xxiv, 5–7.
9 Denmark is not, of course, an island but it has a very narrow land frontier with Germany.
10 The Schengen Agreement (1985) and Schengen Implementation Agreement (1990), Articles 95–100.
11 Schengen Agreement, Art. 92 (1).
12 Schengen Agreement, Art. 95 (2).
13 For a discussion of the general issues see Monica den Boer and Neil Walker (1993: 7). The detailed provisions are listed in the Treaty on European Union, Title VI, Provisions on Cooperation in the Fields of Justice and Home Affairs, K.1–9.

14 Treaty on European Union, Article K.1 (9).
15 Ibid., Final Act, Declaration on Police Cooperation.
16 For the background to the idea see Cullen (1992: 78–81). For a discussion of the difficulties in securing legitimacy for such a plan, see den Boer and Walker (1993).

References

Allason, R. (1983), *The Branch – A History of the Metropolitan Police Special Branch 1883–1983*, London, Secker and Warburg.
Anderson, M. (1989), *Policing the World. Interpol and the Politics of Police Cooperation*, Oxford, Clarendon Press.
Boer, M. den and Walker, N. (1993), 'European Policing after 1992', *Journal of Common Market Studies*, **31**, 1.
Campbell, D. and Connor. S. (1986), *On the Record*, London, Michael Joseph.
Chatterton, M. and Rogers, M. (1989), 'Focused Policing', in R. Morgan and D. J. Smith (Eds.), *Coming to Terms with Policing*, London, Routledge.
Cullen, Peter J. (1992), *The German Police and European Co-operation*, A System of European Police Cooperation after 1992, Working Paper II, Edinburgh.
Dintino, J. and Martens, F. (1983), *Police Intelligence Systems in Crime Control*, Springfield Ill., Charles C. Thomas.
Geysels, F. (1990), 'Europe from the Inside,' *Policing* (Spring), **6**, 1.
Godson, R. (1987), 'Intelligence: An American View,' in K. G. Robertson (Ed.), *British and American Approaches to Intelligence*, London, Macmillan.
Gregory, F.E.C. (1990), 'Policing and Border Controls', Public Administration Committee Conference, York.
Gregory, F.E.C. (1991), 'Police Co-operation and Integration in the European Community: Proposals, Problems, Prospects,' *Terrorism*, **14**.
Hewiit, P. (1980), *Privacy – the Information Gatherers*, London, National Council for Civil Liberties.
Horton, C. and Smith, D.J. (1988), *Evaluating Police Work: An Action Research Project*, Policy Studies Institute, Report No. 687.
Marx, G. (1988), *Undercover*, London, University of California Press.
Porter, B. (1987), *The Origins of the Vigilant State*, London, Weidenfeld and Nicolson.
Porter, B. (1989), *Plots and Paranoia*, London, Unwin Hyman.
Price, P. (1991), 'Intelligence and the Fight Against Drugs', in Susan Flood (Ed.), *Illicit Drugs and Organized Crime – Issues for a Unified Europe*, Chicago, Office of International Criminal Justice.
Robertson, K.G. (1987), 'Intelligence, Terrorism and Civil Liberties', in P. Wilkinson and A.M. Stewart (Eds.), *Contemporary Research on Terrorism*, Aberdeen, Aberdeen University Press.
Robertson, K.G. (1989), *1992 – the Security Implications*, London, Institute for European Defence and Strategic Studies.
Robertson, K.G. (1991a), 'Terrorism – Europe without Borders', *Terrorism*, **14**.
Robertson, K.G. (1991b), 'Crime Frontier Controls and 1992', in Susan Flood (Ed.), *Illicit Drugs and Organized Crime – Issues for a Unified Europe*, Chicago Office of International Criminal Justice.
Shulsky, A. (1991), *Silent Warfare – Understanding the World of Intelligence*, Washington, Brassey's.

DATA PROTECTION

POLICE COOPERATION: THE PROSPECTS FOR PRIVACY

Charles D. Raab

As is documented in this book, European national governments and their police and security forces have devoted much effort to developing effective, cooperative counter-measures to criminal activity of many kinds. However, the increasing internationalisation of crime follows a trajectory which police cooperation finds difficult to overtake despite, or perhaps because of, the pursuit of cooperation through a kaleidoscopic variety of formal and informal networks and groupings, of which Trevi, Schengen and the proposed Europol are some, among others, in a crowded international policy space.

The trajectory of police cooperation is itself strongly affected by another one, that of the development of adequate information systems across, and indeed within, jurisdictional boundaries. Better cooperation depends heavily upon better information exchanges, but the achievement of these is not at all certain. Reports of the Home Affairs Committee of the United Kingdom Parliament have, for example, indicated the formidable agenda of work that lies ahead in regard to all aspects of European police cooperation, not the least of which involves the computerisation and standardisation of criminal information of several kinds (House of Commons, 1990a, 1990b). This agenda is not merely a matter of finding technical solutions to commonly understood problems, but one of hard organisational politics, public policy and consensus-building. The importance of rapidly communicated, secure, accessible and ample information to the goals of policing across borders is already stimulating the further harmonisation or integration of information and intelligence systems, and perhaps their supranational centralisation in arrangements that range from the general to those that are specific to particular types of criminal activity, such as drug trafficking, financial fraud, terrorism, or art and antiques theft, as well as to the large-scale movements of people across borders. Progress towards more efficient and effective information systems is evident internationally, as exemplified by the development of the Schengen Information System (SIS), as well as within countries, as is illustrated by the formation in the United Kingdom of a National Criminal Intelligence Service (NCIS) and of a more centralised system for criminal records.

Nevertheless, many of these innovations lag behind the hopes of their progenitors and proceed at a pace that is dictated in large part by the vagaries of closer political unification or cooperation in Europe. Technological determinist assumptions about the inevitability of blanket 'informatisation' across a vast geographical space ignore the obstacles presented by conflicting purposes and processes, and enjoy the luxury of vagueness about time-scales. Progress along this trajectory remains slow and halting for reasons that are perhaps as much organisational, sociological, legal and political as they are technological. In this sense, the informatisation of the police bears resemblance to that of public administration generally, despite the hopes of practitioners and the fears of criminals or civil libertarians.

This chapter describes a fourth trajectory: that of data protection, or the establishment of effective national and international systems both for protecting individuals' privacy from intrusion by the practices of information users, and for safeguarding the confidentiality of communicated data and the integrity of the processes through which such information flows. Among these users are those involved in policing and related activities. As the chapter shows, attempts to insert not only a concern for privacy but effective laws and systems of data protection as well have been arduous enough in areas of lesser significance and sensitivity than policing. It is necessarily more difficult in regard to the latter, especially at the international level; thus the trajectory for data protection is halting and piecemeal, and the substantive results meagre. This poses the question whether the growth and robustness of data protection are adequate to the tasks of safeguarding privacy and facilitating information flows in a borderless and dangerous Europe in which the pressures for integrated policing – however slow its development – strike resonant chords in countries that perceive their societies, markets and states to be threatened by crime or by the international movements of displaced persons.

The likely answer to this question gives voice to pessimism, rather than to the facile functionalism of a moving equilibrium or an unsynthesised dialectic between problems (crime), solutions-as-problems (cooperative, informatised policing) and further solutions (data protection). The reason for this may lie in the greater political salience of public safety and the maintenance of public order than of protecting individuals from the effects of what Flaherty (1989) has termed 'surveillance societies'. These policy imperatives lie in some of the least publicly accountable areas of state activity, where deference is often paid, albeit with much justification, to officials' or the police's desire for speedier, more effective, and more covert information processes, whilst offering lip-service to the privacy values that data protection systems attempt to safeguard. Where the fear of crime mounts in response to perceived or real increases in violence and unlawful conduct, public opinion is more easily mobilised in support of technological solutions that pose challenges to privacy.

Flaherty (1989: 76) notes that data protection agencies in a number of countries have trod lightly in the sensitive area of computerised police records, although he considers that German data protectors have had 'impressive successes . . . in the police and security fields' as compared, for example, with the French. Such agencies wield relatively little influence over policy, whilst the development of policing methods that depend upon advanced information and communications technology gains strength. Proposals, for example, to include photographs on driving licences, to expand the use of surveillance technology, and to create DNA indexes put to a severe test data protection regulations that were founded upon what are now outmoded technological assumptions. In particular, they call into question the ability of data protection systems to protect privacy in an 'information society' at the international level in which public order and combating illegal activities have become principal objectives.

What is data protection?

Before we can outline the contours of recent policy-making for data protection and assess the prospects for safeguarding privacy in a cooperatively policed Europe, it is helpful to address differing views of the meaning of 'data protection' and thus to point up the way in which it is considered in current discussions of police information systems. These discourses have been shaped by activities and events going back some 20 or more years to the passage of the first data protection legislation in Europe. Insofar as data protection is an idea in good European currency, it is the Council of Europe's (CE) Convention (1981) that has provided its most effective and widespread backing until the present time. The Organisation for Economic Cooperation and Development (OECD) also provided prestigious and influential auspices through similar guidelines for privacy protection and transborder data flow (OECD, 1981), and the idea gained some ground as well in the European Commission and Parliament during the 1970s and early 1980s (Mellors and Pollitt, 1984). Whilst the European Community (EC) had less interest in the subject than did these other organisations, recent developments towards a Community-wide system of data protection constitute a considerable advance on those beginnings and help to form the current context of international debate about data protection with which police cooperation must come to grips.

National data protection legislation from the 1970s to the 1990s partly anticipated, but mostly reflected, an international convergence on a number of principles of data protection that were given force in the CE's 1981 Convention (Bennett, 1992). That Convention sought to remedy the inadequacies in the protection of privacy that had been afforded by the European Convention on Human Rights, and to ease the restrictions on international communication of personal data that the first generation of national laws had imposed. The principles that the Convention enunciated have established a benchmark of minimum requirements that form a common core to which national laws are intended to subscribe, in order to establish a safe international zone for the transmission of personal data across borders, thus reconciling the free flow of information with the requirements of privacy protection.

The principles concern procedures as well as the quality of data by stipulating that they should be obtained and processed fairly and lawfully, stored only for legitimate and specified purposes and not used incompatibly with them, that they should be adequate, relevant and not excessive for these purposes, and that they should be accurate, up-to-date and not held for longer than is necessary. The security of the data is also an important principle, as is the ability of persons as 'data subjects' to have access to the data and to rectify any errors. Taken together, these principles establish a broadly based injunction of 'good practice' upon users of personal data to act responsibly in the interests of the privacy of those persons who are the subjects of the data in question, as well as encouraging conduct that can contribute to the efficiency and legitimacy of data usage. They also promote the empowerment of data subjects in relation to those who handle personal data.

In many respects, it is unfortunate that the term 'data protection' has come into common and official use to refer to what is more properly construed as the protection of individual privacy, rather than of personal data as such. As Raab and Bennett (1994) argue, privacy is the fundamental value in data protection. Its promotion protects individuality against intrusions and empowers persons to control information that relates to themselves. It also increases organisational accountability by enjoining greater transparency upon information processes, and enhances the quality of decision-making about individuals by improving the quality, relevance and security of personal data.

Understanding data protection as privacy protection conflicts with an interpretation that is more frequently encountered in organisational circles, including policing. Data protection is there often construed simply as data (or computer) security, in which protection is afforded by safe-guarding hardware, data-bases, and information systems through physical devices that prevent hacking, unauthorised access, corruption of data, or other damage. As we have seen, security is an important principle of data protection, but it is only one. To be sure, security assists privacy, but the motive and purpose of computer security normally has less to do with the privacy interests of those whose data are held than with organisations' functional need to maintain the confidentiality of information that they hold in face of the possibility of leakage or destruction. In many cases, this information is the result of surveillance activities carried out by organisations in the field of national security and public order that need to maintain a high level of security even whilst communicating data to others in the common pursuit of their objectives. Although it should not be surprising that 'data protection', in these circumstances, comes to mean the protection of data rather than the protection of privacy, it should not be forgotten that alternative meanings implicitly challenge those practices of such data users that are non-transparent and inimical to privacy.

Some would argue that data protection does not aim to prevent surveillance but to manage it or to reconcile privacy with other objectives, including those pursued through policing. In fact, data protection or privacy legislation, although born of a concern for the protection of individuals, typically seeks a reconciliation of values, especially between the claims of personal privacy and others that are predicated upon the unimpeded flow of information between data users within or between countries. Laws, guidelines and principles that have been adopted in the field of data protection typically subscribe to a normative assumption of 'balance' between privacy and other desirable values. This is a questionable approach that is open to criticism, not the least because it potentially compromises the ability of data protection law to protect the privacy of individuals rather than to further the interests of those who would seek to invade it for justifiable or unjustifiable reasons (Raab, 1993a; Raab and Bennett, 1994). Normally, privacy considerations are set aside where national security, public safety, crime control and the monetary interests of the state are concerned, but the factual basis for overriding privacy is not easily contested where it is asserted, partly owing to the very secrecy of the administrative or policing milieux in which such decisions are taken.

There is a sense in which data protection can contribute to the achievement of non-privacy values, insofar as public confidence in the police or in other organisations is strengthened by the belief that personal data are well protected, and through some level of transparency and accountability that data protection might enjoin on the forces of law and order. On the other hand, the constraints that data protection laws might place upon police activities, as upon the information practices of public and private organisations generally, are more likely to provoke resistance. Flaherty (1989: 12–13, 15) observes that it is very unlikely that governments, as custodians of data, will abandon intrusive measures unless forced to, if surveillance seems justifiable in the public interest, given their concern with administrative efficiency rather than with the protection of privacy.

It was therefore to be expected that, for example, the police as well as the Home Office resisted the development of data protection legislation in Britain in the late 1970s and early 1980s (Martin, 1982). This is not to say that custodians of data do not want data protection, but that they are more likely to want it on their own terms; that is, a system that satisfies certain minimal requirements that lend legitimacy to personal-information processes without creating operational difficulties. Whether this interpretation of balance results in only negligible tokens of data protection or in something more effective depends upon data users' calculation of their interests, and also in considerable part upon the process of implementing the law, including the influence that official data protectors, pressure groups, and the political system more generally can bring to bear, especially in regard to the learning processes that are set in motion through data protection systems (Flaherty, 1989; Raab, 1993b).

Balancing is often resolved in favour of non-privacy concerns, a resolution that is envisaged in the typical exemptions in national legislation that privilege police and national security objectives and that therefore set limits to the extent of privacy protection that can be afforded. The leading general European official documents on data protection, such as the proposed European Community directive on data protection (Commission of the European Communities, 1992), the Council of Europe's 1981 Convention and the Council's 1987 police-data Recommendation No. R (87) 15 (CE, 1988) all allow exemptions and derogations for police activities in suppressing crime and related purposes.

The Recommendation is particularly interesting in the present context. Its explanatory memorandum described its rationale in terms of the need to establish police-sector guidelines, balancing individual rights with legitimate police activities, in the face of terrorism, drug delinquency and increased criminality. It argued that the derogation in the Convention had left a hole that needed to be plugged by 'a special set of data protection principles for the classic and crucial tasks of the police' (CE, 1988: 14), principles that would, however, be adapted to the requirements of police work. Thus, within the framework of a balance, the Recommendation drew a tighter circle around the scope of the derogation for society's anti-crime and public-order interests, by referring to 'the prevention of a real danger or the suppression of a specific criminal offence' (para. 2.1 of Recommendation). Nevertheless, the Recommendation is not binding and its exhortations do not necessarily enjoy the assent of national governments. Spencer (1990: 63), indeed, points out the British government's unique reservations about the provisions both for informing individuals about data collected without their knowledge, and for severely restricting the collection of particularly sensitive information about personal characteristics, beliefs and behaviour.

The Council of Europe's Convention as a means of privacy protection

The Convention lies at the heart of a model of international data protection that is based upon the acceptance of common standards as reflected in national laws, and upon a mainly advisory centre. It leaves it largely to the workings of national systems to implement principles and to encourage good practice, although it establishes the grounds upon which the flow of personal data to countries with inadequate data protection can be restricted. This acephalous state of affairs pleases those who fear any stronger measures that might impede such flow, although it is regarded as insupportable by those who see weak data protection as threatening the commercial and other interchanges that are presupposed in a more integrated Europe (Simitis, 1989). These, it is argued, cannot be left to be regulated by an approach that sees international data transactions as an exception that requires only some random rules.

The force of this argument can be appreciated by noting how different are the national systems of data protection despite their convergence on

Convention-type principles (Bennett, 1992). Among other variations, they differ in terms of their coverage of manual or automated systems, of their applicability to the private and public sectors, of their requirements for registration, and of their regulatory and enforcement processes and powers. In addition, the terms of countries' subscription to the Convention vary through the declarations they make when signing or ratifying it (CE, n.d.). Article 3, paragraph 2(a) allows a country to exclude certain types of files from the Convention's application. Ireland, for instance, excludes data kept for reasons of state security, and Italy excludes the automated centres of the police, which are governed by national law but are not subject to any general Italian data protection rules. Article 9 of the Convention allows exceptions that constitute 'a necessary measure in a democratic society in the interests of . . . protecting State security, public safety . . . or the suppression of criminal offences . . . '.

Moreover, the rate at which ratification took place raised doubts that the Convention was a sufficient instrument for promoting international data protection. The Convention came into force in 1985, at the point when five states had ratified it: Germany, Spain, France, Norway and Sweden. Austria, Denmark, Ireland, Luxembourg and the United Kingdom have been among those who have done so since then. Spain's ratification was regarded sceptically, as it was only based upon a constitutional provision, but Spain has come more clearly into line with the Convention, and indeed with Schengen, through its 1992 legislation. One of the original Schengen countries, Belgium, is likewise a newcomer to data protection, although Italy remains without a general law; such lacunae have for several years called into question the ability of the SIS to afford adequate data protection. Raab and Bennett (1994) argue that another gap that was left by the Convention itself was the lack of effective international machinery to implement it in the international arena. Effective data protection owes much to administrative or regulatory organs, but the Convention established only a powerless and intermittently convened Consultative Committee and not a regulatory agency with authority to investigate and impose sanctions. Nevertheless, the CE's intergovernmental committee of experts on data protection has done much seminal thinking and reporting on issues and problems, among which is the question of data protection in the police sector.

The future development of European data protection was shaped by policy debates and activities in several issue networks in the late 1980s (Raab and Bennett, 1994). Within the European Community, the Convention – for all its shortcomings – was still regarded as the ground for future development of European data protection, with the single market and the growing market in information services particularly in mind. If information was to be allowed to flow across borders, adequate protection would have to be in place, and with this aim in mind the Commission of the European Communities (CEC) put in hand internal discussions about the means. Whilst opinion was divided over how far the Convention could play a part in an EC approach, its prestige was such that it could not be ignored, especially if it were applied more uniformly and across a larger number of countries. The policy context for EC deliberations was also influenced by the question of implementing immigration and visa policy, with EC ministers seeking a legal framework guaranteeing privacy (Spencer, 1990). We shall see later on how the proposal for an EC directive on data protection emerged in the early 1990s.

Data protection and the Schengen Convention

Meanwhile, in 1989 the data protection commissioners, a highly influential network of officials who are responsible for implementing legislation in their respective countries, urged a European-wide approach to better data protection. Support for new international rules also came from a leading OECD source (Gassmann, 1989). In proposing alternative models for a more integrated system, Jacques Fauvet, President of France's Commission National de l'Informatique et des Libertés (CNIL), drew attention to the advent of Schengen and its proposed information system (Fauvet, 1989). The 1990 Schengen Convention, discussed elsewhere in this book and by Korff (1990) and den Boer (1991), had galvanised the world of the data protectors towards a more effective approach within Europe. Its proposed abolition of border controls, and the development of cooperative arrangements for policing and for sharing sensitive criminal information caused concern over the lack of privacy safeguards. It is interesting to note that the sequence of trajectories outlined earlier was evident in the Schengen process itself: provisions for police cooperation preceded the plans for an information system, and these in turn preceded provisions for data protection.

Although, as Thyraud (1989) notes, Schengen had been announced in the French *Journal Officiel* in 1987, Fauvet (1989) declares that it was 'not without surprise' that, at the 1988 Oslo conference of data protection commissioners, CNIL delegates learned from German colleagues about its existence, for it had been devised behind closed doors by the five originating states. If the countdown to the 1993 single market in the EC had concentrated the minds of data protectors (and their adversaries) upon the question of information flows across borders, the prospective implementation of the SIS – and, indeed, other information systems involved in police cooperation, as envisaged in the 1990 Trevi Action Programme (Trevi, 1990) – has played a large part as well. It has stimulated the search for high-quality international data protection and the assessment of the bases upon which that can be built.

The chronology of policy development towards this was that, in the year following the promulgation of the CE's Recommendation No. R (87) 15 for the police sector, the commissioners at their Oslo meeting established a working group under French chairmanship to study the Recommendation's consequences (Thyraud, 1992). Following two meetings, the attention of some members was distracted to preparing a joint position on SIS, 'which their governments presented to them as a *fait accompli'* (ibid.: 176). This preparation was organised at meetings early in 1989, held under the auspices of Luxembourg's Consultative Commission on Personal Data Protection, that included French and German counterparts as well as representatives from Belgium and the Netherlands, although the latter two countries had not yet legislated for data protection (Thyraud, 1989; Faber, 1992). As a result of the majority agreement that Schengen had taken insufficient account of the need for data protection, France, Germany and Luxembourg adopted a common declaration at the second meeting, concerning minimum data protection prerequisites for the SIS (Thyraud, 1989; Korff, 1990) and urged their position on the Schengen sub-group that dealt with the exchange of information. This was evidently successful in the eventual Schengen Convention (den Boer, 1991: 7). In December, 1989, the CE adopted principles to the effect 'that the procedures on cooperation between administrations first ensure the protection of individuals with regard to the use of personalised data banks' (Trevi, 1990: para. 15.2).

The Schengen Convention includes provisions for data protection that have found favour with some commentators, although not without reservations of varying degrees of strength (Spencer, 1990; Korff, 1990, 1992; Scheller, 1992). Korff (1990), who welcomes the kind of basic requirements that Schengen would appear to satisfy, but who prefers a higher level (Korff, 1992: 157), shows the importance of a detailed appraisal of how norms and principles may be incorporated into practice, and of how their subversion may be avoided. Scheller (1992: 166–168) worries about the ambiguity of the term 'purpose' in regard to Schengen's limitation of the usage of data to the purpose for which it was gathered, and about the relationship between two sets of data protection regulations in Schengen, one for the SIS and one for other exchanges of information outside the SIS, including information about covert surveillance.

Schengen is grounded in the CE's 1981 Convention and in Recommendation No. R (87) (15). These are specified in Article 115 as forming the bases for the work of the central supervisory authority for the SIS, and in Article 117, which enjoins on each Schengen country the requirement to enact domestic legislation at least equal to that arising from the principles of these CE documents, but Korff (1990) points out that the Recommendation explains that this need not mean the adoption of general data protection if a country has an independent, police sector-specific supervisory authority. As we have seen, however, the limitations of the CE Convention does not provide a high degree of reassurance about its efficacy in underpinning safeguards for police data; nor does the variation in national data protection systems across Europe and amongst the Schengen states in particular.

As to the robustness of the CE's police Recommendation in the Schengen context, Thyraud's (1992) analysis notes the reservations, mentioned previously, entered by Ireland and the United Kingdom, among others. He enquires about the implementation of the proposal that national supervisory authorities should oversee compliance with legal provisions covering police data. With particular reference to France, Thyraud also touches on the Recommendation's points concerning the collection of data (including 'sensitive' data), its relevance and quality, the manner of its sorting, deleting and updating, its exchange between forces, transparency and subjects' access rights. Differences in practice between countries are in part explicable by differing types of investigation and differing organisational functions, as well as by different laws. His conclusion is that the non-mandatory Recommendation will not be as successful as the 1981 Convention, particularly with respect to *ad hoc* files and to the sort of international exchanges of data that Schengen envisages. The exigencies of police work using *ad hoc* files that collate data from various sources make the Recommendation's procedures for notifying the monitoring agency cumbersome and unrealistic.

Deliberations and appraisals of the status of data protection in the midst of new departures have continued in various fora and informally amongst the policy community. René Faber (1992), the President of Luxembourg's Consultative Committee, notes with satisfaction that the commissioners' views found their way into the Schengen text, but remarks that the absence of a central data protection authority leaves a deficit in the performance of certain verifying, troubleshooting and controlling functions. Following their meeting in The Hague late in 1991, the commissioners of Denmark, Ireland and the United Kingdom joined those of the original Schengen countries in commending the 'coherent' set of data-protection provisions, but underscored the need for adequate national provisions before Schengen could come into operation (European Community Data Protection Commissioners, 1991). They also established an *ad hoc* working group of the original five in order to facilitate their mutual consultation over all organisational matters relating to Schengen and to its relevant parts. In 1992, further developments are believed to have included the formation of an omnibus working group of the EC's data protection commissioners or their counterparts, to consider data protection issues in Schengen, Trevi, the proposed European Information System (EIS), the European Drugs Unit (EDU), Immigration and Customs.

The European Community's directive

Action within the EC towards an ostensibly higher level of data protection grew from concerns that were felt over what might be called a potential 'privacy deficit' in the post-1993 single market. There was unease about the level of data protection amongst member states in view of the abolition of frontiers and the development of police cooperation and exchanges of information through the Schengen Convention. These developments pointed towards the imperative of establishing a common level of data protection among the states of the EC. However, when the European Commission published its draft 'directive concerning the protection of individuals in relation to the processing of personal data' (CEC, 1990) in

September, 1990, based on Article 100A of the Treaty of Rome, it aroused a torrent of criticism from a wide variety of special interests. Following a period of vigorous lobbying, an unprecedentedly large number of amendments was consolidated and proposed by the European Parliament, and a revised draft was produced in October, 1992 (CEC, 1992). Subject to possible further amendment, final adoption is not expected until sometime in 1994, and national implementation will take place some two years later. The draft was accompanied by another one concerning data protection in public digital telecommunication networks, and by a draft proposal for information security.

The origins of the draft directive and some of its provisions are discussed at greater length elsewhere (Raab and Bennett, 1994). In general, the draft directive purports to champion privacy in the face of the activities of data users, despite some relaxation of its provisions between the two versions. Its approach is to establish in all member states an equivalent, high level of protection that surpasses the basic principles that it adopts from the general currency of data protection. It defines the conditions under which personal data can be communicated to non-EC countries where data protection is not 'adequate'. The directive would apply both to manual and automatically processed data, and eliminates the conventional distinction between the private and public sectors. Individuals would have to be informed about collections and disclosures of data.

National action would be required for implementation, as with the CE's Convention, but the directive requires much more of national governments in this regard. On the other hand, many exceptions or derogations are permitted, and these may be seen as weakening the effect of the putative harmonisation that is the EC's objective. Whilst some central machinery is proposed, in the form of a working party and an advisory committee, these are not vested with substantial regulatory powers The directive would have implications for the transmission of data across borders and repercussions upon existing national data protection systems, which would have to be modified to a greater or lesser degree in accordance with the EC requirements.

Although the Treaty of Rome does not give the EC legal competence in respect of policing, the relationship between the draft directive and police information is not entirely clear, and the articulation between it and national data protection rules is complex, as is its position in relation to international or bi-lateral rules of the Schengen variety. Recent airing of the question in the United Kingdom is illustrative on this matter. As H.M. Carter of the Home Office's Legal Branch observed in his evidence to the House of Lords (HL) Select Committee that considered the draft directive in its 1992–93 session, there is room for argument on what is within or outside the scope of EC law (HL, 1993a: 5). Article 3 says that the directive will not apply 'to the processing of data in the course of an activity which falls outside the scope of Community law' (CEC, 1992: 67). In the accompanying explanation, the 'secret services' are instanced as an example of the excluded activity (CEC, 1992: 12); the illustration in the 1990 version was the 'intelligence services' (CEC, 1990: 21). Neither version thus explicitly excludes police activities as such. Moreover, the revised draft permits countries to restrict subjects' rights to direct access, consent and transparency where, for example, reasons of national security, criminal proceedings or public safety supervene (Article 14). 'National security' is interpreted as meaning 'the protection of national sovereignty against both internal and external threat, and 'public safety' covers 'all the policing functions of public authority, including crime prevention' (CEC, 1992: 24).

These stipulations lend weight to the view that police data in member states are in some respects affected by the proposed directive, except where they are excluded; although an assessment of these exclusions is that police activities are inadequately controlled in the interests of privacy. If policing were wholly outside the scope of the directive, it could be argued that there would be no eason for Article 14's provision that, where direct subject access is restricted for reasons that include public safety, the member state's data protection authority must, on request, inspect the relevant file on the subject's behalf in order to verify the lawfulness of processing: such files are likely to be police files. Carter argued, however, that the United Kingdom took national security to be wholly outside Community law, whereas Article 14 gave the impression that the EC took it to be within (HL, 1993a: 5).

On the other hand, in his evidence to the House of Lords, Ulf Brühann, the EC official in Directorate-General III who has had responsibility for drafting the directive, affirmed that Article 3 merely clarified what was obvious and that Article 14's exceptions did not involve any question of Community competence in regard to public safety and the like (HL, 1993a: 85) It is important to note that the 1990 package of proposals contained a draft resolution of ministers that would have member states 'undertake to apply the principles contained in the Council Directive . . . to those parts of the public sector which do not fall within the scope of Community law' (CEC, 1990: 73). This resolution, to which Recital 11 of the revised draft directive refers, implies that national security and policing might thus come within the purview of EC data protection, although only in respect of the principles that are derived from the CE's 1981 Convention.

In the United Kingdom, the human rights organisation, Liberty (1991), interprets the resolution as applying to the police. Consistent with this, the House of Lords' opinion in its report on the draft directive makes a special point of urging the resolution's adoption, thus extending data protection principles to 'police, counter-terrorism, intelligence and defence' (HL, 1993b: 34). This is in view of the harm caused to persons through the misuse or inaccuracy of data for these purposes; thus individuals needed to be 'protected from conviction abroad on the basis of suspect police evidence or from mistaken arrest as a supposed terrorist' (HL, 1993b: 34). Noting that the Schengen countries were already discussing these matters, the report recommends a wider scope for the directive, albeit with appropriate transparency exemptions, but applying to police and security matters the fair obtaining and accuracy requirements of good data protection. In proposing this, the report seems implicitly to adopt a stance that resembles the CE's police Recommendation R (87) 15, whose inclusion in the resolution was advocated by Liberty in its written evidence (HL, 1993a: 47), in keeping with the Recommendation's acceptance within Schengen and Trevi.

Conclusion: towards the future

The EC draft directive has raised knotty issues that, in the first half of 1993, still remained to be resolved. The directive was still some distance away from adoption in its final form, beyond which will lie the long process of implementation at EC level and within the member states. In that process, arguments will be opened afresh at the level of single countries, concerning the relationship between the police as data users and the laws and systems that will have to be restructured to provide data protection at the new European standard. The draft directive leaves many avenues open to national decision-making in this respect, including derogations and exceptions, and therefore the outcome of those arguments is likely to fall short of radical change in the terms under which the police use information. Concomitantly, variations across states will remain, as harmonisation of data protection fails to achieve the consistency or equivalence for which many proponents had hoped. Nonetheless, in some respects police activities will be further legitimised and exchanges of information subjected to further safeguards.

The question of the resolution extending data protection principles to areas not covered by EC law had, early in 1993, not begun to be be tackled within the EC machinery. This question has long been overshadowed by the development of police cooperation and information exchange through bi-lateral or multi-lateral arrangements that circumvent the formal machinery of the EC. The secrecy and unaccountability of this development have, of course, invited complaints about a democratic deficit within Europe, insofar as the European Parliament is excluded from a role in the resultant arrangements. On the other hand, a privacy deficit has to some extent been limited, on paper at any rate, through the adoption of data protection provisions in Schengen and by the acknowledgement elsewhere of data protection as a necessary adjunct to police cooperation. For this, much is owed to the efforts of policy networks of data protectors and others whose influence has been exerted strategically over the years.

A late illustration of the insertion of data protection into cooperative policing can be found in the establishment of the Europol Drugs Unit (EDU) by agreement of the Trevi Ministers at Copenhagen in June, 1993 (Trevi, 1993). The EDU – intended as the first step towards Europol as a European criminal intelligence office dealing with a wide range of criminal activity – will involve liaison officers working as a team for exchanging and analysing intelligence regarding drug trafficking and related money-laundering activities. They will each have access to their national criminal information and intelligence, and will communicate information within the limits of national rules. The ministers 'emphasise the necessity of protecting all information from unauthorised access and destruction, including ensuring the physical protection of data processing systems and links' (Trevi, 1993: 3). Beyond this enunciation of data security, however, a broader appreciation of data protection is underscored in the stipulation that liaison officers must act within the terms of their national laws on data protection, including the keeping of a disclosure log if required by that legislation, and in the rejection of any storage of personal information within the EDU itself. Moreover, national data protection authorities are invited to supervise and inspect the work of liaison officers and of the EDU, and are ensured of the cooperation of the officers.

It will be some time before any assessment can be made of the efficacy of this departure in terms of policing and in terms of data protection, as with Schengen, whose SIS is yet to become operational. There is no *a priori* reason to be sanguine about the privacy protection that might be afforded, given the political and policing imperatives that drive the process of cooperation, however intermittent progress may be along that curve, and given the state of data protection in Europe at present and in the years to come. The advent of the Maastricht Treaty, its likely future, and its relationship to interministerial and other arrangements outside the formal EC institutional structure, also exert a powerful influence over the agenda of police cooperation and hence over the way in which data protection can be brought to bear upon it. Maastricht envisages closer police cooperation and thus embraces existing initiatives that involve exchanges of personal and other information in the context of criminal and other investigations. However, the implications of this for the EC's proposed resolution on extension of the data protection principles to those parts of the public sector that do not fall within the scope of Community law are uncertain.

To conclude, the trajectories of police cooperation and of data protection must be examined in relation to one another, for they overlap within the same policy space. It is important to disentangle the alliances, groups and organisations that form and reform, but there are many unfolding processes that intersect or conflict, and there is much that is covert and inaccessible. These analytical problems present challenges that are worth meeting. So too does an evaluative question: how would we know whether data protection is successful? But then, how would we know whether police cooperation is successful?

References

Bennett, C. (1992), *Regulating Privacy*, Ithaca and London, Cornell University Press.
Boer, M. den (1991), *Schengen: Intergovernmental Scenario for European Police Cooperation*, A System of European Police Cooperation after 1992, Working Paper V, Edinburgh.

Commission of the European Communities (CEC) (1990), *Proposal for a Council Directive Concerning the Protection of Individuals in Relation to the Processing of Personal Data*, (COM (90) 314 Final – SYN 287), Brussels, 13 September.

Commission of the European Communities (CEC) (1992), *Amended Proposal for a Council Directive on the Protection of Individuals with Regard to the Processing of Personal Data and on the Free Movement of Such Data*, (COM (92) 422 final – SYN 287), Brussels, 15 October.

Council of Europe (CE) (1981), *Explanatory Report on the Convention for the Protection of Individuals With Regard to Automatic Processing of Personal Data* [includes Treaty No. 108], Strasbourg, Council of Europe.

Council of Europe (CE) (1988), *Regulating the Use of Personal Data in the Police Sector* [includes Recommendation No. R 87 (15)], Strasbourg, Council of Europe.

Council of Europe (CE) (n.d.), *Convention for the Protection of Individuals With Regard to Automatic Processing of Personal Data – Declarations*, Strasbourg, Council of Europe.

European Community Data Protection Commissioners (1991), 'Statement, November 29, 1991', The Hague.

Faber, R. (1992), 'Système d'Information Schengen (SIS)', in Council of Europe (Ed.), *Data Protection, Human Rights and Democratic Values* – XIII Conference of the Data Protection Commissioners, 2–4 October 1991, Strasbourg, Council of Europe.

Fauvet, J. (1989), *Privacy in the New Europe*, Paper presented at the 11th Annual Conference of the Data Protection Commissioners, Berlin.

Flaherty, D. (1989), *Protecting Privacy in Surveillance Societies*, Chapel Hill, N.C., University of North Carolina Press.

Gassmann, H.–P. (1989), *Privacy Protection and Computer Network Operation Rules – A Challenge for the '90s*, Paper presented at the 11th Annual Conference of the Data Protection Commissioners, Berlin.

House of Commons (1990a), *Criminal Records*, Third Report of the Home Affairs Committee, Session 1989–90, HC 285, 3 April, London, HMSO.

House of Commons (1990b), *Practical Police Cooperation in the European Community*, Seventh Report of the Home Affairs Committee, Session 1989–90, HC 363–I, 20 July, London, HMSO.

House of Lords (HL) (1993a), *Protection of Personal Data – With Evidence*, 20th Report of the Select Committee on the European Communities, Session 1992–93, HL Paper 75, 30 March, London, HMSO.

House of Lords (HL) (1993b), *Protection of Personal Data – Report*, 20th Report of the Select Committee on the European Communities, Session 1992–93, HL Paper 75–I, 30 March, London, HMSO.

Korff, D. (1990), 'The Schengen Information System: Also a Question of Data Protection', in G. Mols (Ed.), *Dissonanten bij het Akkoord van Schengen*, Deventer, Kluwer.

Korff, D. (1992), 'Data protection and implications for cross-border policing', in M. Anderson and M. den Boer (Eds.), *European Police Cooperation: Proceedings of a Seminar*, Edinburgh, Project Group European Police Cooperation, Department of Politics, University of Edinburgh.

Liberty (1991), *Memorandum on the European Commission Proposals on Data Protection*, London, National Council for Civil Liberties.

Martin, F. (1982), 'Lindop and After', in C. Raab (Ed.) *Data Protection and Privacy – Proceedings of a Conference*, London, Social Research Association.

Mellors, C. and Pollitt, D. (1984), 'Legislating for Privacy: Data Protection in Western Europe', *Parliamentary Affairs*, **37**, 2, 199–215.

Organisation for Economic Cooperation and Development (OECD) (1981), *Guidelines on the Protection of Privacy and Transborder Flows of Personal Data*, Paris, OECD.

Raab, C. (1993a), 'The Governance of Data Protection', in J. Kooiman (Ed.), *Modern Governance*, London and Beverly Hills, Sage Publications.

Raab, C. (1993b), 'Data Protection in Britain: Governance and Learning', *Governance*, **6**, 1, 43–66.

Raab, C. & Bennett, C. (1994), 'Protecting Privacy Across Borders: European Policies and Prospects', *Public Administration*, **72**, 1 (forthcoming).

Scheller, S. (1992), 'Legal Problems of the Schengen Information System', in M. Anderson and M. den Boer (Eds.), *European Police Cooperation. Proceedings of a Seminar*, Edinburgh, Project Group European Police Cooperation, Department of Politics, University of Edinburgh.

Simitis, S. (1989), *Data Protection: Transcending the National Approach*, Paper presented at the 11th Annual Conference of the Data Protection Commissioners, Berlin.

Spencer, M. (1990), *1992 and all That*, London, The Civil Liberties Trust.

Thyraud, J. (1989), *Communication by Senator Jacques Thyraud on the Report on the Schengen Agreement*, Paper presented at the 11th Annual Conference of the Data Protection Commissioners, Berlin.

Thyraud, J. (1992), 'Recommendation No. R (87) 15 of the Committee of Ministers of the Council of Europe Regulating the Use of Personal Data in the Police Sector', in Council of Europe (Ed.), *Data Protection, Human Rights and Democratic Values – XIII Conference of the Data Protection Commissioners, 2–4 October 1991*, Strasbourg, Council of Europe.

Trevi (1990), *Programme of Action Relating to the Reinforcement of Police Cooperation and of the Endeavours to Combat Terrorism or Other Forms of Organized Crime*, June 1990.

Trevi (1993), *Ministerial Agreement on the Establishment of the Europol Drugs Unit*, Copenhagen, 2 June 1993.

8

WILL SIS BE EUROPE'S BIG BROTHER?

Martin Baldwin-Edwards and Bill Hebenton

Any fact becomes important when it's connected to another. The connection changes the perspective; it leads you to think that every detail of the world, every voice, every word written or spoken has more than its literal meaning, that it tells us of a Secret. The rule is simple: Suspect, only suspect.

(Umberto Eco, 1989: 377–378)

The issues surrounding the collection, maintenance and storage of personal data in information systems are both complex and rich.[1] Information throughout the Western world has come to be regarded as a resource, and the tool which has facilitated this is the computer. Policing, like other forms of activity, has been transformed in recent years by the advent of these computerised information systems (Ackroyd *et al.*, 1992). Although initially presented as a resource-led measure to increase efficiency and deal with perceived increases in crime levels, it is clear that police computerisation and the collection, storage and use of personal information has developed its own, separate trajectory. Lagging behind is the attempt to create systems to protect privacy of personal data in such police systems.

Even given the amorphous character of the concept of 'privacy' which most people hold, the protection of privacy regularly emerges in public opinion surveys and in general discussion as an all-encompassing notion used by individuals to express their anxieties. The attempt to deal with privacy through data protection in respect of policing is a specialised, sectoral aspect of general data protection in the public sector, albeit perhaps the most difficult to achieve because police work is less transparent and closer to the 'regalian' functions of the state than are many others in the public domain (Bittner, 1970; Klockars, 1985).

In seeking to explore data protection within the context of what some commentators describe as the 'unfolding of a transnational policing system' (McLaughlin, 1992: 484) one can properly question whether values such as autonomy of information use (privacy) can make headway against the 'tyranny of convenience' that appears to drive other political developments in this arena. Nevertheless, it is clear that police cooperation in the European Community is a complex, multi-layered affair which tends to resist analysis in terms of clear purposes and linear progress (den Boer and Walker, 1993: 24). As such, issues of data protection are far from settled and it is important to examine the detail of existing arrangements as well as the interstices where problems lurk unseen, or at least dormant, at this stage of integration of policing at the European level. This chapter sets itself that task.

The focus of the chapter is the European exemplary *par excellence* of police transborder transfer of data, namely the proposed Schengen Information System (SIS). Our chapter, however, can be seen as divided into three parts: we begin with the background to the Schengen Agreement (1985), the implementing agreement known as the Convention Implementing the Schengen Agreement (1990), and then describe and consider the structure of SIS. In the second part, we examine the proposed operation of Schengen and SIS. Part three looks at the complex interrelationship between international, European Community, national and Schengen legislation. We conclude with an assessment of Schengen's likely impact on the privacy of the individual.

The Schengen Convention and its background

Schengen, alongside Interpol, Trevi and the proposed Europol, is one of the four major structures relevant to the European Community and police cooperation. Indeed some commentators have stated that cooperation along the form of Schengen is the most likely scenario for transnational cooperation within the EC. For example, Fijnaut is of the opinion that 'it is not an exaggeration to say that in the "Europe of 1992" police cooperation will be built up after the model of "Schengen 1990"' (Fijnaut, 1990: 1). So what is Schengen? In this section we map out the background to and nature of the 1985 Schengen Agreement, and proceed to consider the 1990 Convention devised to allow for implementation of the earlier Agreement.

To begin with, it is worthwhile noting that an analysis of the origins of the 1985 Schengen Agreement on the gradual suppression of border controls points to the fact that its primary rationale was seen by the Contracting Parties as enhanced economic advantage.[2] Movement of goods was to profit from the elimination of control procedures at the respective borders, and mutual trade was expected to receive a substantial boost. The 1985 Agreement's provisions on free movement of persons are much less elaborate than the provisions on goods and transport.[3]

The Agreement was signed originally on 14 June 1985 in Schengen (Luxembourg) by France, Germany, Belgium, the Netherlands and Luxembourg. As O'Keeffe (1992) points out, there was clearly a desire by the countries involved to achieve greater progress than had then been achieved within the context of the European Community. It is essentially a first attempt at realising the objective of creating in Europe an area without internal borders. Some have argued (e.g. Hondius, 1991) that it was an enlargement of the earlier 1958 agreement among members of the Benelux Economic Union, lifting their internal border controls and instituting a common Benelux tourist visa. The two other countries who joined them, France and Germany, were for their part linked in cooperation under the Franco-German Treaty. However, as Steenbergen (1991) forcefully argues, the Schengen process does not 'fit' with previous Benelux law and is of a somewhat different nature dealing primarily with the movement of nationals of third states, that is non-EC nationals.

The Agreement, a short document of 33 articles is divided into two Titles. Title I deals mainly with the movement of goods and services. It entered into force on 1 January 1986 except in the Netherlands where it entered into force on 2 March 1986. Title II, on the freedom of movement of persons, was more in the nature of a statement of intent and clearly was aimed at long-term future negotiations. It sought the complete abolition of controls at the common frontiers and their transfer to the external frontiers of the Schengen territory. The context for this, of course, is that the original Schengen 'five' are countries with extensive land borders which are impossible to police effectively, and consequently possess traditions of relatively strong internal policing controls. A number of compensatory measures were envisaged:

They agreed to approximate their visa policies, to combat drug trafficking, to cooperation between police and customs authorities in the fight against crime, unauthorised entry and residence, customs and tax fraud and smuggling. In the long-term, in order to facilitate the abolition of controls at the common frontiers and their transfer, they agreed to harmonise the regulations governing the exercise of checks at the external frontiers (including measures to safeguard security and combat illegal immigration) and to improve police and judicial cooperation (including the possibility of a right of hot pursuit) (O'Keeffe, 1992: 187).

As Schutte (1991) indicates, a negotiating structure was established immediately following the signing to bring about the detailed implementing regulations required by the Agreement. This structure consisted of four working groups: police and security; free movement of persons; free movement of goods; transport. These working groups reported to a Central Negotiating Group, a committee of very senior officials, which was charged with the preparation of decisions to be taken by the political level, meetings of State Secretaries. The whole structure of negotiations was serviced by the existing Secretariat of the Benelux Economic Union, which was especially enlarged for this purpose. The European Commission has had observer status at these meetings in central group since 1988.

The protracted negotiations failed to achieve consensus for the 1 January 1990 deadline set by the 1985 Agreement. Eventually, on 19 June 1990 the detailed document was ready for signature – it had the full title 'Convention implementing the Schengen Agreement of 15 June 1985 between the Governments of the States of the Benelux Economic Union, the Federal Republic of Germany and the French Republic, on the gradual abolition of checks at their common borders'. (An unofficial English translation of the Convention is published as an annex in Meijers *et al.*, 1991.)

The 1990 Convention contains some 142 Articles under eight Titles, a final Act with six declarations, a Protocol with three declarations, a Common Declaration containing enumeration of subjects for future negotiations and a separate Declaration by the Ministers and Under-secretaries of State. For our purposes, the more important elements feature in Title III 'Police and Security' (the longest Title in the Convention), Title IV the 'Schengen Information System' and Title VI 'Protection of Personal Data'.

Hondius describes the Convention as a 'typical law enforcement instrument. It quotes the price for liberalising internal borders, namely, stringent rules on the controls at external borders' (Hondius, 1991: 302). Title III, in relation to police cooperation and information exchange, illustrates that view nicely. Under Article 39, police shall render mutual assistance upon request, for the purposes of detecting or preventing crime. As O'Keeffe (1992) points out the notion of assistance is not defined but is taken to include the *provision of information* and all other forms of assistance. This obligation is subject only to the general limitation that police must act in compliance with *national* legislation and within the limits of their responsibilities. A series of important innovations in written international public law is introduced, and as Schutte (1991) correctly suggests the Convention first regulates in general terms mutual and direct police cooperation on request. However, as we detail subsequently, Article 46 permits the provision of unsolicited information and does not provide minimum guarantees as regards the transmission of information which has been obtained illegally. Article 46 merely refers to *national* law, which clearly varies from country to country, thus giving varying levels of protection.

The Schengen Information System

Described by Schutte as the 'most spectacular novelty' (Schutte, 1991: 559) in the Convention and by O'Keeffe as 'one of the most innovative features' (O'Keeffe, 1992: 204), the SIS is a joint computerised information system to be set up and maintained to enable national authorities to access reports on people and objects for the purpose of border checks and police inquiries. SIS is not a system linking existing police information data-bases or computer systems, but a separate international register. Structurally, therefore, SIS consists of a central data-bank and materially identical national data files, connected to the central information system.

Article 93 of the Convention sets the purpose of the SIS to be to maintain public order and security and for use in connection with the movement of persons. As O'Keeffe (1992) insightfully points out, the Convention's provision is that it mixes detailed rules as to the functioning of the SIS with prescriptive rules on immigration and asylum. This nexus demonstrates the key position of the SIS within the Schengen framework.

Once SIS has been installed, at all places where external border controls are to take place there should be terminals connected with SIS.

The Convention details the six categories of data file to be entered on SIS:

a) data relating to persons who are wanted for arrest for extradition purposes. Such entries into the system are to be accepted as requests for provisional arrest as intended in applicable extradition treaties, although the Convention requires the state making an entry to submit the necessary additional information supporting the request for provisional arrest to the other countries through traditional channels (Article 95);

b) data relating to aliens, reported for purposes of refusing their entry into the territory of the Parties to the Convention. If such an alien is found within that territory he or she has in principle to be removed (Article 96);

c) data relating to persons whose whereabouts are to be reported. This may concern missing persons who are to be served with judicial writs (Article 97);

d) data relating to witnesses/suspects summoned to appear before a court in criminal proceedings (Article 98);

e) data relating to persons who are to be kept under discreet (covert) surveillance or specifically checked, in order to get information about their movements or behaviour (Article 99);

f) data relating to objects sought, for the purpose of seizure (Article 100).

An SIS information report by the police on an individual is to include only:

– name;

– identifying physical features;

– date and place of birth;

– sex;

– nationality;

– whether violent;

– whether armed;

– reason for the report; and

– action to be taken.

In general, access to SIS is reserved for authorities responsible for: (a) border checks and (b) other police and customs checks carried out within a Schengen state, and the coordination of such checks.

In terms of structural responsibilities, national SIS is to be overseen by a national central authority to be established by the Schengen state concerned. The central SIS, located in Strasbourg and for which France has responsibility, will oversee and monitor input; it will be the only part of the system with information held from all Schengen countries. This central component of SIS (referred to in the Convention as the 'technical support function') will be supervised by a Joint Supervisory Authority comprised of representatives of the national supervisory bodies. It has two tasks: to check that the Convention provisions with respect to central SIS are properly implemented; to examine and mediate on problems arising from the application of SIS.

While the above structure may appear clear-cut, the proposed operation is far from simple to interpret. It is to these matters that we now turn.

The operation of Schengen and SIS

The sole rationale for the Schengen process is to strengthen collaboration between Schengen states. The mutual exchange of personal data forms an integral part of this process and as such the Convention in addition to specifically establishing a joint information system (SIS) also provides for possibilities of mutual exchange. In what follows, we distinguish between arrangements that the Convention sets out for the operation of SIS and exchange of personal data outside of SIS.

SIS

The SIS originally dealt with by the Police and Security Working Group (Working Group 1) is now handled by a separate Steering Committee , which reports directly to the Central Negotiating Group. National SIS in each country are networked to the central SIS (C-SIS) in Strasbourg. The Strasbourg C-SIS began work in 1990, with an initial target date of 1 March 1993. According to Cruz (1993), C-SIS has reached operational status amongst the five original signatories, but technical problems remain, for instance in harmonisation of regulations on surnames. *Statewatch* (1992, vol. 2: 5) reports that two regions of the Netherlands, Rotterdam and Arnhem, used the test version of SIS in October 1992.

Articles 102–118 set out provisions for the protection of personal data and security of data on SIS. One of the initial and most important points to note in this regard is that the Convention provides that, insofar as it does not lay down *specific* provisions, the legislation of the Schengen state shall apply to the data included in the national SIS. In an attempt to deal with disparity of national legislation, the Convention states that prior to its coming into force, Schengen states must achieve a level of personal data protection at least equal to that resulting from the principles of the 1981 Council of Europe Convention for the Protection of Individuals with Regard to Automatic Processing of Personal Data and the Committee of Ministers of the Council of Europe Recommendation (87) 15 'Regulating the Use of Personal Data in the Police Sector'. While these principles set the 'default' values, a number of detailed provisions are set out in the Convention, and we now proceed to describe and comment on these.

USE OF PERSONAL DATA

Here, the concept of purpose limitation applies. As a general rule of data protection it means that information may be used only for the purpose for which it was gathered. The Convention states that data recorded in SIS may be used only for the purposes laid down for each type of report. This is clearly an important principle; however, it is not clear whether this notion of 'purpose' refers to purpose as indicated in an individual's data record under 'reason for report' (for example, criminal prosecution) or to the more general six categories of data file. Scheller (1992: 167) concludes from her analysis of the relevant provision (Article 102) that it refers to the latter. If this is the case then its effectiveness as a safeguard is severely limited. States can derogate from the 'purpose limitation' principle where it can be justified 'by the need to prevent an imminent serious threat to public order and safety, for serious reasons of state security or for the purposes of preventing a serious offence' (Article 102). On this, O'Keeffe comments that 'derogation . . . could render guarantees about the use of data nugatory' (O'Keeffe, 1992: 207).

The Convention also sets out who may have direct access to data on SIS. While authorities responsible for border checks and other police and customs checks are included, this is only a very general indication which has to be supplemented by national lists to be drawn up by Schengen states. In addition, Verhey points out that authorities responsible for the implementation of aliens regulations have direct access in accordance with Article 96 (Verhey, 1991: 124).

DATA SUBJECT ACCESS

In principle, subjects are accorded right of access (Article 109). Importantly, the Convention clearly indicates that such access can only be exercised in accordance with the law of the Schengen state in which the right is invoked. Thus any person is at liberty to determine to which state he will address his access request. The principle of right of access is however constrained, and not only by the national law. The Convention provides that prior to agreement on access, the *reporting* state should be given the opportunity to contest the matter. Quite how this process of legal challenge to right of access would work is left unstated as is any analysis of the problem of how a difference of view between *requested* and *reporting* state would be resolved. In addition, access can be refused if it undermines the execution of the legal task relating to the SIS report, or in order to protect the rights and freedoms of others, or in relation to the task of discreet (covert) surveillance.

It is open for any person to have factually inaccurate data relating to him/her corrected and to have legally inaccurate data deleted. Verhey (1991: 125) sees as highly significant the provision which allows a person to bring an action to correct, delete or provide data or obtain compensation before the courts or the competent national legal authority. Final decisions taken are binding. Thus, for example if a German court finds an SIS report recorded at the behest of the French authorities to be unlawfully stored, they would have to delete the report from SIS. However, there is no direct legal remedy for the data subject offered by the Convention at either the national or supranational level.

SUPPLY OF PERSONAL DATA

While the Convention provides that national SIS reports may not be copied to other national data files, it is left unclear whether this excludes supply of personal data to third parties where the data being stored is not specifically in a personal data file. Furthermore, because it is left unstated, can it be presumed that national domestic law would govern such supply of data originating from SIS?

REPORTING ON SIS

As we have set out earlier, there are six general categories of data file on SIS. However, the category dealing with reporting for the purpose of discreet (covert) surveillance is worthy of more detailed examination (Article 99). According to O'Keeffe it allows reporting on SIS for aims which 'are both vague and arguably too wide' (O'Keeffe, 1992: 207). In particular, concern has been expressed that it provides that a report may be made where an 'overall evaluation' of the person concerned gives reason to suppose that he will commit serious offences in future. Indeed, in April 1991 the Council of State of the Netherlands in its opinion on the Convention took the view that such a provision may well be in conflict with Principle 2.1 of the Recommendation (87) 15 which states that the collection of personal data for police purposes 'should be limited to such levels as is necessary for the prevention of a *real danger or the suppression of a specific criminal offence*' (our emphasis). The Dutch Council of State felt that such a provision on reporting on SIS could lead to fundamental infringements of personal privacy.[4] A further matter of reporting on SIS is the vagueness of the provision relating to aliens (Article 96). Here aliens can be reported for the purpose of being refused entry on the basis of a threat to public order or national security and safety which the presence of an alien in national territory may pose. In addition, a particular case referred to in Article 96, namely 'an alien who has been convicted of an offence carrying a custodial sentence of at least one year' is unclear on the distinction between serving a term of imprisonment and the length of sentence which an offence may carry.

Information exchange outside of SIS

As mentioned earlier, the Convention generally aims at enhancing collaboration on mutual exchange of personal data. In particular, it refers specifically to exchange on:

– processing of asylum requests (Article 38);

– police cooperation on preventing and investigating crimes (Article 39 and Article 46);

– mutual assistance in criminal matters (Article 48 *et seq.*);

– control of the acquisition and possession of firearms (Article 91).

As O'Keeffe (1992: 207) indicates, Title VI of the Convention was added at a late stage in negotiations and covers the protection of data other than on SIS. The provisions are very intricate: it is not at all clear why they are so complex and why they allow for the range of exemptions specified.

The primary distinction made is a tripartite one which recognises three forms of information exchange:

(a) automated processing of personal data (Article 126);

(b) personal data recorded in a non-automated personal data file (Article 127); and

(c) personal data recorded in another manner (Article 127).

Differing levels of *general* protection are specified for each of the three forms of information exchange and this is supplemented by other specific provisions. In terms of general levels of protection, the first two forms are subject to a level of protection equal to the principles of the 1981 Council of Europe Data Protection Convention. The third form receives a lesser degree of protection. Additionally, exchange of data in the police sector is subject to the principles of the 1987 Council of Europe Recommendation (87) 15.

Specific provisions (Article 126) in relation to automatic processing of personal data relate to: compliance with the principle of purpose limitation, accuracy and legality of supply, confirmation of liability in cases where inaccurate data is transmitted and the obligation to record each transmission and receipt of personal data. However, as Verhey (1991: 117) notes, these measures do not apply in all circumstances. For example, neither the general level of protection nor the specific provisions apply to the transmission of data on handling asylum applications. In addition, other *partial* exemptions include exchange of data on extradition, mutual assistance in criminal matters and the application of the *non bis in idem* (no double jeopardy) principle.

In relation to non-automated data files the measures mentioned above are in principle also applicable in the case of the transmission of non-automated to non-automated data file, and with the same exemptions. The data protection provisions do not apply at all to extradition, mutual assistance in criminal matters and the application of the *non bis in idem* principle.

The third form of data exchange involves application of the Schengen provisions as for automated data, although with no requirement of national protection equivalent to the 1981 Council of Europe Data Protection Convention. In addition, there are supplementary provisions. They relate to: the obligation to keep records of transmission and receipt, the use of personal data and access to data. A crucial exception, which O'Keeffe refers to somewhat ironically as 'unfortunate', is given in Article 127 (2a) which in our view effectively nullifies any obligation. As with the non-automated form of exchange, these provisions do not apply to extradition, mutual assistance in criminal matters and the application of the *non bis in idem* principle.

In relation to information exchange outside SIS two other provisions regulate purpose limitation. Article 126 (3a) states that personal data may only be used for the purposes for which transmission of such information is provided for in the Convention, thus allowing for very wide interpretation.

In respect of data exchange in relation to unrequested data in the police sector (Article 46) there are specific provisions (Article 129). These provide that: data may only be used for purposes set out by the Schengen state supplying the data, data may only be disclosed to police and other authorities, and that a supplying Schengen state may request a receiving Schengen state to indicate what use was made of the data and the subsequent results.

This, however, may lead to problems, if national legislation and implementation practice differ greatly in, for example, covert surveillance (Article 99). Under Article 99, the requesting state does not even apply the law of the state which carries out the measure but exclusively its own. Therefore, one state may supply information on behalf of Article 99 and this information is then used, let us say, in a minor case, in which covert surveillance could not have been carried out in the supplying state. Scheller describes this as 'circumvention of national law by international cooperation' (Scheller, 1992: 168).

A particularly puzzling provision exists in relation to *liaison officers*. Article 47 authorises bi-lateral secondments of police officers for the purposes, inter alia, of information exchange and mutual police assistance. Curiously, Article 130 specifies application of the Convention's data protection provisions *only* in relation to data flows back to the liaison officer's country of origin. It would appear that data flows *from* the country of origin are not covered.

A separate code is introduced via Article 38 for the exchange of data concerning asylum seekers, which in certain areas offers less protection than the general rules to be found in Title VI. Specifically, there is no protection for non-automated personal data, no legal remedies and no liability of the Schengen states for inaccurate data. Cruz (1993) points out that the Schengen group has given assurances that the SIS will never serve as a network of exchange of information on asylum seekers. But nothing has been said on rejected asylum seekers served with expulsion orders to leave Schengen 'territory'. Failure to comply with such orders renders one a clandestine immigrant. Article 96 provides for the inclusion in SIS of personal data on any 'alien [who] has been the subject of a deportation, removal or expulsion measure which has not been rescinded or suspended, including or accompanied by a prohibition on entry or, where appropriate, based on non-compliance with national regulations on the entry or residence of aliens'.

Schengen and its relationship with other legal arrangements

The two Schengen treaties occupy an anomalous position with regard to other legal arrangements. First of all, the aims in most respects replicate European Community ambitions, although proceeding at a much faster pace. Despite apparently requiring EC membership of its signatories (Article 140), Schengen is an agreement in international law between originally five, now nine, EC countries and is potentially in conflict with EEC law. Secondly it should be noted that Schengen in some instances stipulates *modus operandi*, and in others leaves the precise operation to (very) different national legal systems: this makes almost impossible any characterisation of the arrangements as either 'harmonising' or 'coordinating'. Finally, there is no envisaged judicial authority to interpret and implement the treaties; although an intergovernmental Executive Committee is to perform this role, it is not a Court and 'operates completely outside the constraints of domestic or supranational law' (Hathaway, 1992).

Altogether, the 1990 Supplementary Agreement refers to no fewer than 12 other treaties (Hondius, 1991: 303): the Treaty of Rome 1957, the Geneva Convention of 1951 and its 1967 Protocol, three UN Conventions on drugs (1961, 1971, 1988), the Benelux Treaty on mutual assistance in criminal matters 1962, the 1967 Convention on mutual assistance between customs administrations, and five Council of Europe Conventions on personal data (1981), extradition (1957), mutual assistance in criminal matters (1959), transfer of sentenced persons (1983), and the control, acquisition and possession of firearms by individuals (1978). A glaring omission in this catalogue of international arrangements is any reference to the 1951 European Convention of Human Rights; yet each member state is a signatory to the ECHR, and within the framework of EEC law the European Court of Justice (ECJ) is bound to respect basic human rights provisions (O'Keeffe, 1992: 210). This could lead to incompatibilities with national Constitutions or European Community law, either of which would present serious problems.

The Schengen arrangements, although innovatory in abolishing internal border controls and strengthening external ones, display a certain degree of continuity with existing arrangements. Thus it is possible to view

Schengen as consisting of two antithetical ideas: on the one hand, *facilitating conditions* for, inter alia, mutual assistance in criminal matters, extradition arrangements, and customs arrangements. On the other, are *limiting conditions* such as the 1981 Data Protection Convention, the 1987 Recommendation on personal data in the police sector, and possibly the European Convention on Human Rights. All of these matters are currently regulated by international agreements; thus to some extent, Schengen is a rationalisation or ordering of existing international cooperation. However, it is evident that the balance of these two interests is very strongly weighted in favour of the facilitating conditions, at the same time as permitting each member state to retain almost complete national autonomy. Clearly it is the latter aim which has precluded serious entertainment of a supranational court, to interpret and enforce the treaties analogously to the role of the ECJ in EEC law.

Relations with international legal instruments

As noted above, Schengen aims explicitly to supplement and facilitate many international conventions in relation to policing, immigration and customs. Here we shall concern ourselves with the limiting conditions – in particular, the Council of Europe 1981 Data Protection Convention and the 1987 Recommendation on data in the police sector. It should be noted that although frequent reference is made to the standards of the 1981 and 1987 legislation, there is no requirement actually to ratify these. However, Articles 117 and 126 do require the introduction of national levels of equivalent protection (to the Council of Europe legislation), and no data transmission until those have been achieved. (There are specific exceptions to this provision, for example in the case of certain types of data and also with respect to asylum-seekers, as noted above.) We examine below the significance of this requirement.

The 1981 Council of Europe Convention for the Protection of Individuals with Regard to Automatic Processing of Personal Data attempts to achieve some limited degree of harmonisation of standards, principally for the purpose of freeing transborder flows of data (Article 12.2).

The Convention establishes certain principles (Articles 5–8) which the Parties are required to implement in domestic legislation (Article 5). These include principles relating to quality of data, use of 'sensitive' data, data security, personal access to and correction of data.

Even though formal reservations cannot be entered, the Convention permits in Article 9 (2) derogation from Articles 5, 6 and 8 (dealing with quality of data, sensitive data and protection of data subjects, respectively); such derogation can be on the grounds of national security, monetary state interests, suppression of criminal offences, and protecting data subjects or others' freedoms. Also, Article 3 allows a declaration to be submitted, exempting certain categories of data. The UK declaration includes employment data, accounts records, and information publicly available. France has extended coverage to manual files; in practice, both Germany and the Netherlands regulate such data. With respect to transborder data movements, the Convention regulates only export of data (Article 12), since it assumes that national regulation will be sufficient for imported data.

Nugter (1990: 261) identifies three serious deficiencies of the Convention as being:

- different territorial scopes of national data protection laws, resulting in conflict of laws or no applicable law;

- divergent national rules with regard to data protection; and

- divergent national rules with regard to the protection of the data subject.

Vassilaki (1993), in a more recent study, concludes that the general character of the Convention's norms does not provide legal certainty. Even where both sending and receiving states have corresponding legislation, 'small differences between national provisions which determine the transport of data are enough to cause questions and uncertainties' (Vassilaki, 1993: 36).

Thus the Convention seems to have achieved relatively little in promoting a European 'data area'; furthermore, several EEC countries have failed to ratify it. These are Belgium, Greece, Italy, the Netherlands and Portugal: of these, only the Netherlands has long-standing domestic data protection legislation.

The 1987 Recommendation on personal data in the police sector supplements the 1981 Convention, but does not have binding force. In particular, it calls attention to the 1981 Convention and the provisions of Article 8 of the ECHR and lays down ground rules for the protection of individuals' rights. An independent supervisory body, outside of the police sector, should be established. Rules governing the collection, storage and communication of data are enunciated, along with data subjects' rights of notification, rectification and erasure. Alone of Council of Europe members, the UK has entered reservations on Articles 2.2 and 2.4 – informing data subjects (retrospectively) of data-holding and sensitive data, such as race, sexual behaviour and political opinions.

With regard to data protection and policing, the most specific norms are contained in the Recommendation (87) 15, which has been drawn up within the framework of the broader 1981 Convention, and which seeks to adapt the general principles contained in that Convention for the police sector. However, neither instrument can be relied upon directly by individuals in national or international proceedings. Both the Recommendation and the 1981 Convention are furthermore (primarily) restricted to data which is processed automatically. By contrast, the ECHR allows for the possibility of bringing proceedings at an international level, by individual petition.

Relations with European Community law

The potential for conflict with EEC law has, to a certain extent, been acknowledged in the 1990 Agreement. Thus an 'alien' is defined as a person who is not a national of an EC member state, thereby recognising exclusive Community competence with respect to free movement of persons (Schutte, 1991). Yet even with respect to third country nationals, it has been argued that the EC has limited competence (see e.g. Plender, 1990). Two Articles of the Implementing Convention attempt to deal with the problem of compatibility with Community law – Articles 134and 142.

Article 134 states that the Convention will apply only insofar as it is compatible with EC law. O'Keeffe suggest that the main areas are likely to be firearms, where an EEC directive is almost identical to the corresponding section in the Convention, checks on hand baggage, and – most crucially – data protection (O'Keeffe, 1992: 210). Also there is possible conflict with Article 8A of the EEC Treaty, since Schengen fails to distinguish between borders with EC member states and those with non-member states. Two other areas of difficulty are with human rights, as noted above, and third country nationals who are family members of EC nationals. Under EEC law, family members of EC nationals have the full protection of Community law: no such provision is made in Schengen, but this matter could be covered by Article 134.

Article 142 is a provision to allow for adaptation of Schengen to future EC arrangements, including conventions drawn up outside the formal EC framework. This includes the Dublin Convention and the unsigned External Frontiers Convention, for example. O'Keeffe suggests that duplication of material at EC and Schengen levels is likely, and Article 142 does not then require repeal of Schengen provisions (O'Keeffe, 1992: 211).

The Maastricht Treaty's third pillar, dealing with intergovernmental arrangements, could provide an alternative path. In particular, provision exists to attribute legal competence to the European Court of Justice to interpret any particular convention within that framework (Article K3 (2)). There is some pressure to provide ECJ jurisdiction over Schengen, particularly from the Netherlands and the European Parliament (see Cruz, 1993: 11; *Migration News Sheet*, 12/92: 2). However, it has been suggested that the Court of First Instance would be overburdened, and a new court – dealing specifically with the third pillar (immigration, aliens, policing, customs) – and new procedure would be needed (O'Keeffe, 1992: 213).

Relations with national legal systems

Much of Schengen leaves legal responsibility and liability at least partly in the hands of domestic legal systems of the Schengen states. However, there are also specific Schengen safeguards, along with multiple exceptions, thus making the relationship with national legal systems far from straightforward. We examine this relationship in the two areas of data exchange – SIS itself, and general Schengen.

SCHENGEN INFORMATION SYSTEM

In the operation of SIS itself, the specific data protection provisions of Schengen are generally applicable (Articles 102–118). These provisions are inextricably linked with national laws in the following manner:

- national law shall apply to reporting and data included in each national section of SIS; where Schengen requires specific action, national law of the Schengen state shall apply (Article 104);

- an individual's right of access to data shall be governed by the Schengen state before which that right is invoked (Article 109), although there are specific exemptions if the contracting state is not the reporting state, if access would impede the legal task specified in the report or damage the rights and freedoms of others, or in the case of discreet surveillance;

- an individual's rights to correction, deletion and provision of information, along with compensation in connection with a report, shall be in accordance with national law (Articles 111, 116);

- if action is taken under domestic law, the final court decision is binding on all Schengen states (Article 111);

- national supervisory authorities are to be set up, in accordance with national law, to supervise data files in national sections of SIS (Article 114);

- a joint supervisory authority is to be set up to supervise the technical support function of SIS, in accordance with the 1990 Convention, the 1981 Data Protection Convention, the 1987 Recommendation, and the national law of the Schengen state – in this case, France (Article 115);

- each Schengen state shall make national arrangements 'to achieve a level of protection at least equal to . . . the (1981 Convention and the 1987 Recommendation)' (Article 117).

Thus, in relation to the operation of SIS, it seems that there are limited harmonising elements – for instance the minimum data protection standards required by Article 117, the acceptance across Schengen of any national legal decision stipulated by Article 111, and the actual provisions of Schengen itself (for instance Article 102). But these standards are minimal, when contrasted with the possible diversity of national laws and data protection standards: individuals' data protection rights are *wholly* dependent upon invoking national legal rights, which may even be non-existent. Against this may be posited the argument that 'shopping around' for the most user-friendly legal system for the right of access to data is not precluded by Article 109; in practice, there may be substantial financial and practical difficulties in so doing.

NON SIS DATA EXCHANGES

Such exchanges are governed by Articles 126–130 of the Convention. As noted above, there are three principal types of data exchange outside of the SIS; also there is a major exception in the case of asylum-seekers, and minor differences with respect to mutual assistance in criminal matters, the application of *non bis in idem*, extradition, and the transfer of execution of criminal judgments. Additionally, more stringent requirements are laid down with respect to the police sector.

Generally, exchange of automatically processed data requires the following:

- each Schengen state shall adopt national provisions to achieve a level of protection at least equal to that of the 1981 Convention (Article 126 (1));

- personal data may not be transmitted until such national provisions in the Schengen states involved have entered into force (Article 126 (2));

- transmitted data may be used only for purposes stipulated in the Schengen Convention, except where prior authorisation has been given by the sending state and in compliance with the laws of both sending and receiving states;

- the transmitting state is responsible for the accuracy and provision of data; where the data is inaccurate or should not have been transmitted, it must inform the receiving state(s). They must correct or destroy the data;

- each Schengen state is liable under its national legislation for inaccurate data; where damages are awarded against a receiving state for using such data, the full amount must be refunded by the sending state;

- transmission and receipt of personal data must be recorded;

- a national supervisory authority must be established, to ensure compliance with the Convention; transmission may not take place until both parties have achieved this.

Broadly similar provisions apply to non-automated personal data. In the case of personal data recorded in 'another manner', slightly different rules apply:

- less stringent recording requirements (Article 127(2));

- the guarantee of a level of protection in the recipient state according to its national legislation;

- access to data to be governed by the national law of state to which the person applies;

- for personal data not recorded in a data file, supervision is dependent on national legislation but should observe any requirements of the Convention (Article 128(2)).

With exchange of data in the police sector, the following also applies (Article 129):

- a level of protection equivalent to the 1987 Recommendation.

Where *unrequested* data is sent, as authorised by Article 46, 'to prevent future crime or threats to public order and security', the following conditions apply:

- data to be used by the recipient solely for the purposes and under the conditions stipulated by the sending state;
- data may be forwarded only to police authorities, except with the prior authorisation of the sending state;
- the recipient state, shall when requested, inform the sending state of any use made of the data and results obtained.

With asylum applications, Article 38 regulates data exchange. Purpose limitation and right of access to data are well formulated, but the principles of the 1981 Convention are inapplicable to non-automated data files and liability of the state for inaccurate data is largely circumvented (Verhey, 1991: 119).

Thus it can be seen that the 'harmonising' aspect in this part of Schengen is almost non-existent, consisting principally of requirements to respect the principles of the 1981 Convention and the 1987 Recommendation, and the setting up of national supervisory authorities to ensure compliance with the Convention. Insofar as the police sector is concerned, there is not even a requirement for domestic legislation to implement the 1987 Recommendation (Verhey, 1991: 119).

Liability for accuracy of data is posited with the state of origin, but there is no actual requirement for effective domestic remedy in that state: this is totally dependent on its own national data protection provisions.

Essentially, here Schengen is relying on the effectiveness of the Council of Europe legislation to promote transborder data exchange, whilst respecting individual privacy. All available evidence suggests that *coordinating* provisions are insufficient to achieve this: the result is either impeded data flows or damaged individual liberties.

Conclusions

There is a major difficulty in attempting to provide an overall assessment of Schengen's impact on the privacy of the individual. This stems from the almost impossible task of characterising how the Convention will operate given that it relates so much to national arrangements and allows such a range of exceptions across types of *case* – exceptions almost Byzantine in complexity.

An important conclusion which can and must be drawn, however, is the very real lack of judicial control accorded. There is a 'structural frustration of judicial or semi-judicial control' (Boeles, 1991: 146) and an obvious reluctance to concede domestic jurisdiction to any supranational authority. Even the Executive Committee may turn out to be only advisory, since it is difficult to see any mechanism for enforcement. Equally, Schengen imposes no formal requirement to ratify the Council of Europe legislation, or to put in place any meaningful standards of domestic remedy.

Although Schengen requires the adoption of national provisions in conformity with the principles of the 1981 Convention, it is questionable how effective these provisions are in establishing any adequate harmonisation of standards. This is because, as both Nugter and Vassilaki identify, the character of the 1981 Convention's norms is such that it fails to provide legal certainty and can lead to widely divergent application of the Convention in national systems. The requirement to implement the principles of Recommendation (87) 15 with respect to data in the police sector does not even necessitate the passing of national legislation. It is unclear how onerous this obligation will be.

Schengen is often portrayed as a complete break with current patterns of police cooperation. We choose to emphasise its continuity with existing practice, at the same time as acknowledging certain innovatory features. The principal innovation is of course SIS, which imposes certain limitations on users. These restrictions include rights of access for the data subject, restricted items of data and purpose limitation with respect to data. They do not include the right to know of communication of data, and furthermore have a general derogation for matters of state security (Article 99). Even the seemingly very limited list of items of personal data allowed under SIS (Article 94) allows for more flexible use in practice. For example, 'objective and permanent physical features' could easily encompass skin colour.

In respect of data exchanges under Schengen but outside of SIS, minimum standards of transmission are secured, but minimum standards on collection and storage (including data illegally obtained) are implemented through Council of Europe legislation. We have already established that these arrangements are far from satisfactory; furthermore, again there is a general derogation under Article 99 for matters of state security.

Broadly speaking, Schengen operates as a coordinating instrument with few harmonising obligations and with no single judicial body to interpret and enforce the Schengen treaties. A consequence of this intergovernmental approach is that not only are there variable standards of data protection across the Schengen area, along with no supranational judicial control, but also that Schengen has put in place a system of cumulative controls. Thus the reporting mechanism of Schengen will, to all intents and purposes, categorise an offender of one state's *ordre public* as an offender of Schengen's security – even where the alleged offence may not be an offence in any other Schengen state.

Perhaps the least clear aspect of Schengen is the exchange of data with non-Schengen countries. Presumably, the 1981 Convention is seen as adequate for this purpose. The 1981 Convention regulates only the *export* of data, and leaves many issues unresolved. Scheller (1992: 168) notes the possibility of 'circumvention of national law by international cooperation' with respect to Schengen: interaction with the less regulated environment outside of Schengen seems even more unpredictable in outcome. Increasingly, to secure both free flow of transborder data and to provide minimum standards of personal data protection, it seems necessary to envisage supranational regulation.

Interestingly, when the European Commission's revised draft Directive on Data Protection (COM (92) 422) was debated in the UK House of Lords, the view was taken that any legislation on data protection must have effective controls on the police sector. The House of Lords Select Committee stated:

The Council should not adopt an EEC directive to protect personal data in areas within Community competence which leaves on one side the potential application of its rules to police and government . . . It is in the nature of things that these areas are the ones where real harm is most likely to result to individuals. There is little benefit to the individual in being protected from an unwarranted charitable appeal, from unfair loading of his insurance premiums or denial of credit, if he is not also protected from conviction abroad on the basis of suspect police evidence or from mistaken arrest as a suspected terrorist . . . (House of Lords, 1993: 34).

If the EC should choose to venture into this sensitive area (which seems unlikely at the moment) then the whole Schengen project is in danger. Despite the provisions of Articles 134 and 142, the contradictions of effective judicial control at the EC level and the random implementation of Schengen through national systems would be intolerable. Perhaps a more likely scenario is that envisaged by O'Keeffe (see above). The third pillar of Maastricht could turn out to be the sort of compromise between supranational regulation and retention of national jurisdiction which could satisfy most parties.

Currently, France appears set on retaining full border controls and not participating even in Schengen, let alone in anything more advanced. Across Europe, opinion seems to have shifted in favour of traditional inter-governmental cooperation such as Interpol.[5] This has the 'advantage' of precisely no judicial control or data protection, and would facilitate the exchange of 'soft' or unsubstantiated data across a far wider area than Schengen.

Police information systems continue to raise anxieties among the public, the media and academic commentators. The difficulty posed by the use of personal data in the Schengen process is that some of the advantages which appear to accrue through the loosely structured use of such data are visible and immediate – catching international criminals, dealing with unwelcome aliens – whereas the disadvantages are intangible and distant – respect for a key element of individual autonomy. Moreover, the impact of police investigations on privacy is not easily measurable. This is particularly intense with respect to law enforcement agencies which attempt to argue that they require more access to data generally and increased capacity to store personal data.

The real danger lies not so much in the arcane details of data protection provisions but in what Schengen presents as the key practice of policing in the future: essentially this focuses on 'unwanted and undesirable' individuals and groups as the end-point in European police-work. In our view, effective policing requires public confidence: this can only be achieved with appropriate standards of transparency, accountability and judicial review. The standards of Schengen will amount in practice to little more than a complex, almost impenetrable, legitimation of state and inter-state invasion of personal privacy. The underlying trend is without doubt towards 'Big Brother'.

Notes

1 See Flaherty (1989) for a magisterial introduction to the general field of government surveillance and privacy.
2 For elaboration on this point, see Steenbergen (1991). An alternative view is given by Cruz (1993).
3 For the text of the 1985 Schengen Agreement, see House of Lords Select Committee on the European Committees, *1992 Border Controls*, Session 1988–89, 22nd Report, London, HMSO, 1989, Report Appendix 3.
4 Opinion of the Council of State No. WO2.91.0018 of 8 April 1991, on two Schengen Agreements.
5 *Fortress Europe*, May 1993: 1–3.

References

Ackroyd, S., Harper, R., Hughes, J., Shapiro, D. and Soothill, K. (1992), *New Technology and Practical Police Work*, Milton Keynes, Open University Press.
Bittner, E. (1970), *The Functions of the Police in Modern Society*, Chevy Chase, Md., National Institute of Mental Health.
Boeles, P. (1991), 'Schengen and the Rule of Law', in Meijers, H., Bolten J.J., Cruz, A., Steenbergen, J.D.M., Hoogenboom, T., Swart, A.H.J. and Boeler, P.
Boer, M. den and Walker, N. (1993), 'European Policing after 1992', *Journal of Common Market Studies*, **31**, 1, 3–28.
Cruz, A. (1993), *Schengen, Ad Hoc Immigration Group and other European Inter-governmental Bodies*, CCME Briefing Paper 12, Brussels, Churches Committee for Migrants in Europe.
Eco, U. (1989), *Foucault's Pendulum*, London, Secker and Warburg.
Fijnaut, C. (1990), *The Europeanisation of the Police*, Paper presented to the Congress of the International Sociological Association, July.
Flaherty, D.H. (1989), *Protecting Privacy in Surveillance Societies*, Chapel Hill, N.C., University of North Carolina Press.
Hathaway, J.C. (1992), *Harmonizing for Whom? The Devaluation of Refugee Protection in the Era of European Economic Integration*, Toronto, mimeo.
Hondius, F.W. (1991), 'Legal Aspects of the Movement of Persons in Greater Europe', *Yearbook of European Law*, **10**, 1990, 291–307.
House of Lords (1993), *Protection of Personal Data*, Select Committee on the European Communities, Session 1992–93, 20th Report, HL Paper 75, London, HMSO.
Klockars, C. (1985), *The Idea of Police*, Beverly Hills, Sage.
McLaughlin, E. (1992): 'The Democratic Deficit', *British Journal of Criminology*, **32**, 4, 473–487.
Meijers, H., Bolten, J.J., Cruz, A., Steenbergen, J.D.M., Hoogenboom, T., Swart, A.H.J., and Boeles, P. (Eds.) (1991), *Schengen: Internationalisation of Central*

Chapters of the Law on Aliens, Refugees, Privacy, Security and the Police, Deventer, Kluwer.

Nugter, A.C.M. (1990), *Transborder Flow of Personal Data within the EC,* Deventer, Kluwer.

O'Keeffe, David (1992), 'The Schengen Convention: A Suitable Model for European Integration?', *Yearbook of European Law (1991),* **11,** 185–219.

Plender, Richard (1990), 'Competence, EC Law and Nationals of Non-member States', *International and Comparative Law Quarterly,* **35,** 531–566.

Scheller, S. (1992), 'Legal Problems of the Schengen Information System', in M. Anderson and M. den Boer (Eds.), *European Police Cooperation: Proceedings of a Seminar,* Department of Politics, University of Edinburgh.

Schutte, J.E. (1991), 'Schengen: Its Meaning for the Free movement of Persons in Europe', *Common Market Law Review,* **28,** 549–570.

Steenbergen, J.D.M. (1991), 'Schengen and the Movement of Persons', in Meijers, H., Bolten, J.J., Cruz, A., Steenbergen, J.D.M., Hoogenboom, T., Swart, A.H.J., and Boeles, P., 1991.

Vassilaki, Irini (1993), 'Transborder Flow of Personal Data', *The Computer Law and Security Report,* **9,** 33–37.

Verhey, L.F.M. (1991), 'Privacy Aspects of the Convention Applying the Schengen Agreement', in Meijers, H., Bolten, J.J., Cruz, A., Steenbergen, J.D.M., Hoogenboom, T., Swart, A.H.J., and Boeles, P., 1991.

CONCLUSION: IDEOLOGY AND DISCOURSE

9

THE EUROPEAN INTERNAL SECURITY FIELD: STAKES AND RIVALRIES IN A NEWLY DEVELOPING AREA OF POLICE INTERVENTION

Didier Bigo

Much discussion has taken place on the economic and financial integration of Europe, the implication of a single market and currency, the harmonisation of various taxes, and monetary policy; very little, until recently, has been said about European internal security, the free movement of persons, police measures to stem a possible increase in crime resulting from reduced border controls, on the need to coordinate behaviour patterns, policies and action in relation with European countries signatories to certain agreements (Schengen, Trevi, etc.), and with other countries; on the new concepts of sovereignty that all this implies; and many other matters.

Yet, the latter series of problems represents a 'European work site' of equal importance to the first. The problems are closely linked with inherent prerogatives of the state, its legal role in restraining violence, and democratic control over methods used. Unquestionably, Europe and its internal security is an especially rich field of research for political scientists: sovereignty, citizenship rights, emergence of novel types of group loyalties and group violence, new concepts of internal security under the impulse of Maastricht, Schengen, Trevi, the Pompidou group, the future Europol, the need to coordinate policies for asylum seekers, and so on.

The subject covers the full range of political science: analysis of legal texts concerning freedom of movement, and of police and security countermeasures (with study of penal policies, constitutional liberties, the legal foundations of European integration); sociology of organisation – the study of novel forms of police organisation within each European country, and the growing links that point toward a transnational network of police officials operating within a nascent European internal security field; sociology of conflict – analysis of new methods of controlling political and criminal violence, which have caused the police to adopt a major role in previously marginal fields of activity (like the control of migration) as a result of the restructuring their fields of investigation and creating new types of offences; political philosophy – to the extent that the EC as a future political agent, competes with the nation state, at least in its Jacobin version, with its monopolistic and exclusive relationship with the citizen, notably in its dominating role over 'intermediary group solidarity'.

Towards an internal European security field: some working hypotheses

In order to explore some of these questions, the Centre d'Etudes et de Recherches Internationales (CERI) set up a research team (Didier Bigo, Daniel Hermant, Rémy Leveau) with the initial terms of reference: 'Anti-terrorism and Europe'. These were soon extended to 'Internal Security and Europe after 1992'. The change of terms of reference followed the adoption of several working hypotheses: these need explaining in order to understand the stakes and the rivalries of the various agents involved.

The first hypothesis arises from the relative lack of relationship between terrorism and European reaction against terrorism; neither Euro-terrorism nor Middle Eastern threats are at the origin of the creation of European structures (Trevi, Schengen, etc.). Practically all agents involved in anti-terrorism agree that the answer to increasingly transnational acts of terrorism lies at the European level; to call this into question – which is possible after careful examination of events between 1983 and 1986 – would undermine the practical justification of European-level arrangements. However, practitioners admit that the supposed 'threat' of those years was out of proportion with the real risks involved. Moreover they agree that occasional and informal collaboration has been more effective than action by any pertinent European institution. Hence, rather than to argue that a 'European police' is the answer to 'Euro-terrorism', it would be more correct to consider that terrorism has prepared the ground for building and consecrating the anti-terrorist structures of Europe. This also applies to the alleged 'Middle Eastern threat' (Bigo and Hermant, 1985; Colard, 1989; Bigo, 1991).

The emergence of European cooperation in police and security matters does not appear to stem from a genuine necessity to increase cooperation against terrorism, drug traffic, or 'cross-border crime'. In order to make this judgment, the analyst must, of course, distance himself from the spontaneous (or deliberate) justifications used by the social agents, which is not always as easy. Indeed, the social sciences have a tendency to accept categories created by agents, and to elevate them to the status of concepts. Much academic discussion has taken place of such 'new realities' as international terrorism, cross-border crime, drug traffic, or the new term of 'internal security'. Little effort is expended on checking the extent to which these categories are borrowed directly from the agents (Clutterbuck, 1990; Latter, 1990). Such behaviour results in a self-reinforcement of questionable theses; police and 'anti-terrorist experts' help each other in establishing a terminology which, as we shall see, essentially serves the tactical interests of actors in a political game.

If there is a lack of connection between what we may call the 'internal-security Europe' and a genuine response to various threats, what is the real reason for the rapid progress in this 'second European work site'? This leads to the second hypothesis: this construction of 'internal security Europe' is closely linked with a professional-defensive (corporatist) reaction of the various Ministers of the Interior and of Justice when they perceived that Europe would upset routine activities as a result of the free movement of persons (including those of third countries) within Europe. Some informal consultative structures have existed since 1971 (Clubs of Berne and Vienna, Pompidou group, Trevi group, etc.), but it was mainly after 1984-5 that coordination structures at the European and sub-European level were created. These opened new fields of activity, linking free movement of persons and abolition of internal borders with police activities, strengthening external border controls, and control of migratory flows. In June 1984 the Fontainebleau Council created the Adonnino Commission, which was followed by the Franco-German agreement of Saarbrücken in July 1984, the Schengen Agreement in June 1985, and the signature of the Single European Act in February 1986.

This new field of activity has been consolidated by the adoption of texts that deal with all these problems (February 1989 – Group for the Coordination of free movement; June 1990 – Trevi Action Programme and Convention for the implementation of the Schengen Agreement; February 1992 – Third Pillar of the Treaty on European Union providing for Cooperation in Justice and Home Affairs), which was in line with the interests of certain states. The 'Europeanising' of issues such as clandestine immigration and rights of asylum has, to some extent, changed the internal political landscape. Ministers of the Interior and of Justice, in those countries where governments have decided to promote European integration, do not wish to appear anti-European. Thus, while giving lip service to freedom of movement, they create, through increasingly frequent informal contacts among their top officials, a series of measures that are first labelled 'safeguards', later 'compensatory' and finally 'complementary'. These are supposedly to accommodate and make more effective freedom of movement, but are based on a philosophy that opposes free movement and is more in keeping with the earlier, 'cruder' terminology. Five years of intensive contacts between different ministerial services (mainly Ministries of the Interior, Transport and European Affairs with little involvement of Foreign Affairs) have created a new way of looking at the subject and of working on police questions. The Europeanisation resulted in subjects being dealt with other than those traditional at the national level – because relationships seemed plausible and certain phenomena stood out (cross-border crime: car theft, antiques traffic, arms traffic; drug traffic; terrorism; hooliganism; clandestine immigration; national minorities, etc.). Older issues were dropped (economic responsibility of employers, effects of the media, counter-productivity of repression, and so on).

Thus the concept of a *European internal security field* emerged, which is not only a new field of activity, but also a battleground of bureaucracies – on a European scale. There are stakes involved which arise from a specific corporatist ideology that restructures police activities and links separate activities (drug-related terrorism, hooliganism and extreme rightists; mafia and financing of terrorism; drugs and clandestine immigration; crime and illegal immigration; smuggling, etc.). This can lead to a 'security continuum' that stretches from terrorism to regulation of asylum rights, including drugs, action against crime, clandestine immigration, and migratory flows. However, by bringing together previously isolated problems and by adopting new rules and procedures, the concept of the subject under consideration has altered (Deleuze, 1991). Thus, by sliding from police and immigration questions to 'internal security' issues, there is a change of paradigm which directly concerns citizens' rights, state–citizen relations, and group relations of Europeans among themselves and towards third countries. This change of paradigm is carried out by agents who are not fully aware of who is involved, though fully conscious of the power game.

There was a refusal, in the mid-eighties, to emphasise such dilemmas as security vs. freedom, national sovereignty vs. Europe. These could, it seemed, be resolved by appropriate technical measures: control ommissions for police data banks, intergovernmental cooperation. The central question of the decade became: security – European integration – immigration. The appropriateness of this new approach can be questioned. While it may be useful for the agents in the game, this is not necessarily so for academic research. Let us emphasise, however, that this is not a sinister plot of ministerial power-seekers to attack civil liberties. At the basis there is the serious concrete problem that politicians do not wish to tackle relations with the emigration countries and the need to act with diplomacy and efficiency. The elaboration of a common immigration policy – easily as complex as that of a common currency – has been handed over to officials of the Interior, Justice, Transport and European Ministries, who only vaguely perceived the extent of their task, wishing to build on 'concrete foundations', they used their empirical knowledge. As a result, the policy agenda concerning immigration control and political asylum is more security-led than economic or social in approach. When the problems needed to be disaggregated, officials created as many sub-groups as there had been problems.[1] By breaking down certain boundaries between issues, they changed ways of thinking and approaches to immigration and asylum rights, unaware that they were engaged in philosophical and political issues; they simply acted in accordance with their experience. Thus the issue was no longer, on the one hand, terrorism, drugs, crime, and on the other, rights of asylum and clandestine immigration, but they came to be treated together in the attempt to gain an overall view of the interrelation between these problems and the free movement of persons within Europe.

This continuum has led to a 'transfer of illegitimacy' which allows, in the name of anti-terrorism and anti-drug action, the adoption of measures mainly concerning asylum policy and migratory flows, issues that those in power hesitate to tackle directly. The transnational networks thus partly free the senior civil servants, the main agents in the field, from those national and/or political constraints which often make it difficult to deal with controversial matters which nonetheless have to be settled speedily. These senior officials thereby gain autonomy. One is tempted to speak of a revenge against the world of politics – the possibility of opposing, via Europe, unwanted government policy options. Top police officials have been concerned that they can no longer control migratory flows. This apprehension is strengthened by the events of 1989, the paralysis of political leaders, growing contacts between Europeans in all streams of life: it has developed into an internal security 'ideology', based on the idea of a 'permanent security deficit' resulting from the disappearance of internal borders. This article of faith is not challenged by the agents involved; outside its immediate field of application it nonetheless raises many questions. Its basic tenet is that the reduction of border controls will inevitably increase different types of crime, unless it is offset by safeguards at the external borders of Europe.

Statistics are produced on clandestine immigration, the number of asylum seekers, drug traffic, highlighting the role of border police, customs and immigration officials. These figures are supposed to show that more than half of these criminal flows have been stopped at the national borders. Other studies speak of less than 20 per cent success rate and even suggest that the new mobility might be beneficial and could lead to the abandonment of obsolete forms of control.[2] Europe might thus have a chance to modernise national police forces and break down trade-union and other corporatist obstacles to change.[3] Moreover the transfer of additional police resources to external borders implies redeployment – possibly even strengthening – rather than a reduction of police forces. What remains unsaid is that these new control functions will serve essentially to police clandestine immigration, whereas this aspect was previously of minor importance in police priorities. Thus, the belief in the 'security deficit' is not well-based; it is not necessarily wrong, but it has not been satisfactorily proven. It serves essentially – consciously or unconsciously – to conceal the change of emphasis in police functions within the European zone, and the fact that it is the control and management of migratory flows that will have a priority role in the European internal security field (see also den Boer in this volume).

This corporatist ideology obscures political responsibilities; it is based on the proposition that the 'security deficit' needs counter-measures. It is linked to wider beliefs, especially the threat of a tidal wave of immigration from our closest neighbours – the South (North and Black Africa) and the East (Romanians, Gipsies, ex-Yugoslavs, Albanians). European societies are in the process of distilling propositions that brings together widely diversified phenomena – differential demographic potential, migration, religious fanaticism, ideological links with country of origin, threat to the secular nature of our countries, Middle Eastern-type terrorism, spread of drugs and AIDS through foreign minorities. This is not without consequence on external security thinking, widely developed in military circles[4] and significant among arms manufacturers since the end of the bi-polar world. The new enemy is not clearly identifiable nor associable to a particular state with a given border, and, therefore, potentially omnipresent, transnational, and already infiltrated; the police (and especially the secret services) are the obvious agents of defence against a threat which leaves the army powerless. The Gulf War, which provoked fantasies of generalised terrorism, showed the extent to which this type of thinking erodes the frontiers between internal and external security, and confuses the responsibilities of ministries of the Interior, of Defence and of Foreign Affairs. Moreover there is increasing emphasis on the danger of differential birth rates and demographic growth between North and South, thus justifying stronger controls at the European borders.[5] This ideology is not the exclusive property of the political right; it has affected many others, even the EC Commission.[6] It has also created a feeling of solidarity among agents in different countries, bringing closer together different lines of reasoning and has led, despite national antagonisms, and after many internal controversies, to agreement and the adoption of texts. The in-fighting has been of an intensity which makes it a field of power struggle, rather than a negotiation or a consensus, let alone the finding of a compromise on ideological differences.

The emphasis on the free movement of persons in the Maastricht Treaty, together with the fear of a tidal wave of immigration, has created a European field of action which goes beyond occasional cooperation. It is not sufficient to explain this by reference to the ideology of the agents, for this would indicate a common will, a project, perhaps even a plot: European internal security had its origins in the desire to settle pressing bi-lateral or multi-lateral issues, like Franco-Spanish problems with the Basque separatist movement ETA, the definition of dangerous drugs, and similar matters. This explains how the security system was created: European internal security is not a community, but an intergovernmental project. Political, police or legal border issues (extradition, asylum, immigration, drugs) were settled through 'generalised bi-lateralism', frequently concealed in the language of the legal agreements adopted. Many provisions are the result of transactions and power-play between two or three of the states concerned, tacitly approved by the others. Bi-lateral measures are thus 'Europeanised'. To view this process as a natural, linear development towards supranational European integration is naive. There is no law of historical development. Individuals, bureaucracies, or states are behind this Europeanisation, at a given moment, or in a given sector, because it helps them settle internal or bi-lateral problems. European internal security has thus been developed in a piecemeal and opportunistic manner. Ideology has, however, provided a homogeneity and quasi-legitimacy when the security continuum emerged out of the political hazards of bi-lateral and multi-lateral relations between states. Without going into detail, this field of activity is strongly affected by similarities and/or differences between national services, bureaucratic struggles, and national positions of the EC member states. Dominance in internal security depends not only on the content of the agreements, but as much on the level at which the question is dealt with (Schengen, the Twelve, Brussels Community, Council of Europe, even NATO). No matter how

European internal security is dealt with at the level of five, eight, twelve or more, this new field of activity restructures power relations, and previously dominant agents are displaced.

Strategies and rivalries between agents in the European internal security field

Because of the opposition of the UK, Ireland and Denmark, and an initial mistrust of southern Europe (Greece, Portugal, Spain and Italy) by northern Europe, the other countries felt obliged to create the 'Schengen zone' among themselves, outside community structures. We shall deal with this later because there is evidence that, while duplicating certain structures, each multi-lateral authority aims at controlling the whole of the European internal security framework.

One should consider sceptically the quasi-consensus between European countries regarding developments towards coordinated European internal security. Behind the monolithic surface, only slightly marred by an occasional British or Danish outburst, there are serious struggles between countries and institutions to dominate the process, and to determine its objectives on matters such as the admission of third parties. Each state, national institution or service, plays its hand according to its own interests, and within a moving framework of alliances. Moreover, some agents, like the European Commission, complicate the problem by not treating it as a pure intergovernmental matter. Also, informal and semi-official networks have been established – more flexible than formal institutions, but also less controllable by citizens (and even governments). A new problem of transnational links among police forces at the European and the pan-European levels is created by these networks.

The history of all the agencies shows that many have been developed – institutionally or informally – to deal with the whole field, and that they soon started competing (Bigo, 1992). The push towards a single European security concept is exemplified by the fact that all reject specialisation. Each body, regardless of its original purpose (drugs for the Pompidou group, terrorism for Trevi, major crime for Interpol, defence for NATO, etc.) aims at control of the whole field of internal European security; they create research groups and committees in order to provide data complementing the intelligence which they have in their original field, and to identify related problems (Trevi on terrorism is complemented by Trevi II on maintaining of order and hooliganism, Trevi III on criminality and drugs, and Trevi '92 on the free movement of persons). Thus, a body extends its role, through a series of committees, over the whole spectrum of internal security. Inevitably this leads to duplication, entanglement, competition, and bureaucratic struggles to ensure permanency and independence from politicians. This explains the overwhelming significance of apparently unimportant details, such as the creation of a permanent secretariat and its location.

Competition between agencies

To explore the entanglement of agencies, a distinction can be made, on the one hand, between criteria such as the field of cooperation, type of data provided and work carried out by the agency, its degree of institutionalisation, and on the other, between the strategies adopted by states, national police services and new European bodies.

First, the organisations can be grouped in *concentric circles*, starting with the bi-lateral (UK–Ireland agreements), and continuing through: intra-European at the level of the Twelve or some of them (Schengen Agreements); intergovernmental between some of the Twelve and others (agreements with northern countries, Club of Berne, Club of Vienna); intergovernmental among the 12 EC member states of the European Community (Trevi, *Ad Hoc* Group on Immigration, Mutual Assistance Group '92, K4 Committee and arrangements included in the Third Pillar of the Treaty on European Union); the Community including other European countries (Police Working Group on Terrorism); European in the wider sense (Council of Europe, European Regional Secretariat of Interpol, West European Union); and finally intercontinental agreements (NATO, Helsinki agreement, G7).[7] The questions of the compatibility of the agreements, and their hierarchisation, are immediately ignored. Lawyers are working on this important question, which also has its relevance to citizen's rights and possibilities of redress of wrongs by agencies against individuals.

Second, distinctions can be made between the purely technical aspects of police activities (informal European cooperation groups on terrorism, Stars group, Clubs of Berne and Vienna, MAG 92, Interpol), those more legal in nature (follow-up groups on international conventions and treaties), the diplomatic and political (EPC, EC Commission, Council of Europe, WEU, NATO, G7), finally the mixed groups (Trevi, Pompidou group). The areas of activity of these various bodies, the origin of their officials (Interior, Justice, Foreign Affairs, political staff, international officials, etc.) create problems of circulation of information, duplicate structures, 'false hierarchies' where supposedly authoritative structures merely serve to endorse research being carried out. Care has to be exercised not to restrict our vision to the clearly institutionalised groups (as legal experts are inclined to do), neglecting so-called technical or operational groups, which are of fundamental importance in the elaboration of practical measures of internal security. A sociological rather than a legal-institutional approach is usually more effective in distinguishing innovative groups from others.

Third, bodies can be distinguished according to their degree of institutionalisation, periodicity of meeting, and effectiveness of cooperation. Some bodies lack official recognition (tripartite group), some are recognised unofficially (Club of Berne, Vienna, Quantico), some, though officially recognised, are not institutionalised (Trevi), others are (Interpol). Most authors consider that there has been a movement from the informal to the institutional, from diversity to unity: an institutionalised body should logically take the place of earlier multiple informal groups. This is a 'naturalist' approach to European integration. According to this approach, the national pattern should be smoothly integrated into a higher level of development towards gradually strengthened cooperation. Government strategies and partisan action in favour of Europe can indeed be explained as a deliberate step-by-step procedure: to avoid direct conflict (sovereignty vs. federation), each step has to be treated as a discrete decision. This also explains the use of terms labelling proponents of national sovereignty with being 'outdated', 'attached to past values', 'out of touch with history'. This is political-ideological ammunition and has little to do with reality. There is no evidence that informal bodies tend to disappear: rather, they multiply, create networks that stifle institutional bodies, prepare the real decisions, and create a team spirit among officials of different countries that presages a 'bureaucracy beyond the state'.[8] The interests of this bureaucracy may no longer correspond to those of the nation, nor may it see any advantage in a supranational political accountability. The intensity of consultation and cooperation between bureaucrats of different countries, attending meetings which, although not normally confidential, are nonetheless unpublicised and of limited attendance, suggests a tendency in this direction. The fact that individuals are present in several bodies decreases competition between them. Networks of personal friendship determine the efficiency of cooperation and exchange of data. All this has little to do with the gradual absorption of informal bodies into institutions. Indeed, the institutional bodies only work because of the vitality and the links of friendship established in the informal bodies. The proliferation of bodies, the distribution of persons within them, and the absence of democratic control of their activities, will create difficult problems if the professional interests of the European internal security community leads to an abandonment of national ideologies without a satisfactory European substitute. The creation of a self-motivated bureaucracy, free of national control but not yet subject to supranational control, is a possibility. Transnational police networks, more or less outside political control – even though their efficiency may be great – can only be detrimental to democracy.

The multiplication of bodies, 9 Schengen, 12 EC, 23 (soon 26 or 28) Council of Europe and 35 Greater Europe countries creates ever more working groups, proposals, rules and regulations and promotes a Europe of bureaucrats, not of citizens. The principle of 'non-contradiction' (rather than harmonisation) of legislation thus becomes a solution to avoid the imposition of harmonisation. Most analysts and agents mute specific criticisms of either the lack or the excess of coordination, and propose pragmatic, 'technical' solutions, but few call into question the strategy of these bodies. Lack of a proper synthesis, or absence of rigour are the accepted excuses in policy-making, but an analysis of the strategies clearly shows the reasons and purposes of such overlapping arrangements.

The strategies of the agents

A proliferation of bodies is not due to simple lack of organisation or a cheerful 'empiricism'. Each state, according to the time and its interests, promotes one or another body because the place of discussion (i.e. the scope of possible alliances) is often as important as the subject matter itself. Some states, like the United Kingdom, have always tried to paralyse certain groups at the European Community level, not so much because they are against Europe, but because they are opposed to supranationality and federalism. On the other hand, they have firmly supported intergovernmental bodies, including Trevi, and promoted a redefinition of the NATO terms of reference which would lead to a greater involvement of that organisation in internal security, and thus not only harmonise European, but Western, policies. France has been more supportive of the Community, all the more because of the close personal relationships between Jacques Delors and François Mitterrand. But it would be naive to assume that interests of France and the EC converge in the long run. France has often been the most reticent country when it came to abandoning sovereignty over internal security, and sided with those who refused the participation of the EC Commission in discussions concerning it. France thus promoted bodies and agreements of the intergovernmental type, pretending that they were a step – and not an obstacle – towards the Community. The Netherlands, on the other hand, has always played the Community card and has considered that the different agreements might constitute an obstacle to full implementation of the Community. This has led to a lively debate in the Netherlands between the Council of State on the one hand and Parliament and government on the other. Italy initially considered itself marginalised by Schengen and assumed a more positive stance towards the Community and federalism than France. But Italy remains very sceptical about Europeanising internal security, and has no desire to abandon sovereignty over the police. Belgium – which is considered very pro-Europe – fears the loss of its fragile identity and has often defended a nationalist position.

The United States, although outside the Community, is very active in European affairs; represented in many informal groups, it often dominates discussions thanks to its highly efficient information sources. The US suggests, *inter alia*, that there should be little distinction between member and non-member states in Trevi so as to be fully involved in negotiations; a position supported by the United Kingdom, Germany and the Netherlands. France, Greece, Spain and Belgium are opposed to this suggestion, in order to preserve the homogeneity of the Twelve; they do not want Trevi to become an international anti-terrorist forum, following a parallel course to the Pompidou group where the multiplicity of participants has hampered its development. The various strategies towards the United States are relevant to the general discussion on the widening and deepening of European structures. Some states favour widening despite the risk of being swamped by a new 'Northern Empire'. Others, like

France, prefer deepening the political structures of the Twelve and, if necessary, creating a second circle of 'associate states' with special relations to, but not membership of, the Community. Germany would like to include Central Europe, but unlike the United Kingdom, does not want to water down European Community political structures. The games of governments are complicated by the entrance of new players on the scene: the European Commission and European Parliament. The Commission develops its own policies and is becoming increasingly influential with governments, extracting concessions for them unimaginable a few years ago. Hampered by its lack of official competence in police matters, the Commission has in the past avoided intervening in this domain and even requested states to use intergovernmental channels, but it is increasingly concerned by the implications of this abstention. The implementation of the Maastricht Treaty may result in the Commission converting itself, via free movement of persons, into the role of promoter of both police and human-rights issues. If this happens, Maastricht would be an example of the power of influence becoming power of decision.

Obviously, these political moves have a direct influence on various arrangements and institutions of police cooperation. When a proposal is put forward, one or another arrangement will be preferred. For example, some informal structures were established between regions in two or three member states in order to cope efficiently with border problems. Germany used this form of cooperation to promote the idea of Europol, even before a Europol proposal had been officially put forward. France brought up the idea of a European Interpol, mainly because Interpol happens to be located at Lyons. There are many other examples. To describe these political games as originating exclusively at the state level would be erroneous. There is no such thing as a French, a British, a German, or a Dutch policy. To limit analysis to the state level would be tantamount to believing in the rationality and single-mindedness of states and governments; organisational sociology, however, has shown the multiplicity and interpenetration of internal forces in foreign policy, and the power of bureaucratic interests in decision-making (Allison, 1971). One thus has to inquire at the level of each service of each bureaucracy in each country to understand how decision-making works in different formal and informal groups, how alliances and controversy are fostered, and how an ideology of internal security is developed.

In the present state of knowledge, we can only sketch some of the outlines of the game being played. For example, the strongest opponents of the European idea are British HM Customs and Excise, the HM Immigration Service, the French Gendarmerie, and the Spanish Guardia Civil. It so happens that these services have no natural 'correspondents' at the European level, and they depend on ministries (Defence for the Gendarmerie, Treasury for HM Customs and Excise) and are, in a manner of speaking, 'prisoners' within their own state.[9] They feel that European integration will sacrifice them, or at best relegate them to second-rate tasks. In budgetary conflicts, in order to cut them down to size, competitors for funds have used the argument that they do not 'fit' into

Europe. British and French police are more 'European' than the French Gendarmerie or HM Customs and Excise. Inside each of the police forces, differences in attitude relate to their structure: British and Dutch police enjoy considerable local autonomy, but European harmonisation emphasises the role of the national level which has been constantly opposed in the United Kingdom and in the Netherlands, because harmonisation leads to centralism and to authoritarian changes. As pointed out earlier, fields of activity are also significant. The different police units engaged in the 'drugs war' differ from 'ordinary police' because they have frequent international contacts and carry out investigations in different countries. Intelligence services are used to international contacts, but they are mistrustful of Europeanisation; their professional ethic is based on total loyalty to the national idea, which makes them suspicious of European integration.

Those most favourable to Europe are inside ministerial cabinets or in the informal coordination structures between major services; their role gives them power over the services which they coordinate, and they have their own correspondents, interests, and political outlook.[10] Those favourable to Europe inside bureaucracies have this outlook because of their location in these bureaucracies within the European and national internal security fields. The analysis of their role and influence could be carried further by looking into relational factors with emphasis on the topology of inter-service relations (Bourdieu, 1989). On the basis of proximity analysis, it could be determined why apparently distant and apparently competing groups managed to achieve agreement (Schengen Implementation Convention, Trevi Action Programme, and more recently cooperation in justice and home affairs in the Maastricht Treaty). More investigation along these lines is necessary.

Notes

1 See the organisation of the groups that negotiated the Schengen Implementation Convention of Schengen or Trevi Action Programme.

2 The harsh battle of figures can be explained by the struggle between competent services, not only for their budget, but sometimes their very survival. For example see the statistics on 'irregular immigration' published by the French Police de L'Air et des Frontières, or those on drug traffic by HM Customs and Excise. Viewed in the context of global migratory flows, these figures are of marginal importance in relation to the 'risk' which is to sharpen the attitudes of our fellow citizens toward other Europeans, or North and Black African nationals.

3 Discussions with police officials emphasise the need to modernise structures and rely on the European idea to bring to fruition essential projects that have been gathering dust for years on national shelves.

4 See 'Menaces du Sud: images et realités', *Cultures et Conflits* (1991), **2**.

5 See *a contrario* the last report of INSE and the annual report of the permanent observation system on migration of the OECD.

6 See papers of the Committee on the Abolition of controls of persons at in-community borders, 7 December 1988, and 11 October 1991, the latter dealing especially with the subject of immigration.
7 This reflects the ideas expressed in Report No. 1 1990 Home Affairs Committee (House of Commons).
8 I.e. a body whose professional aims go beyond the state.
9 For an excellent analysis of the attitude of British services, see Gregory, 1990.
10 Personnel links, generational phenomena, transfers between posts can often be used practically to reduce risks of conflict and competition between services.

References

Allison, G.T. (1971), *Essence of Decision: Explaining the Cuban Missile Crisis*, Boston, Little, Brown.
Bigo, D. (1991), 'Les Attentats de 1986 en France: un cas de violence transnationale et ses implications', *Cultures et Conflits: Réseaux internationaux de violence*, **4**.
Bigo, D. and Hermant, D. (1985), 'Résurgance du terrorisme en Europe', *Esprit*.
Bourdieu, P. (1989), *La Noblesse d'État*, Paris, Minuit.
Clutterbuck, R. (1990), *Terrorism, Drugs and Crime in Europe after 1992*, London, Routledge.
Colard, D. (1989), 'Les Dissensions entre alliés occidentaux dans la condamnation du terrorisme', *Ares*, **2**.
Deleuze, G. (1991), *Qu'est-ce que la philosophie?*, Paris, Minuit.
Gregory, F. (1990), *Policing and Border Controls*, Paper of Public Administration Committee Conference, University of York.
Latter, R. (1990), *Crime and the European Community after 1992*, Steyning, Wilton Park.

10

THE QUEST FOR EUROPEAN POLICING: RHETORIC AND JUSTIFICATION IN A DISORDERLY DEBATE

Monica den Boer

The recent explosion of initiatives in the field of international police cooperation may be regarded as a reaction to the abolition of internal border controls within the European Community. The rationale which underlies the creation of new structures and institutions, such as the Schengen Agreement and Europol, is that the abolition of border controls accompanying the completion of the Single Market will pose a threat to Europe's internal security and, more specifically, will lead to an upsurge in international crime and illegal immigration. In line with this philosophy, senior police officers and policy-makers often argue that an intensification of cross-border police cooperation would compensate for the loss of border controls which have traditionally been relied upon as 'crime-filters'. However, the quest for these compensatory measures and their underlying rationale remain virtually unchallenged, even though there may be serious implications for public finance, democratic control and civil liberties.

This chapter will look at developments in European police cooperation as a distinct policy-making field, within which arguments are exchanged and initiatives realised by the members of a 'policy community'. Hence, the method of inquiry is discourse analysis, which enables us to deconstruct and reconstruct a number of justificatory domains which are supported by the members of that policy community. Discourse analysis functions as an explanatory tool of analysis, but discourse itself – the 'interlocutions' produced by agents who are involved in the policy-making process – is evidence of the ideological structure underlying the evolution in European police cooperation. This chapter examines the perspectives and opinions of the different interest groups involved in the debate on the quest for European policing. The principal objective is to unravel some of the dynamics of this new policy area, and to locate the policy decisions and innovations in the international political context and in a new era of internal security thinking.

European police cooperation as a policy-making process

The arena of 'European police cooperation' is here defined as a *discursive field* within which opinions are exchanged on the future shape of international police cooperation. The idea which underpins this definition is that all policy-making processes, whether national or international, are linguistic in character. As Majone (1989: 2) notes: 'We miss a great deal if we try to understand policy-making solely in terms of power, influence, and bargaining, to the exclusion of debate and argument.' Policy-making is a dynamic process in that it is conducted by means of a 'rhetoric of persuasion', which is an interchange between the parties involved, a method of mutual learning through discourse (ibid.: 7, 8).The adoption of discourse analysis as a method of inquiry allows us to view policy-making as a process conducted by a group of people (rather than one individual or unit), whose objectives may not always coincide. It allows us to look behind the final products of decision-making, and to take into account the various moments in the policy-making process, which are crucial to the formation of opinion about plans and proposals.

This methodology appreciates the dynamic character of policy-making and acknowledges that ideas seldom preserve their original form: this is reflected in the variable nomenclature: 'New meanings and interpretations emerge at each stage, leading to new formulations of the underlying issues ... Instead of producing single, well-defined solutions, the policy debate leads to a sequence of issue transformations and to a corresponding expansion of the boundary of the policy community' (ibid.: 164f.). An illustration of issue-transformation in the area of European police cooperation is the semantic career of 'Europol' (den Boer, 1992: 6). During the Luxembourg Summit in June 1991, 'Europol' stood for a 'European Criminal Investigation Office',[2] while in the final text of the Treaty on European Union it stands for 'European Police Office'. Although this terminological shift may seem quite innocent, the latter term allows more flexibility in the determination of Europol's remit: although the role of Europol will be restricted to that of an information- and intelligence-gathering agency initially, it may in the future be given modest operational powers if and when an international consensus can be established. A similar tale can be told of Europol's predecessor organisation, namely the 'European Drugs Unit', which has been established with the support of a national Drugs Unit in all EC member states. It is significant that even this conception has undergone a name-change, as the word 'intelligence' was scrapped from the original 'European Drugs Intelligence Unit'. Once again this could imply that the remit of the Unit may not remain confined to the exchange of information and intelligence. Another issue-transformation in the area of European police cooperation has become apparent from the creation of a Coordinating Committee (Article K.4, Title VI, Treaty on European Union) which will be the umbrella body for all the pre-existing topical structures. The reasons for this creation must not be sought exclusively in a bid for improved efficiency, but also in the now more widely adopted theory that crimes and criminals cannot be classified in simple terms; the acknowledgement of the existence of active links between different fields of crime has inspired a shift from specialist crime-combating to generalist crime-combating (den Boer, 1992: 10, 11).

When we take a closer look at the evolution of international police cooperation, we see yet another transformation. Although with the creation of Interpol police cooperation was perceived as directed against one target, namely international crime in its most general sense, the target became gradually more differentiated and crystallised. Europe witnessed the creation of institutions, bodies and branches, each of which specialised in a specific form of international crime. The Pompidou group's main concern has been drugs, the UCLAF's main concern has been fraud, and until some years ago, Trevi's main concern was the fight against terrorism (Fijnaut, 1993: 109). Today however, there is a movement back to 'generalism', and to a concentration of efforts. Senior police officers and top civil servants argue that there are now very strong links between 'fields of crime'. For example, more and more evidence points to terrorist groups being involved in illegal drugs or arms trade, and subsequent money-laundering enterprises. This connection between terrorism, drug trafficking and money laundering[3] intensifies the strategy in favour of police cooperation which concentrates on criminally active groups, rather than on crime fields. The proposal to set up Europol is an example of a generalistic approach to the combating of international crime, but the future might show a tendency back to specialisation and differentiation. It should therefore be concluded that the evolution of police cooperation is subject to a series of *conceptual transformations*, which are inspired by a changing evaluation of the efficiency and accountability of existing institutions and forms of cooperation, resulting in a demand for renewal. The policy-making process in the field on European police cooperation can be marked as a form of *evolutionary politics*. A more suspicious interpretation of these conceptual transformations is that the resetting of the policy agenda is in some ways related to the market-expansion and market-differentiation of the police organisations in Europe (cf. van Outrive, 1992: 20).

Developments in international police cooperation are often displayed as a natural evolution, from a position with inherent deficiencies to a position with new achievements. Our language, says Hirschmann (1991: 9) is under the influence of the belief in progress: 'it implies that the mere unraveling of time brings human improvement, so that any return to an earlier period would be calamitous.' Perhaps Hirschmann's use of 'calamitous' is exaggerated. However, a common frame of mind often suggests that only progress, not stagnation, is seen as satisfactory. This type of language emerges in the debate about European police cooperation. In that debate, structures of the past are rejected as insufficient to deal with 'the new phenomenon' of international crime. The repercussion of this rejection is that institutions which were created in the past for the fight against international crime, like Interpol, are currently the subject of criticism despite vigorous efforts at modernisation. The rejection of the 'obsolete and antiquated' creates the rhetorical ground for the justification of innovation and renewal. As the old institutions become too slow and cumbersome to deal with international crime, new ones, capable of a more efficient response, are promoted. Policy-making, which includes the creation of new opportunities for international policing, is

a repetitive, incremental activity: under such conditions yesterday's experiences are continually incorporated into today's decisions, so that tendencies toward perversity stand a good chance of being detected and corrected (Hirschmann, 1991: 42).

The observation that recent developments in international police cooperation are generally regarded as a natural evolution from a policy vacuum to a satisfactory situation, fails to explain fully the recent explosive concentration on the issue by police, politicians and media. Here Giddens' (1984: 251) general concept of a 'conjuncture of circumstances' (interaction of influences) can be usefully applied in the analysis of the development of European police cooperation. It seems to be the case that we are currently situated in an 'ideal climate' for the launching of new ideas and proposals on European police cooperation.

The supranational debate on European police cooperation, which has recently emerged on the fringes of the European Community, is conducted by the members of various international *policy communities*:

A policy community is composed of specialists who share an active interest in a certain policy or set of related policies: academics, professionals, analysts, policy planners, media and interest-group experts. The members of a policy community represent different interests, hold different values, and may be engaged in different research programs, but they all contribute to policy developments by generating and debating new ideas and proposals (Majone, 1989: 161).

Policy communities are loose-jointed structures consisting of individuals with their own professional, intellectual and ideological commitments. In the case of European police cooperation, the members of this policy community represent a variety of professions (police, politics, academia, civil service). Membership and participation fluctuate according to the specific topic to be discussed, and the national and institutional priority given to that topic.[4] Therefore, not only the policy-making process has a dynamic character, so does the policy community which performs that process. This fluctuation and dynamism does not detract from the relative *institutionalisation* of the members of the policy community active in the field of European police cooperation, to the extent that they have coined their own rules and procedures. The definition of the discursive field as a series of 'interlocking' (cf. Wessels, 1990), semi-institutionalised policy-making agencies allows us to take a broader view of the policy-making process – one that does not exclusively focus on state interests, but in particular also on the interface between (institutionalised) interests. As Peters (1992: 107) writes:

An institutional analysis of the European Community must recognise the several different but interconnected 'games' being played simultaneously within the

Community. The idea of a two-level game is too simplistic to capture the complexity of motives and interactions.

Peters argues that at least three different games are being played: the national game, the institutional game (e.g. between the Commission and the Council of Ministers), and the bureaucratic game, the latter 'becoming an important subtext' within the EC and characterised by boundary conflicts caused by the competition for policy space (Peters, 1992: 107). It is the latter, more or less formalised, bureaucracy which is of relevance to our inquiry.

The use of the term 'disorderly' in the title of this chapter is related to the rather unsystematic character of the policy-making process and the policy community (cf. Peters, 1992: 118). The evolution of international policies on European police cooperation has lacked a homogeneous sense of direction and planning: it can be considered fortuitous that apparently consensus can be achieved about policy purposes across the national, cultural and institutional differences of opinion. The unsystematic character of the debate is due to a number of factors, such as the lack of control by central authorities over the steering of that debate. The complexity of the debate may however be a typical reflection of the organisational landscape, which may be characterised as a *crowded policy space* (see also Weidenfeld, 1992: 18), in which 'policies are initiated at all levels of an organisation or policy-making body, not just at the top . . . a particularly common phenomenon . . . where implementation problems are compounded by interdependencies and policy overlaps' (Majone, 1989: 160). Different interest groups are responsible for laying emphasis on different areas of police cooperation. For instance, the *Ad Hoc* Group on Immigration has been prominent in drafting agreements on asylum and external border controls,[5] the Trevi group expanded its remit from terrorism to include matters such as police training and European police cooperation (Trevi, 1990; Fijnaut, 1993: 109) the Pompidou group has done work to increase cooperation against drug trafficking, and there are a number of other working structures. Most of the intra-EC working structures will be merged under the Coordinating Committee, which will be set up as a consequence of Article K.4 of the Justice and Home Affairs provisions of the Treaty on European Union, provided this Treaty will be ratified and implemented. Not only arguments concerning different topics such as drugs, terrorism, organised crime, fraud, money laundering and illegal immigration are exchanged within the policy community on European police cooperation, but also arguments of a different nature (political, organisational, humanitarian and legal) are the subject of that exchange.

Hence, developments in international policing may be observed from a multiplicity of perspectives as regards the ultimate social values which are at stake. In the range of perspectives, the extremes are likely to be occupied by the police and by the civil libertarians respectively. This may however be too simple a picture. The police themselves embrace a wide variety of views, often coloured by their personal interest and experience with aspects of international policing. Civil libertarians come in grey shades as well. Some adopt ultra-radical positions and reject anything related to cross-border policing, while others manage to find both pros and cons in the development of international policing after rigorous scrutiny. It is crucial to note, however, that almost all participants in the debate about international policing are members of established interest or pressure groups. Police officers, politicians, civil libertarians, immigrant advisors and policy-makers are all people who promote or criticise developments in international policing through the ideological grid supplied by their particular interest groups. The debate about international policing can therefore be described as 'multi-layered and interest-bound'.

As a result of the fragmentation of policy-making and politics in the European Community in general, discussion, coalition formation and bargaining are conducted at various levels, and across various fora, which usually correspond to already existing structures and arrangements in respect of European police cooperation (cf. Peters, 1992: 117). In order to render the analysis of the disorderly debate about European police cooperation comprehensible, one may divide this discursive field into two axes, one which represents the continuum between national and international debate, and another which represents the continuum between generalist and specialist organisations. On the first axis, national levels of debate ought to be distinguished from international ones. The national level of discussion about European police cooperation is in itself worthy of comparative study: the interaction with regional and local levels varies from country to country, depending on factors such as whether the national model of policing is more or less centralised, and modes of consultation, information and training. At the international level, we can distinguish fora like the European Council (with debates about Europol, and intergovernmental cooperation in judicial and home affairs), the Schengen Working Groups, the intergovernmental K4 Committee, and Interpol. It should be noted that the Schengen Working Groups have been the only ones to interact (i.e. consult, negotiate) directly with the local and regional level in the signatory countries.[6] On the second axis, we can distinguish between the generalist and the specialist fora. The generalist fora are again the European Council, Trevi, Schengen and the K4 Committee, whilst specialist fora include the Pompidou group, the *Ad Hoc* Group on Immigration, UCLAF, CELAD and CELAT. There are many intersections between national and international groups, and between the generalist and the specialist groups, most notably because the same personalities participate in different working structures (such as representatives from Ministries of Justice or the Interior, or of organisations such as the Interpol National Central Bureaux). Inspired by a need for more coordination, the early nineties are witnessing a move towards generalisation and centralisation.

A key characteristic of the debate of international police cooperation is that it has been performed in the intergovernmental arena (Leyendecker, 1992: 379ff.; van Outrive, 1992: 19f.) and its relative closure from public scrutiny. The intergovernmental character of of the policy-making process is largely due to the boundary problems thrown up by limited competences of the European Community in the area of justice and home affairs (Timmermans, 1993: 359), and politically sensitive intervention in the sovereignty of the nation state (see Walker in this volume). Intergovernmental policy-making is sometimes equated with the 'hidden dimension of government' (Muskie, in Wright, 1982: 6), which is often characterised by a labyrinth of administrative interactions (cf. Wessels, 1990: 238), the lack of a clear sense of direction (Wright, 1982: 22), and a curious mixture of cooperation and competition (ibid.: 40; van Reenen, 1989). The debate has been and still is primarily conducted by senior police officers, senior officials and civil servant representatives of relevant ministries, and mostly without the participation of representatives from various interest groups in society. A justification often given by the participants in these meetings for the general lack of consultation and negotiation is that the involvement of several parties could result in an infinite debate due to the difficulty of building an overall consensus. Another possibility is that the intergovernmental character of the fora within which European police cooperation is being discussed, by institutionalising the clash between sensitive national interests, necessarily precludes the opening of its doors to the public. The relatively opaque character of the debates means, however, that the proposals which flow from them are based on the opinions of a narrow sector of society, and that they are unlikely to achieve the status of formal agreements embedded in a coherent international constitutional and administrative structure.

Agreement about forms of international police cooperation is a result of political power-plays at the negotiating table and not always based on maximal consensus. Some reports about the Luxembourg summit in June 1990 suggest that the Danes were forced to retract their criticisms of Chancellor Kohl's proposal after he threatened to re-discuss every detail of the items on the agenda. Meanwhile, the British were against Europol but could not resist a looser, intergovernmental arrangement, and the Dutch remained surprisingly silent despite profound criticism of the proposal at home.[7] Other narrative versions, however, suggest that the Europol proposal was presented late in the evening when the attention-level of the delegates was at its lowest. The view shared by both narrative versions is that the proposal was based on a narrow consensus between the EC member states. Not only does this mean that the creation of new international policing institutions is being based on a lowest-common-denominator form of bargaining, but it also means that disagreements about location, remit, staffing etc. are carried through in the policy-implementation process. As a result of this constellation, the public has been, and will be confronted with a series of *faits accomplis*, without having been offered the opportunity to exercise democratic control through its parliamentary representatives (although there are *post hoc* parliamentary controls at the national levels; van Outrive, 1992: 19).

In policy-making circles evolving around European police cooperation, there is, however, increasing sensitivity that the debate on international policing should be shared with the electorate, since their approval is the recipe for the acceptance and success of new developments. Lack of public support for international policing initiatives may result in the spotlight becoming fixed on the possibly negative implications of international policing for civil liberties, societal costs and democracy, thus demanding that initiatives in the sphere of international policing should be subject of parliamentary and judicial control, both at a national and at an international level. The centralisation of control is paramount, because it will assist in (but not guarantee) consolidating the order, structure and transparency of international policing. The move toward centralisation raises the question whether the 'formalists' are winning. While formalists argue that the creation of institutional structures and formal-legal agreements improve the quality and effectiveness of police cooperation as it prevents unwieldy growth and lack of quality control, the 'informalists' are wary of regular, binding, and unduly restrictive institutional structures. The compromise the formalists have to accept is that although the informalists have provisionally agreed on the creation of formal institutions, they are not willing these to be tightly embedded in democratically accountable structures. In turn, this puts the long-term integrity of these initiatives at risk.

It will take some time for genuine *subsidiarity* in this policy-field to materialise (Leyendecker, 1992: 378f.). The arguments are presented by people whose level of specialisation is so high that the danger of exposure to profound and well-targeted criticism is very low. Does the rarefied quality of the policy debate about policing, coupled with the dominance of professional law enforcement prospectives in respect of access to policy-making structures and media outlets, imply a gradual indoctrination of the electorate with the ideology of a 'Fortress Europe'? Although the answer to this question may on first consideration appear to be negative as no explicit manipulation is at work, the public is nevertheless becoming progressively familiarised with the introduction of new instruments of international and supranational control.

Policing in the context of European internal security

The reason why the debate on European police cooperation has had the chance to flourish is because it has become embedded in an international cooperative framework of a more general nature, thereby rendering the debate and the proposals more formalised in character. The debate on cross-border policing – although still disorderly and opaque – has the opportunity to tie into existing precedents in the field of international cooperation. The proposals on European police cooperation are parasitic on the more general experience of international cooperation in the sphere of financial and monetary matters, taxation, foreign policy, etc. The 'ideal climate' is predominantly supported by mutual trust, which is facilitated by the entrenchment of permanent international arrangements. Although the EC member states steadfastly cling to their national hobby-horses, such as sovereignty and local democracy, a genuine reciprocal acknowledgement of these principles becomes apparent from the overtness of some of the disagreements.[8]

One of the other contextual incentives behind European police cooperation is the interdependence between states. International integration and cooperation find a natural extension in the areas of home affairs and internal security. Europe is faced with the challenge of creating an entirely new structure of international relations, and policing is only a fragment of that. However, it could well be that the future of European police cooperation, as it hinges upon developments within the political context, will remain relatively undefined for some time to come. Hanrieder (1991: 410) writes in this context:

The new Europe we see emerging is in some respects also a very old Europe, with a troublesome and flawed historical genealogy and an onerous legacy of economic mistakes, political crimes, and unattended grievances. The emerging state system in Europe (and the world at large) is a peculiar amalgam of the past and the present, moving towards an uncertain future. It is multidimensional, contradictory and in transition.

When trying to come to grips with the arguments and justifications which stimulate the growth of cross-border police cooperation in Europe, it is instructive to look at the wider context of European integration. The most significant changes have been the shift from a bi-polar international political system to a multi-polar political system (van Ham, 1993: 206),[9] and the formation of a 'supranational community' within the European Community as a result of the abolition of border controls. These developments have partly crystallised in the creation of a new European 'security apparatus' (Pastore, 1992: 11). As the definition of the internal security concept in Europe is currently undergoing a number of transformations (Dalby, 1992: 95; Denis, 1992: 19; Rupprecht and Hellenthal, 1992: 61; Weidenfeld, 1992: 9), so does the concept of policing. When we look at the development of policing in the post-Cold War period, the analogy with defence can only be partial (Overbeek, 1993: 1). For instance, the adversarial situation has been replaced by the extensive fracturing of the territory on one side of the former divide and by diverse tensions resulting from it. We are now envisaging a new Europe, which by virtue of its absorption of East European countries, has not only paralysed the old enemy image, but also introduced another. The danger to the stability of our system is no longer perceived as a homogeneous external 'enemy' which was identified with the communist system, but with terrorism, drugs and illegal immigration. Not only has this new moral panic congealed in the public mind, there has also been a material response in the sense of building an 'impregnable' Europe. While the exterior menace has undergone a metamorphosis, Europe has initiated an attempt to confront the enemy within; after communism it is principally immigration that is perceived to be a destabilising factor:

Societies appear to be subject, every now and then, to periods of moral panic. A condition, episode, person or group of persons emerges to become defined as a threat to societal values and interests; its nature is presented in a stylized and sterotypical fashion by the mass media; the moral barricades are manned by editors, bishops, politicians and other right-thinking people; socially accredited experts pronounce their diagnosis and solutions; ways of coping are evolved or (more often) resorted to; the condition then disappears, submerges or deteriorates and becomes more visible. Sometimes the object of the panic is quite novel and at other times it is something which has been existence long enough, but suddenly appears in the limelight. Sometimes the panic passes over and is forgotten, except in folklore and collective memory; at other times it has more serious and long-lasting repercussions and might produce such changes as those in legal and social policy or even in the way the society conceives itself (Cohen, 1980: 9).

The mobilisation of social anxiety through media reports in particular has created a fertile ground for the introduction of pragmatic, *ad hoc* agreements which seek to provide solutions which are no more than temporary expedients (den Boer, 1993a: 44). International security agreements increasingly cover the control of migratory movements (Bunyan, 1991: 19; Bigo and Leveau, 1992: 9, 29).

This ideological shift implies that the tendency towards the internationalisation of policing can be displayed and justified as a natural reaction to an ever growing threat. The analogy with the Cold War era returns here: the need for police action in reaction to a perceived upsurge in international crime and immigration falls neatly within a premeditated plot which has been put forward by the various interest groups with the support of institutional structures of power. The objective of international policing institutions to eradicate the rotten and dangerous criminal core in European society quietly massages the definition of their task as repressive and authoritarian, which in turn closes the door upon the introduction of international forms of community policing ('the police as your best friend' in football-matches, tourism, traffic).

Therefore, much as some would like to think that Europe is beginning to achieve stability by means of cooperation through international machinery, Europe at large is also facing uncertainty and perhaps even an era of relative instability, caused by regional fragmentation and a resulting tension in the administrative frameworks. For the purpose of analysing this wider political context of European policing we may examine the four possible scenarios for the future of Europe as sketched by the Federal Trust for Education and Research (1991). The most apocalyptic scenario portrays a frustrated pressure to emigrate from the poorer regions, leading to instability among the Community's members, and resulting in the progressive disintegration of Europe and the worsening of internal security problems. In the light of this possibility, two questions should be raised: first, do the proposed structures of European police cooperation take account of or even anticipate emerging forms of regionalism, forms which could potentially alter the currently popular analysis of cross-border cooperation and/or external border controls? (den Boer, 1992: 10); and, second, does the loss of the bi-polar divide between East and West mean that the demand for internal security might become encoded in a quite different language, namely that of internal policing instead external, military defence?

In response to the first question one may note that recently concluded international agreements with chapters on European police cooperation, such as the Schengen Implementation Agreement (June 1990)[10] and the Maastricht Treaty (December 1991) include clauses which express a cautious attitude with regard to emerging internal security problems. Notwithstanding that cautious note, the tone of the EC treaties seems to be one of mutual trust and one which regards instability as an exceptional situation. But pressing questions remain: Will Europe be wide but weak, or narrow but strong? Is it conceivable to widen police cooperation to East European states who do not (yet) possess a fast, reliable and technologically modern infrastructure? What does the future of Europe's political structure and constitution hold? Does the quest for regional autonomy throughout the European Community (Scotland, Basque Country, Corsica, etc.) pose a threat to current international policing arrangements? If East and Central European states, Austria, Switzerland and the Scandinavian countries remain unassociated with the work of Europol, will internal security gaps soon begin to emerge? (den Boer, 1992: 10).

In response to the second question posed above, one may note that policing rhetoric has not established itself as a substitute for defence rhetoric; rather, it has marginalised defence as a model for the solution of international conflicts and instability. Police checks and border controls have certainly become closely associated with defence: these controls will be re-introduced when 'public policy and public safety in connexion with national policies on immigration, aliens, drugs control etc.' are at stake (Timmermans, 1993: 357),[11] and for the determination of which criteria constitute an internal security risk, we may have to rely on future rulings by the European Court of Justice which has traditionally adopted a fully open-ended approach. Police organisations throughout Europe will be more and more entrusted with internal security tasks as terrorism, right-wing extremism and white-collar crime endanger the stability of European states.

Rhetoric and justification: prophecies of doom

Will the recent proposals in the field of European police cooperation fill the organisational vacuum or will they be the answer to a perceived 'internal security gap'? Can we be certain how well the European internal-security apparatus is equipped to deal with features of international crime? The wide spectrum of international crime-fighting bodies suggests that immense efforts have been undertaken already, albeit in a rather disorderly and disconnected mode.

Closer scrutiny of the discourse on European policing reveals that the rationale for international policing is no longer questioned or analysed. Rather than investigating whether the intensity of international crime justifies the expense that goes into creating new institutions, the threat thrown up by international crime is very much an accepted fact. On the one hand, there has been a lack of properly conducted feasibility studies into the need, organisation, accountability structure and location of new institutions (in particular Europol). On the other hand, there has been insufficient scrutiny of the *raison d'être* of these institutions and their effective potential to combat forms of international crime. In other words, the discussion about causes, means and ends has not had a chance to develop, and the disruptions caused by this are manifest, for example, in the delay in the implementation of the Schengen Agreements and the production of the Europol Convention. In a world where the deep structures of international crime and (illegal) immigration are hardly addressed because of their intrinsic connection with embedded political and social–economic structures, the newly created forms of international policing may well amount to cosmetic changes in a much more complex world.

In the virtual absence of systematic scrutiny, European police cooperation has started to take on its own momentum (den Boer and Walker, 1993: 10f.); the policy-making debate survives almost as an autonomous discourse, with the exception of occasional political initiatives, authorisations and interventions. One of the dangers inherent in this autonomous discursive spiral is that it has the chance to expand semantically and ideologically, and that the self-policing of its remit allows for creeping incrementalism.

In the remainder of this chapter, we will see that despite the lack of systematic attempts to examine the relationship between international crime and European policing institutions, the public interlocutors in the international policing discourse reiterate and reinforce the public anxiety about the growth of international crime and illegal immigration. The demand for the creation of international police organisations is reinforced by *justifications*. In fact, one seldom sees the quest for Europol or ED(I)U very often accompanied by explicit arguments concerning why they should be created. But the perceived growth of international crime, the wave of illegal immigration and the mobility of the EC population function as justificatory pockets or semantic clusters within the discursive space where the debate on the intensification of European police cooperation is conducted. In other words, demands for international police organisations are indirectly coupled with public justifications, the importance and magnitude of which is often inflated by the various interest groups which are involved in the determination of international policing policies.

Domains of justification

There are at least three domains of justification at play: (1) the perceived increase of international crime; (2) the relaxation or abolition of border controls; (3) the upsurge in (clandestine) immigration.

(1) A frequent justification for the extension of international police cooperation is the internationalisation, or even the 'Europeanisation' of crime.[12] It is often argued that the introduction of modern technology and the use of fast means of transport has increased the flexibility and

mobility of the criminal. 'Intelligent' criminals are thought to be knowledgeable about loopholes in the various legal systems (in particular rules concerning financial transactions) and which enable them to by-pass legal obstacles. The abolition of border controls in the European Community has encouraged the belief among law enforcement officers that criminal individuals or groups are now widening their playing field beyond national borders. Not only does this belief simplify the complex relationship between national and international criminal justice regulations, it also equates the abolition of border controls with the weakening of Europe's internal security (see also under (2) below). Although the stipulated connection between the increase of international crime and the relaxation of internal border controls has not been the subject of an independent scrutiny, the extension and the intensification of European police cooperation is frequently put forward as a policy to enable the law enforcement officials to act at the same level as that of the international criminal. Statements by key officials underline this point:

Senior Police Officer: For those who are bound by convention, by political influence, by national borders and by laws and procedures the future changes daily. But what of the future of the thoughtful criminal entrepreneur? He has never taken regard for borders, he is not bound by laws. He has regard only for his criminal enterprise. In this respect he has always the advantage and our criminals are already looking for the opportunities presented by the changing face of Europe. If we are wise we need to do the same and with some urgency . . . (Even so it is my belief), shared by many European colleagues, that there are many good class criminals who will be encouraged to expand their activities across internal boundaries in the belief that 1 January 1992 will produce a sudden relaxation in police and customs activity. I accept that the perception may be more significant than the reality, but nevertheless, there is a danger that the criminal will feel less restricted and will act accordingly (Birch, 1992: 4).

Senior Official: Encouraged by the modern means of communication and greater prosperity, people are now crossing borders in huge numbers. In the European Community this will soon take place without any controls. The scope for transboundary crime will therefore continue to increase. The enormous sums of money involved in organised crime make complicated transactions in numerous countries attractive and feasible. This requires coordinated action by police and judicial authorities, extending across borders (Grosheide, 1993: 71).

Senior Official: Modern criminal policy is no longer conceivable if it does not also include an international element. At a time when the mobility of the individual is increasing and the separation function of national borders is constantly decreasing, no domestic criminal legislator can afford to treat crime merely as a national phenomenon. The internationalisation of economic activity and of transport goes hand-in-hand with a dramatic internationalisation of crime. Each day, it becomes painfully clear to the police and the judiciary how great the energy, speed, mobility and sophistication of offenders are and, by contrast, how difficult it is to overcome the barriers created for the police and judiciary out of differences in national legal systems and out-moded concepts of national sovereignty (Wilkitzki, 1991: 8).

It cannot be denied that the internationalisation of crime has been assisted by increased access to information technology, computers and fax-machines, and by increased mobility. The burden of international crime has, however, been with us for many years, despite the impression created by senior law enforcement officers that it is a relatively new phenomenon. A significant factor in creating this impression is the propensity of law enforcement institutions to apply discrete labels when analysing international crime; most recently, the international attention has turned to 'organised crime' (in particular in East Europe) and to 'environmental crime'. A new label for old phenomena may assist the policy-makers in finding approval for new proposals. The question should therefore be whether, if objectively assessed, international crime establishes a greater threat to the internal security of EC member states than a decade ago, or whether mass attention for phenomena related to international crime acts as an instrument in the justification of new investment.

(2) The existence of internal border controls within Europe has frequently been hailed as the most preferred and effective means to detect suspected criminals or to prevent them from leaving the country (Rupprecht and Hellenthal, 1992: 43, 133).[13] The philosophy behind this is that borders function as an eel-basket, in which elusive and slippery international criminals find themselves entrapped. According to Rupprecht and Hellenthal (1992: 89), the internal security of EC member states is potentially compromised by a combination of the abolition of internal border controls and the following conditions:

- the abolition of police and customs presence at the internal borders;

- the abolition of checks on persons and goods;

- internal checks are based only on prior suspicion;

- the police presence on national territory is not as concentrated as at the borders;

- the difference between police laws, aliens and asylum laws, detection methods and measures, means of communication and language;

- unsatisfactory rules on hot pursuit;

- the lack of a broader right to enter the neighbouring country armed and in uniform;

- unsatisfactory opportunities for surveillance abroad in the event of emergencies;

- lack of integration between police forces in the neighbouring country in the types of circumstances where crime has an international dimension;
- unsatisfactory legal and civil assistance (i.e. insufficient practical contact).

Rupprecht and Hellenthal (1992: 100ff.) predict that: the chances to arrest wanted or suspected persons will decrease; organised crime will benefit from the post-1992 situation and international criminal links will be encouraged; drugs and arms trafficking will increase; economic and environmental crime will be boosted; asylum policies will be more open to abuse by non-EC citizens; the fight against illegal employment and counterfeit production of identity documents will become more difficult; and the traffic situation in Europe will be affected adversely.

These gloomy predictions may be instrumental in generalist policies which favour the compensation of the abolition of border controls by intensified international police cooperation:

> *Senior Official*: Border controls are a classic instrument for member states' policies regarding aliens, drugs, crime prevention/terrorism, etc. Abolishing all internal frontier controls between member states to complete the internal market, more particularly as far as the free movement of persons is concerned, must therefore be balanced by accompanying measures replacing these controls (Timmermans, 1993: 353).

> *Senior Police Officer*: We need also to bear in mind that there has been a massive increase in recent years of goods and passenger traffic through our sea and airports which will continue to rise in excess of any available or desirable increase of manpower employed there. We must accept that even in the UK our controls are perhaps not as effective as they used to be and their efficacy will continue to diminish as traffic increases. It is in our interest, therefore, despite possible retention of border arrangements to look for enhanced police cooperation with our neighbours and other compensatory security measures (Birch, 1992: 5).

> *Politician*: The open frontier system could not be better for the terrorist or for the drug cartel and to counteract them we need more and more exchanges of information. Crimes are now worldwide, let alone Europeanwide, and the spreading of data is a vital way of combating them. There are those who say that this impinges on civil rights. That is not my view.[14]

There are a number of weaknesses in the 'eel-basket'-philosophy. First, it is based on the dubious assumption that in a region *with* border controls, internationally active criminals move around with caution, while in a region *without* border controls, international criminals become rather complacent in their movements. One might call into question whether international criminals start behaving differently when border controls are abolished. Will they start to cross Europe *en masse* from Sicily to Schleswig-Holstein, from Dublin to Kiel? Are internationally active criminals not aware of the international exchange of police intelligence and mobile cross-border controls? These assumptions rather ignore the fact that, in the past, international crime has had the chance to expand despite border controls, and it also ignores the fact that international criminals have actually been able to capitalise on the existence of border controls and on the differences that exist between criminal justice systems in Europe (Levi, 1993: 185). Paradoxically perhaps, border controls and the national differences which they mark, may assist the criminal to escape through the holes in the net: once the border has been negotiated, he or she may well escape detection, prosecution and even extradition and may generally stay well away from the tentacles of the domestic law of the other state.

The second weakness in the 'eel-basket' philosophy is that the argument about the effectiveness of the filter function of borders is silent as to what type of criminals are actually arrested at border control points. Is it realistic to expect border controls to be effective against hard-core criminals? Is it not the case, one might argue, that minor criminals or lower participants in criminal organisations are more likely to be caught at the border than those that run the organisation? Therefore, the *quality* of the relationship between border controls and successful arrests is hardly questioned (Stüer, 1990: 290; Weidenfeld, 1992: 10; Dorn and South, 1993: 79). The 'success' of border controls may be a simultaneous failure, because they may be presumed ineffective against those who control the scene of international organised crime.

The third weakness of the 'eel-basket' philosophy is that it fails to expose the role of intelligence. The use of selective intelligence in combination with possibly intensified border checks remains a mystery. In other words, one may wonder to what extent the intensification of border checks is prompted by a selective and strategic use of intelligence gathered prior to the mobilisation of border officials. One may assume that the police are conscious of the movement of wanted criminals or that they have intelligence about repetitive patterns in international crime, and that they will intensify controls where they anticipate a criminal to leave or enter the country. It is regrettable therefore that although the call for compensation of abolished border controls plays a crucial role in the justification of an expanded internal security apparatus, the relationship between the effectiveness of border controls and the selective and targeted application of prior intelligence remains obscure (Brittan, 1991: 3).

Hence, when exploring this domain of justification, the analysis of the relation between border controls and the mobility of international criminals fails to take account of important contextual factors, such as the rationality of agents (criminals, police), and the role of criminal intelligence.

(3) In the re-conceptualisation of European security and identity, immigrants have emerged as enemy number one. It was noted previously that the external antagonist of communism has been substituted by that of

immigration. This discursive replacement coincides with a growing European cultural and political cohesion, which in turn is coalesced by reinforcing the discourse of 'otherness' and by specifying the internal community in antithesis to external threat (Dalby, 1992: 107). To underline the increasing migratory pressure which rests on the European Community, statistics, charts, and press reports have been drafted to reveal not only a considerable rise in the number of asylum applications, but also an upsurge in the number of clandestine immigrants entering or residing in the European Community. Indicative of the perception of migration as a threat to the internal security of the member states of the European Community is the opinion of the *Ad Hoc* Group on Immigration (1991: 3; EC ministers responsible for immigration): 'Other phenomena indicate the same path, in particular the substantial intensification of migratory pressure now exerted on almost all member states . . . and the massive increase in the number of unjustified applications for asylum, a method which is used – in most cases in vain – as a means of immigration by persons who do not meet the conditions of the Geneva Convention.' The insertion of the term 'unjustified' is significant: the attribution of deviancy, false pretences and criminal objectives is crucial in the labelling of would-be immigrants (Cohen, 1980: 54; see also Albrecht, 1993). This negative discourse of 'otherness' has allowed the term 'bogus application' to slip into the official vocabulary of politicians and policy-makers (den Boer, 1993b: 14).[15] The picture which is displayed is becoming increasingly blurred, because it fails to draw a proper distinction between economic migrants, asylum seekers or refugees, and illegal or clandestine immigrants. In particular the dividing line between asylum seekers and illegal immigrants has rapidly been transformed into a semantically grey area. Many asylum seekers may be re-classified as 'bogus' or illegal immigrants for failing to present valid travel documents, or upon evidence of prosecution in their home country.

It cannot be denied however that the EC member states have come under pressure caused by a mounting number of applications from immigrants or asylum seekers to stay (Dedecker, 1991: 20–23). Hondius (1991: 28) writes:

At the beginning of the 1970s, the average number of applications for asylum made in Western Europe was 13,000, most of whom received in due course recognition as refugees. In the 1980s, this figure increased first ten-fold and later twenty-fold . . . Not only have the numbers increased but also the motivations for this influx have become more complex . . . At present the number of illegal immigrants is on the increase, not only as a result of demographic and economic imbalances between the developed and less developed countries, but also in connection with specific employment opportunities in developed countries. Consequently, it is increasingly difficult to distinguish between genuine refugees and asylum-seekers, '*de facto* refugees' – persons who, although not definitively accepted, are not sent back to their countries of origin for humanitarian reasons – and illegal migrant workers.

Germany was the most drastically affected with over 400,000 people applying for asylum in 1992, which was an increase of 75 per cent over the previous year. In the UK, the number of asylum applications went up from around 25,000 in 1990 to 44,730 in 1991; in the first months of 1992, the number of applications for political asylum dropped by more than half, which according to the Home Office reflected tougher controls and a significant number of 'bogus' requests (*Social Trends*: 35; den Boer, 1993a: 30).

The debate about international police cooperation is relevant for some aspects of migration, such as (a) the impact upon internal instability and the threat to internal security, through the provocation of xenophobic reactions from the native population; (b) police involvement in the performance of internal controls by means of spot checks, the inspection of hotel and employment registers inside the territories of the EC member states for the purpose of checking residential legality; (c) the forced deportation of those who have not been given permission to stay; and (d) the prosecution and/or expulsion of aliens who are undesirable for security reasons. In broad terms, the trend towards compensation of the abolition of border controls through the intensification of internal controls widens the responsibility of the national police organisations for immigration control, and it puts pressure on the police to reinforce inter-agency cooperation with immigration and border officials. The four aspects just mentioned tilt the policing task towards internal controls in the EC member states (checks at ports and airports; spot checks in guest houses, hotels and companies; public order policing in the case of riots; etc.) and/or towards controls at the external frontiers of the European Community. The distance between the fight against international crime and (illegal) immigration is narrowing rapidly. A European internal security continuum has emerged, along which the attribution of illegality can be transferred from crime to immigration (Bigo and Leveau, 1992; Bigo, present volume). Hence, not only do new policies on European police cooperation include proposals on immigration control, these policies are also a product of the same policy-making bodies (e.g. Trevi).

In order to get a clear picture of the closing gap between the policing of international crime and the policing of (illegal) immigration, certain views expressed in recent publications may be examined:

Politicians: Harmonisation of admission policies must be combined with a common approach to the problem of illegal immigration . . . Strict surveillance would be required both at borders and within member states for an approach to be efficient. The first consideration in controlling borders is the long sea borders of the member states. It seems practically impossible to introduce border controls there whichwould entirely eliminate clandestine immigration. . . . Checks within the territory of member states on persons who have entered illegally are also an important feature in the fight against clandestine immigration, although such checks must be carried out without infringing individual freedoms (*Ad Hoc* Group on Immigration, 1991).

Civil Libertarian: It is becoming increasingly common to speak of the 'burden' of the immigration. It becomes increasingly self-evident to want to protect 'ourselves' against 'migrations of the nations'. To substitute border controls for us all by the control of aliens inland. To employ the military constabulary for this purpose. To put up with the duty of identification. To claim that the living situation of the source countries of the immigrants ought to be improved, without doing anything about it (van Es, 1991: 57; author's translation)

Having collated a number of views on the three related justificatory arguments, one may distinguish a strong reiterative pattern in the quotations, which draws on a stereotypical analysis of the consequences of the removal of internal border controls.

When the arguments in the policy-making debate on European police cooperation are selected and presented as above – that is, without a detailed substantiation of the premises which underlie the assumptions – they tend to be mutually consistent in an ideological constellation. But a closer scrutiny of these premises' and statistics' analyses would perhaps reveal a number of frictions or contradictions. The controversy about the filter function of border controls is illuminating in this respect: arguments that most illegal drugs are seized at the borders may be taken out of context, while the argument about the use of criminal intelligence in respect of illegal transactions may be grossly overstated. It would require another research project to examine the actual usefulness of borders. This chapter has indicated a number of potential blind spots in the debate on European police cooperation, which ought to be addressed in the policy-making process. The worrying aspect is whether these blind spots have deliberately *not* been addressed in order to promote a European control culture.

Conclusion

Applying the statement 'All language is rhetorical' (Eagleton, 1991: 201) to the discourse on European police cooperation would suggest that the policy-making process on European police cooperation has a rhetorical dimension; the presentation of facts, statistics, numbers and functionalistic arguments are instruments in a process of negotiation, persuasion and consensus-building.

The semantics of international relations are a powerful influence on this rhetoric. For example, the Western model of terrorism depicts the West as 'an innocent target and victim of terrorism', that it 'only responds to other people's use of force' and that it is 'the aim of terrorists to undermine' institutions and democracies etc. (Herman and O'Sullivan, 1991: 43f.). Western interests and policy are shaped by the constellation of myths and fabrications which fit this 'patriotic model' (ibid.: 44). Ideologies which dominate international relations correspond with ideologies that support developments in Europe's internal security control.

The quest for international policing is a public exchange of rhetorical statements which reveal minimal empirical or analytical scrutiny. The next step forward in the analysis of European police cooperation as a discursive policy-making process is to examine the role of counterfactuals – the way in which socio-political models of European integration affect the position taken by politicians and policy-makers. It is, in other words, necessary to examine the dynamic interaction between the broad ideological horizons of the participants on cross-border policing and their proposals and initiatives. This would, however, require the identification of separate rhetorical contributions by the interest groups represented within the policy community, which is difficult because of the opaque character of the policy-making process and the large number of participants.

What practical recommendtions emerge from the analysis which has been presented? The quality of the policy-making process on European police cooperation could be improved to gain wider acceptance of current proposals and initiatives. The debate about European police cooperation could be made more transparent and accessible; it could be steered more centrally (i.e. limiting the number of administrative bodies responsible for a particular sphere of public policy); it could be distanced from issues such as immigration and be immediately concerned with only a few issues, such as the balance between the extension of international police powers and civil liberties, the financial costs which are involved, and the effects of international crime on daily life. Most crucially of all, it could endeavour to underpin rhetorical claims with empirical evidence and explanations.

Notes

1 I would like to thank my colleagues and friends Dr Neil Walker (University of Edinburgh) and Dr Elizabeth Bomberg (University of Stirling) for their invaluable comments on earlier drafts of this chapter.

2 Secretariat-General of the European Commission, 'Luxembourg European Council', *Bulletin of EC*, 24, (6): 15.

3 See for example *The Independent*, 7 February 1991; *The Observer*, 7 February 1993.

4 For an analysis of the involvement of the government, private sector institutes, think-tanks and experts in the 'terrorism industry', see Herman and O'Sullivan (1991: 52–62).

5 'Convention of 15 June 1990 determining the State responsible for examining applications for asylum lodged in one of the Member States of the European Communities' (the Dublin Convention) and the 'Convention of the Member States of the European Communities on the crossing of their external borders' (External Borders Convention).

6 These working groups are now in charge of studying the implementation of the Schengen Agreement.

7 *NRC Handelsblad*, 10 December 1991.

8 Note for instance the dispute between the United Kingdom and the Schengen countries about the differentiation of controls for Schengen-citizens and EC-citizens (*The Guardian*, 22 July 1992; *The Guardian*, 25 November 1992). Also

significant is the difference of opinion between the EC member states about the toughness of drug policies (*Le Figaro*, 4 December 1992; *NRC Weekeditie*, 9 March 1993; *NRC Weekeditie*, 20 April 1993).

9 'With the demise of the Soviet Union and the relative decline of the United States' economic and political power, the post-war international system of bipolarity has clearly given way to a multipolar one. Whereas bipolarity by definition is characterized as a system wherein two Great Powers dominate, multipolarity is generally defined as a system with five or more Great Powers' (van Ham, 1993: 206).

10 See Article 2, Chapter I, Title II: 'However, if so required by public order (*ordre public*) or national security, a Contracting party may, after consultation with the other Contracting Parties, decide that national frontier controls suited to the situation shall be carried out at the internal frontiers for a limited period. If public order or national security require immediate action, the Contracting Party concerned shall take the necessary measures and shall inform the other Contracting Parties as soon as possible.' From: *Commercial Laws of Europe*, Volume 14, February 1991, Part 2, English Language Texts, 'Schengen Convention on Border Controls 1990'.

11 This reading is based on the exception clauses of public policy etc. of Articles 48 (3), 56 (66), of the EEC Treaty.

12 *The Independent*, 4 April 1991.

13 See also *The Independent*, 10 May 1990.

14 Sir James Scott Hopkins, Conservative MEP for Hereford and Worcester, in: *The £1 Billion Bill for 'Europol'*, John Weeks, 1990.

15 See for example *The Scotsman*, 3 November 1992; *The Guardian*, 23 October 1992.

References

Ad Hoc Group on Immigration, *Report to the European Council Meeting in Maastricht on Immigration and Asylum Policy*, Brussels, 3 December 1991, SN 4038/91 WGI 930.

Albrecht, H.-J. (1993), 'Ethnic Minorities. Crime and Criminal Justice in Europe', in Heidensohn and Farrell, 1993: 84–100.

Bigo, D. and Leveau, R. (1992), *L'Europe de la Sécurité Intérieure*, Rapport de fin d'étude pour l'Institut des Hautes Etudes de Sécurité Intérieure, Paris.

Birch, R., CBE, QPM (1992), 'Policing Europe – Current Issues', *PRSU Bulletin*, Home Office, January, 4–6.

Boer, M. den (1992), *Police Cooperation after Maastricht*, Paper presented to seminar on European Union after Maastricht, 1 May 1992, European Community Research Unit, University of Hull, Research Paper No. 2/92.

Boer, M. den (1993a), *Immigration, Internal Security and Policing in Europe*, A System of European Police Cooperation after 1992, Working Paper VIII, Edinburgh.

Boer, M. den (1993b), *Moving between Bonafide and Bogus: The Policing of Inclusion and Exclusion in Europe*, Leiden, ECPR Joint Sessions, Workshop 'Inclusion and Exclusion: Migration and the Uniting of Europe', mimeo. Forthcoming in: Miles, R., and Tränhardt, D. (Eds.), *Migration and European Integration: The Dynamics of Inclusion and Exclusion*, Pinter Publishers, (1993) London, 1994.

Boer, M. den, and Walker, N. (1993), 'European Policing after 1992', *Journal of Common Market Studies*, **31**, 1, 3–28.

Brittan, Sir L. (1991), *The European Single Market: Implications for Policing*, Newsam Memorial Lecture, Police Staff College, Bramshill, 1 November.

Bunyan, T. (1991), 'Towards an Authoritarian European State', *Race and Class*, **32**, 3, 19–27.

Cohen, S. (1980), *Folk Devils and Moral Panics*, Oxford, Martin Robertson.

Council of the European Communities & Commission of the European Communities (1992), *Treaty on European Union*, Luxembourg, Office for Official Publications of the European Communities.

Dalby, S. (1992), 'Security, Modernity, Ecology: The Dilemmas of Post-Cold War Security Discourse', *Alternatives*, **17**, 95–134.

Dedecker, R. (1991), *Le Droit d'asile dans Schengen. Quelques réflexions a propos de l'avis du conseil d'état néerlandais du 8 avril 1991 sur la convention d'application de l'accord de Schengen*, Brusells, Université Libre de Bruxelles.

Denis, F. (1992), 'Veranderingen in de politiestructuren van het nieuwe Europa', *Politeia*, 21 December, 19–26.

Dorn, N., and South, N. (1993), 'Drugs, Crime and Law Enforcement', in Heidensohn and Farrell, 1993: 72–83.

Eagleton, T. (1991), *Ideology. An Introduction*, London and New York, Verso.

Es, A. van (1991), *Schengen, of de nieuwe deling van Europa*, Amsterdam, Van Gennep.

Federal Trust for Education and Research (1991), *Europe's Future: Four Scenarios*, London.

Fijnaut, C. (1993), 'Police Cooperation within Western Europe', in Heidensohn and Farrell, 1993: 103–120.

Giddens, A. (1984), *The Constitution of Society*, Cambridge, Polity Press.

Grosheide, J.H. (1993), 'Cooperation in the Field of Criminal Law, Police and Other Law Enforcement Agencies', in Schermerr, H.G., Flinterman, C., Kellermann, A.E., Haersolte, J.C., and Meent, G-W.A. van de (Eds.), *Free Movement of Persons in Europe. Legal Problems and Experiences*, Asser Institute, Dordrecht, Martinus Nijhoff, 70–74.

Ham, P. van (1993), *The EC, Eastern Europe and European Unity. Discord, Collaboration and Integration since 1947*, London, Pinter.

Hanrieder, W.F. (1991), 'Germany, the New Europe and the Transatlantic Connection', *International Journal* (Summer), **46**, 3, 394–419.

Heidensohn, F., and Farrell, M. (Eds.) (1993 (1991)), *Crime in Europe* (2nd edn), London, Routledge.

Herman, E.S. and O'Sullivan, G. (1991), '"Terrorism" as Ideology and Cultural Industry', in A. George (Ed.), *Western State Terrorism*, Cambridge, Polity Press, 39–75.

Hirschmann, A.O. (1991), *The Rhetoric of Reaction. Perversity, Futility, Jeopardy*, Cambridge, Mass., The Belknap Press of Harvard University Press.

Hondius, F.W. (1991), 'Legal Aspects of the Movement of Persons in Greater Europe', *1990 Yearbook of European Law*, 10, 1990, 291–307.

Levi, M. (1993), 'Developments in Business Crime Control in Europe', in Heidensohn and Farrell, 1993: 172–187.

Leyendecker, M. (1992), 'Die Europäische Gemeinschaft der Inneren Sicherheit – die europapolitische Perspektive', in R. Rupprecht and M. Hellenthal (Eds.), *Innere Sicherheit im europäischen Binnenmarkt*, Gütersloh, Bertelsmann Stiftung, 371–381.

Majone, G. (1989), *Evidence, Argument and Persuasion in the Policy Process*, New Haven and London, Yale University Press.

Outrive, L. van (1992), *Second Report of the Committee on Civil Liberties and Internal Affairs on the Entry into Force of the Schengen Agreements*, European Parliament Session Documents, A3-0336/92.

Overbeek, H. (1993), *Transnationalisation, Migration and the State*, Leiden, ECPR Joint Sessions, Workshop 'Inclusion and Exclusion: Migration and the Uniting of Europe', mimeo. Forthcoming in: Miles, R., and Tränhardt, D. (Eds.), *Migration and European Integration: The Dynamics of Inclusion and Exclusion*, Pinter Publishers, London, 1994.

Pastore, M. (1992), 'Boundary' Conflicts around and inside the European Community, Paper presented to the 20th Annual Conference of the European Group for the Study of Deviance and Social Control, Padova, 4–6 September, mimeo.

Peters, B.G. (1992), 'Bureaucratic Politics and the Institutions of the European Community', in A.M. Sbragia (Ed.), *Europolitics. Institutions and Policymaking in the 'New' European Community*, Washington DC, The Brookings Institution, 75–122.

Reenen, P. van (1989), 'Policing Europe after 1992: Cooperation and Competition', *European Affairs*, **2**, 45–53.

Rupprecht, R. and Hellenthal, M. (1992), 'Programm für eine Europäische Gemeinschaft der inneren Sicherheit', in R. Rupprecht, M. Hellenthal (Eds.), *Innere Sicherheit im europäischen Binnenmarkt*, Gütersloh, Bertelsmann Stiftung, 23–318.

Social Trends, Central Statistical Office, 1992 edn, London, HMSO.

Stüer, C. (1990), *Personenkontrollen an den Europäischen Binnengrenzen und ihr Abbau*, Berlin, Bonn, München, Carl Heymans Verlag.

Timmermans, C.W.A. (1993), 'Free Movement of Persons and the Division of Powers between the Community and its Member States. Why do it the Intergovernmental Way?', in Schermerr, H.G., Flinterman, C., Kellerman, A.E., Haersolte, J.C., and Meent, G-W. A. van de (Eds.), *Free Movement of Persons in Europe*, Asser Institute, Dordrecht, Martinus Nijhoff, 352–368.

Trevi (1990), *Programme of Action relating to the Reinforcement of Police Co-operation and the Endeavours to Combat Terrorism or other Forms of Crime*, Dublin, Trevi.

Weidenfeld, W. (1992), 'Die innere Sicherheit als europäische Politik', in R. Rupprecht and M. Hellenthal (Eds.), *Innere Sicherheit im europäischen Binnenmarkt*, Gütersloh, Bertelsmann Stiftung, 7–21.

Wessels, W. (1990), 'Administrative Interaction', in W. Wallace (Ed.), *The Dynamics of European Integration*, London, RIIA, 229–241.

Wilkitzki, P. (1991), *Development of an Effective International Crime and Justice Programme – a European View*, International Workshop on Principles and Procedures for a New Transnational Criminal Law, The Society for the Reform of Criminal Law & Max Planck Institute for Foreign and International Criminal Law, May 21–25, Freiburg.

Wright, D.S. (1982), *Understanding Intergovernmental Relations*, (2nd edn), Monterey, Calif., Brooks/Cole Publishing Company.

INDEX